_IAL SERIES, NO. 18   15 DECEMBER 1943

GERMAN WINTER WARFARE

PREPARED BY
MILITARY INTELLIGENCE DIVISION
WAR DEPARTMENT

Published by Books Express Publishing
Copyright © Books Express, 2011
ISBN 978-1-780390-69-7

Books Express publications are available from all good retail and online booksellers. For publishing proposals and direct ordering please contact us at: info@books-express.com

MILITARY INTELLIGENCE DIVISION
WAR DEPARTMENT
WASHINGTON 25, D. C., 15 December 1943

SPECIAL SERIES
No. 18
MID 461

NOTICE

1. Publication of *Special Series* is for the purpose of providing officers with reasonably confirmed information from official and other reliable sources.

2. In order to meet the special requirements of certain headquarters, or in order to conserve shipping space, the distribution of any particular issue may be modified from the standard of 150 copies to a division, 30 to a nondivisional group or regiment, 6 to an independent squadron or battalion, and 2 to an independent troop or company. In an infantry division organized according to T/O & E 7 (15 July 1943), redistribution should be effected as follows:

Div Hq	7		Hq	4
Div Hq Co	2		Hq Btry	2
MP Plat	1		Bns (4)	24
Rcn Tp	2		TOTAL, DIV ARTY	30
Ord Co	2			
QM Co	2		Regtl Hq	4
Sig Co	2		Regtl Hq Co	2
Engr Bn	6		Serv Co	2
Med Bn	6		Cn Co	2
Div Arty	30		AT Co	2
Inf Regts (3)	90		Bns (3)	18
TOTAL, INF DIV	150		TOTAL, INF REGT	30

3. In addition to *Special Series*, publications of the Military Intelligence Division include *Tactical and Technical Trends* (biweekly), *Intelligence Bulletin* (monthly), and *Military Reports on the United Nations* (monthly). Distribution to AAF units and installations is made by the Assistant Chief of Air Staff, Intelligence, Army Air Forces, and quantities sent to AGF addresses are recommended by the Commanding General, Army Ground Forces. Requests for additional copies of any MID publication should be made through channels.

4. Every command should circulate available copies among its officers. Reproduction within the military service is permitted provided that (1) the source is stated, (2) the classification is maintained, and (3) one copy of the publication in which the material is reproduced is forwarded to the **Dissemination Unit, Military Intelligence Division, War Department, Washington 25, D. C.** Comments on this publication and suggestions for future issues may be sent directly to the same address.

PREFACE

This work is substantially a translation of an enemy document which has been edited in the style and format of War Department publications and rearranged in order to present the material in a more logical order than in the original text. All of the illustrations, which were rough sketches in the original, have been redrawn, and have been improved as much as possible.

The handbook was based on the experiences of the German Army during the first two winters of the war in Russia. Essentially it tells a story of efforts to solve two vital problems of winter warfare: mobility and shelter. The handbook was published by the German High Command on 5 August 1942, apparently in a great hurry, in order to help the German forces to prepare for a third rigorous winter on the invaded territory of a formidable foe. The material, evidently collected from the various branches of the German Armed Forces, was put together badly and in some places was almost unintelligible. A considerable portion of the material was in the form of appendices under headings that duplicated section captions in the main text. These appendices have been merged into their logical places. Some material which had no special application to winter warfare was eliminated.

While the handbook was badly arranged, the material itself is considered to be valuable for the insight that it gives into the experiences of an Army under conditions of extreme cold and for its reflection of the degree of improvisation to which the German Army was compelled to resort. The numerous references to "makeshifts," "expedients," and "improvisations" point to the lesson that the problems of winter warfare must be considered and solved long before a force is committed to winter combat. In the manual the German High Command repeatedly emphasizes the lesson that equipment, methods, techniques, and clothing must be specially designed for the struggle against snow, ice, mud, moisture, and bitter cold. Above all, it emphasizes the lesson that the individual soldier must be specially acclimated, trained, and toughened to fight in winter and that he must develop the will to resist its hardships as determinedly as he should resist the enemy.

In paragraph **4**, "Preparation for Winter Warfare," the manual asserts: "In building up endurance against the rigors of the Russian winter, mental discipline is the determining factor." Again in paragraph **6**, "Morale," the manual states: "The coming winter will again severely tax the spiritual stamina of the soldier. All suitable means, commensurate with the situation and combat conditions, will be employed to bolster his inner resilience."

It will be noted that the German High Command does not consider winter as a fixed season of snow and low temperatures. Before and after the winters in Russia there were periods which in most respects raised practically the same problems as snow and cold. The rains of autumn and the thaw in spring brought floods and mud, which, like deep snow, tended to immobilize the German forces on the long Eastern Front.

The text of the *Taschenbuch für den Winterkrieg* begins in Section I. The "Foreword" and other preliminary matter of the German original are also included in order to emphasize the fact that this publication is a translation of a German manual intended for German troops. It is not a manual for U. S. troops, but must be read as an enemy document which is intended to convey information about the enemy's doctrine, techniques, and methods.

Anhang 2 zur H.Dv.Ja
Seite 18a lfd. Nr. 17

Taschenbuch
für den Winterkrieg

Vom 5. August 1942

Title page of original.

Verso of title page of original.

FOREWORD [1]

This handbook is a compilation of practical experience in winter warfare. It is intended to facilitate adaptation to winter conditions in Russia.

Section I gives a general idea of conditions during the winter and the muddy period and of the inferences which may be drawn therefrom. It is intended chiefly for officers of all grades.

The information in this handbook must become the common property of the troops, and a detailed study of it must be made the duty of all officers and instructors. Most of the subjects are suitable for the instruction of noncommissioned officers.

For the more intensive study of the subject of winter warfare, other training publications as well as training films will be used extensively.

---

[1] Translation of foreword of original.

CONTENTS

	Page
Section I. WINTER, MUD, AND THAW	1
1. Influence of Winter	1
2. Duration and Nature of Snow	2
3. Seasons of Mud and Thaw	3
4. Preparation for Winter Warfare	4
5. Winter Combat Methods	7
6. Morale	12
a. General	12
b. Recreational Aids	13
(1) *Reading material*	13
(2) *Lectures*	13
(3) *Radio*	13
(4) *Movies*	14
(5) *Employment of "Strength through Joy" groups*	14
(6) *Competitions*	14
(7) *Improvement of quarters*	14
(8) *Organization of spare time*	15
(9) *Service centers*	15
(10) *Front convalescent camps*	15
II. MARCHES AND ORIENTATION	16
7. Marches	16
a. Reconnaissance	16
b. Preparation for Marches	17
c. March Discipline	18
d. Halts and Rest Periods	19
8. Orientation in Snow-Covered Terrain	20
a. General	20
b. Fundamentals of Orientation	21
c. Methods of Orientation	22
d. Controlling March Direction	25
e. Conduct When Lost	27

	Page
III. ROADS	28
9. Road Marking	28
10. Road Making	30
a. General	30
b. Methods	31
11. Winter Road Service	37
a. General	37
b. Preparations	38
(1) *Weather conditions on the road*	38
(2) *State of repair*	38
(3) *Capacity of roads*	38
c. Clearing Roads	40
d. Snow Fences	41
e. Treatment of Slippery Surfaces	44
f. Transition from Snow to Mud	45
12. Ice Crossings	46
a. Capacity of Ice	46
b. Preparations and Safety Measures	47
c. Crossing	49
d. Reinforcement of Ice Surfaces and Ice-Bridge Construction	50
IV. RAILROAD MOVEMENTS	53
13. General	53
14. Preparations for a Train Movement	53
15. Protective Measures en Route	54
V. WINTER BIVOUACS AND SHELTER	57
16. Bivouacs	57
a. General	57
b. Snow Shelters	60
17. Snow Hole	60
18. Snow Cave	63
19. Snow Pit	65
20. Snow House	65
21. Igloo, Eskimo Type	66
a. General	66
b. Building Equipment	67
c. Condition of Snow	67
d. Preparation for Building	68
e. Cutting the Blocks	69
f. Building the First Four Tiers	70

CONTENTS

V. WINTER BIVOUACS AND SHELTER—Continued.

	Page
21. Igloo, Eskimo Type—Continued.	
g. Completing the Dome	72
h. Finishing Touches	74
i. Furnishings	75
j. Building of Large Igloos	75
22. Plywood Shelters	75
23. Tents	79
24. Circular Tents, Finnish Type	83
25. Lean-Tos and Other Improvised Shelters	83
26. Shelters for Horses and Motor Vehicles	86
27. Permanent Billets	87
a. General	87
b. Factors Governing Construction	91
(1) *Type of construction*	91
(2) *Planning construction*	92
c. Improvement of Existing Buildings	93
d. Water Supply	93

VI. CONSTRUCTION OF WINTER POSITIONS

	94
28. General	94
29. Construction of Simple Positions	95
30. Improved Positions	97
31. Obstacles	100

VII. HEATING FACILITIES

	105
32. General	105
33. Fires	105
34. Making Charcoal	111
35. Danger of Carbon-Monoxide Poisoning	113

VIII. CAMOUFLAGE, CONCEALMENT, AND IDENTIFICATION

	115
36. General	115
37. Camouflage Materials	115
a. Prepared Camouflage Materials	115
b. Improvised Camouflage Materials	116
38. Utilization of Camouflage	117
a. Individual Camouflage	117
b. Means of Identification	118
(1) *Brassards*	118
(2) *Manner of wearing belt*	118

VIII. CAMOUFLAGE, CONCEALMENT, AND IDENTIFICATION—Continued.

38. UTILIZATION OF CAMOUFLAGE—Continued.

	Page
b. Means of Identification—Continued.	
(3) *Ground flags and signals*	118
(4) *Passwords and blinker signals*	119
c. Camouflage of Field Positions	120
d. Camouflage of Trails	123
e. Dummy Installations	126

IX. PROTECTION AGAINST COLD, SNOW, AND THAW — 127

39. GENERAL	127
40. CLOTHING AND EQUIPMENT	128
a. Regulations for Fitting Winter Clothes	128
b. Emergency Precautions against Cold	131
c. Care of Clothing and Equipment	133
(1) *On the march and in combat*	133
(2) *Procedure during rest in permanent billets*	134
(3) *Care of footgear during mud and thaw period*	134

X. RATIONS IN WINTER — 137

41. GENERAL	137
42. FIELD RATIONS IN EXTREME WEATHER	138
43. EMERGENCY RATIONS	138
a. Frozen Meats	139
b. Raw Fish	139
c. Food from the Woods	139
d. Sawdust Flour	140
e. Baking Bread in Mess Kit	140
44. EFFECT OF COLD WEATHER ON FOOD	141
45. TRANSPORTATION AND STORAGE OF FOOD	141
46. FREEZING AND STORAGE OF POTATOES	142

XI. WINTER HEALTH MEASURES — 144

47. HYGIENE IN BILLETS	144
a. Hygiene	144
(1) *Cleanliness and rest*	144
(2) *Prevention of disease*	144
b. *Sauna* (Finnish steam bath)	146

XII. EVACUATION OF WOUNDED ... 149

- 48. General ... 149
- 49. Means of Evacuating Wounded ... 150
    - a. General ... 150
    - b. Hand Sleds and Improvised Means ... 151
- 50. Equipment of Vehicles for Wounded ... 153

XIII. CARE AND USE OF WEAPONS AND EQUIPMENT ... 154

- 51. General ... 154
- 52. Lubricants ... 155
- 53. Recoil Liquids ... 156
- 54. Care of Weapons ... 157
    - a. Rifles and Carbines ... 157
    - b. Semiautomatic Rifles ... 157
    - c. Pistols ... 157
    - d. Submachine Guns ... 158
    - e. Machine-Gun Equipment ... 159
    - f. Machine Gun (*M.G. 34*) ... 159
    - g. Antitank Rifles ... 160
    - h. Tank Guns ... 160
    - i. Antiaircraft Guns (*2-cm Flak 30 and 38*) ... 161
    - j. Artillery ... 161
    - k. Chemical Mortars and Heavy Projectors ... 162
        - (1) *105-mm chemical mortars 35 and 40* ... 162
        - (2) *Heavy projectors 40 (wooden model) and 41 (metal model)* ... 163
- 55. Firing of Infantry Weapons ... 164
    - a. General ... 164
    - b. Rifle ... 164
    - c. Light Machine Gun ... 165
    - d. Heavy Machine Gun ... 165
    - e. 50-mm Light Mortar 36 (*5-cm l.Gr.W. 36*) ... 166
    - f. 81-mm Heavy Mortar 34 (*8-cm s.Gr.W. 34*) ... 167
    - g. Infantry Howitzer ... 167
    - h. Antitank Weapons ... 167
- 56. Storage and Handling of Munitions in Winter ... 168
    - a. Storage ... 168
    - b. Ammunition in Combat Positions ... 170
    - c. Handling of Shell Cases ... 170
    - d. Ammunition of Chemical Troops ... 171
    - e. Special Experiences ... 171

XIII. CARE AND USE OF WEAPONS AND EQUIPMENT—Continued.

	Page
57. Artillery Fire in Winter	172
a. Effect of Weather	172
b. Artillery Reconnaissance	173
c. Firing of Chemical Mortars	173
58. Optical Instruments	174
59. Chemical-Warfare Equipment	175
a. Gas Masks	175
b. Horse Respirators	176
c. Protective Clothing	177
d. Gas Detectors	177
e. Decontamination Materials	177
f. Smoke-Producing Agents	178

XIV. SIGNAL COMMUNICATION — 179

	Page
60. Protection of Signal Equipment	179
a. Housing	179
b. Heating and Insulation	179
c. Lubrication	181
d. Grounding	181
e. Protection of Crew	181
61. Protection of Power Sources	182
a. Storage Batteries	182
b. Dry Batteries	183
c. Converters, Vibrators, and Generators	183
d. Power Units	184
e. Network Markings and Safeguards	184
f. Protecting Lines against Frost, Ice, and Snow	184
g. Laying of Cables	185
62. Telephone, Radio, and Miscellaneous Equipment	187
a. Telephone	187
b. Radio Equipment and Sound Locators	188
(1) *Transmitters, receivers, and cipher equipment*	188
(2) *Aerials and accessories*	188
c. Teletype Equipment	189
d. Blinker and Heliograph Equipment	190
e. Pyrotechnic Equipment	190
f. Supply of Equipment	190

		Page
XV. SKIS, SNOWSHOES, AND SNOW VEHICLES		192
63. General		192
64. Skis, Accessories, and Snowshoes		193
	a. Skis	193
	b. Ski Shoes	193
	c. Army Flat-Terrain Ski Binding	194
	d. Overboot	196
	e. Ski Kit	197
	f. Snowshoes	197
65. Hand Sleds		197
	a. General	197
	b. Akjas	198
	c. Construction of Light Akja	200
	d. Construction of Hand Sled	200
66. Horse-Drawn Sleds		203
	a. General	203
	b. Army Sleds	205
	c. Loading Army Sleds	209
	d. Toboggan Type of Sled	210
	e. Runners and Sliding Troughs	210
	(1) *Runners*	210
	(2) *Sliding troughs*	212
	f. Drags	213
	g. Harnessing	213
67. Pack Harness		213

ILLUSTRATIONS

Figure	Page
1. Sleds cutting trails and roads in an assembly area	8
2. Prepared trails in a defensive position	10
3. Circular trail for the security of a winter position	11
4. Shadow-casting as an aid in following a weak trail	23
5. Example of a march table	26
6. Snow-man type of road marker	28
7. Functions of the trail detail	32
8. Organization and disposition of a road-making detachment	33
9. Sequence of snow plows for clearing roads	34
10. Improvised snow plow	35
11. Improvised snow roller	36
12. St. Andrew's cross used to mark by-passes	39

CONTENTS

Figure	Page
13. Snowdrift factors affecting roads	42, 43
14. Types of snow fences	44
15. Ice-measuring stick	46
16. Load capacity of ice surfaces	48
17. Ice-crossing frame for guns and heavy vehicles	49
18. Ice reinforced with layers of twigs and straw	50
19. Ice bridge for crossing open channels in partially frozen bodies of water	51
20. Making a snow hole without tools	61
21. Types of snow holes	62
22. Cave in snowdrift	63
23. Snow pit for several men	63
24. Snow pit in deep snow	64
25. Snow pit in shallow snow	65
26. Snow house with walls of ice blocks	66
27. Cutting snow blocks	68
28. Pattern formed in cutting snow blocks	69
29. Part of the first tier of the igloo	70
30. Cross section of the igloo, with snow cover, showing lines radiating to the center	71
31. Installing support blocks	72
32. Tunnel entrance and anteroom of the igloo	74
33. Measurements of wooden forms for making snow blocks	76
34. Plywood shelter for 20 men	77
35. The 16-man tent	79
36. Layout of the 16-man tent	80
37. Method of tubing a stove chimney underground	81
38. Circular tent, Finnish type	82
39. Shelter built around a fir tree	83
40. Circular hut made of branches	84
41. Earth hut for 6 men	85
42. Foliage shelter for 10 men	86
43. Hut erected against a hillside	87
44. Shelters for horses	88
45. Tank shelter built against a slope	89
46. Heated shelter for motor vehicles	90
47. Sandbag position	96
48. Log position in snow	96
49. Cross section of covered snow trench	97
50. Cross section of vaulted dugout	98
51. Shelter made of "ice-concrete"	100

CONTENTS   XIX

Figure	Page
52. Antitank obstacle of packed snow	100
53. Barbed-wire fence pickets in snow	101
54. Tripod trestle for barbed-wire fence	102
55. Barbed-wire roll for use in snow	103
56. Antitank trap in frozen body of water	104
57. Long-burning fir-log fire	106
58. Various types of fires, showing (1) pit fire; (2) hunter's fire; (3) star-shaped fire; (4) "invisible fire"	107
59. Fireplace for emplacements and caves	108
60. Insulated trench stove	108
61. Bricked-in stove	109
62. Brick stove with two ovens	110
63. Cross section of two-layer charcoal pile	112
64. Camouflaging trenches with willow frames	120
65. Concealment of installations in a trench system	121
66. Antitank ditch camouflaged to resemble an ordinary trench	121
67. Tank concealed under snow-covered canvas	122
68. Flat-top camouflage of tank in gully	123
69. Supplies concealed under trees and snow	125
70. Method of wrapping foot cloths	130
71. Improvised protector for shoes and boots	132
72. Prefabricated rations hut installed underground for potato storage	142
73. *Sauna* (Finnish steam bath) in log cabin	147
74. Some methods of evacuating the wounded, showing (1) skier dragging an akja, or boat sled; (2) skier dragging a wounded man from a field of fire; (3) akja used for evacuation under fire; (4) method of evacuation in difficult terrain	152
75. Snow plates for machine-gun mounts	166
76. Padded and heated box for a portable radio	180
77. Flat-terrain ski binding and the overboot	195
78. Types of akjas: (1) weapons akja; (2) boat akja; (3) light akja	199
79. Construction of a light akja	199
80. Construction of a hand sled	201
81. Hauling accessories for the hand sled	202
82. Siberian type of sled	203
83. Table of specifications for issued sleds	204
84. Army sled No. 1, with side walls in place	205
85. Army sled No. 3, showing (1) the sled with the body in place; (2) an antitank gun mounted on the sled; (3) a light field kitchen loaded on the sled	206
86. Improvised horse-drawn toboggan type of sled	207

Figure	Page
87. Antitank gun mounted on ski runners	208
88. 105-mm howitzer mounted on sled runners	209
89. Sliding trough for hauling heavy loads	211
90. Drag made of naturally curved tree branches	212
91. Improvised wooden pack saddle	214
92. Pack saddle consisting of a back pad and basket	215

Section I. WINTER, MUD, AND THAW

1. INFLUENCE OF WINTER

The Russian winter brings long-lasting, severe cold (−40 to −58 degrees F.) punctuated by short periods of thaw, snowfalls, storms, and fogs. During the cold months daylight often amounts to but a few hours a day.

In winter, variations in temperature and precipitations exert great influence on the nature of terrain and the mobility of troops. During the early part of winter, severe frosts, before snow begins to fall, make it possible to cross otherwise impassable terrain. Rivers and lakes freeze and may be crossed by vehicles, but swamps which are under a blanket of snow usually have only a thin and weak ice surface. The effect of snow and freezing temperatures varies with local conditions, but generally snow can immobilize wheeled and tracked vehicles of all kinds except on first-class roads.

Even a light snowfall, piled into snowdrifts by the wind, may lead to serious traffic difficulties. Drifts may begin to form early in winter and they may pile very high, especially on the great steppes. Visibility is usually good in clear, frosty weather, and noises carry to great distances. An overcast sky makes observation difficult. Exact terrain appreciation and target designation may become impossible, because elevations and depressions show up only slightly and serious errors occur in estimating distances.

2. DURATION AND NATURE OF SNOW

In European Russia, snow blankets the terrain for about 4 months in the south (the Ukraine and the lower Volga); 4 to 6 months in the central region (Moscow area); and 6 to 7 months in the north (Archangel). The first frosts appear at the beginning of October. The depth of the snow varies with the terrain. The wind sweeps the snow away from open and flat surfaces and heaps it up in front of obstacles and in hollows. In woods it is distributed evenly in depth. An average of 4 to 16 inches may be expected in southern Russia; in the central region and in northern Russia, 20 to 39 inches. Local snowdrifts 6 feet 6 inches to 9 feet 10 inches high are not rare.

The soldier who is unaccustomed to winter conditions, particularly the conditions of winter warfare in Russia, ought to know not only the disadvantages of snow, but also the advantages which it affords and which he may exploit. Snow, when properly employed, provides shelter against cold and wind, yet it is porous enough to permit ventilation in snow shelters. When it is packed sufficiently thick (3 meters, or 9 feet 10 inches), snow affords protection against enemy fire. It is also good camouflage.

In slightly cold weather falling snow consists of large crystals or flakes and forms a loose surface, but in severe cold it falls in fine grains. Wind packs snow hard. A hard crust on deep, soft snow assures mobility; but if the crust is not strong, it becomes a disadvantage. Breaking through such a crust is strenuous for foot soldiers and often dangerous for skiers. Horses may injure their hoofs and dogs their paws. The carrying capacity of snow crusts varies with the temperatures at different times of the day; on sunny days it is likely to weaken considerably.

3. SEASONS OF MUD AND THAW

Heavy autumn rains or snowfalls and the melting snow and floods of the spring thaw also make roads virtually impassable. The first period of mud begins about the middle of October and is frequently terminated by biting frost (in the winter of 1941–42 by a temperature of –31 degrees F.) or by snowfalls. The spring thaw period, beginning in March in southern Russia and progressing northward, brings another spell of mud. In some parts of the country the thaw causes gigantic floods. Temperature, wind, and ground consistency as well as rain and snow are factors which determine the extent to which roads vanish. Light soil, especially sand, permits water to drain off, but the dark humus of the Ukraine turns into well-nigh untraversable, sticky mud.

Wheeled and tracked vehicles are unable to use unpaved roads and highways while the ground is mired. Paved roads which cross depressions, as well as combat positions with deep foundations, may be flooded temporarily. All bridges which are not sufficiently anchored may be damaged or destroyed by floods and floating ice. Airplanes may be limited to airdromes with concrete runways.

It is just as important to maintain the mobility of troops during thaws as it is while snow is on the ground. Positions must be improved and made mud-proof, and they must be stocked to make them independent of supply lines for extended periods (3 to 4 weeks). Unpaved roads must not be used until they have thoroughly dried out. The possible gain in traveling time is out of proportion to the long time and considerable labor that is necessary to recondition such roads. Special roads must be constructed for use during the muddy period, and measures must be taken to make the normal road net serviceable as soon as possible.

Wheeled motor vehicles should be prohibited on muddy roads, and tracked vehicles should be employed only in emergencies. Heavy wheeled vehicles or sleds should be replaced by light carts, high two-wheeled vehicles, boat sleds, or pack animals. If it is impracticable to secure bridges against floating ice and floods, they should be dismantled and supplanted by a ferry service.

Where necessary, units should move to positions free of mud, or construction material should be stocked for the improvement of existing positions. Drainage ditches and seepage shafts should be dug within them. Wounded men and unserviceable mounts must be evacuated promptly. Ammunition, rations, fodder, and heating and illuminating equipment must be stored in advance in dry places. The heavy winter clothing and footgear of the troops must be replaced by articles suitable for wet weather.

4. PREPARATION FOR WINTER WARFARE

Experience teaches us that the German soldier knows how to master the difficulties of the Russian winter, and that he is superior to the enemy even in winter. He is capable not only of defending himself against the Russian but also annihilating him in attack.

Prerequisites for this superiority are as follows: psychological preparation for the hardships of winter warfare, appropriate training and adaptation, familiarity with winter combat methods, and proper equipment and employment of expedients.

In building up endurance against the rigors of the Russian winter, mental discipline is the determining factor.

Many cases of freezing are caused by a slackening of attention and by indifference. The danger of freezing is especially great when one is exhausted after great exertion or after a long period on guard. Then the soldier must summon all his will power in order to keep awake and alert. The code of comradeship demands that soldiers must assist each other in this effort and in stimulating the will to live. The most serious danger begins when confidence in one's own strength is extinguished.

The aim of training must be to convey to the soldier all the knowledge he will need for survival and combat in winter. His field training must condition him to endure extremes of cold, moisture, and snow. His training will include the following important subjects:

a. Protection of the soldier, horse, vehicle, weapons, and equipment against cold and snow.

b. Training—hardening and conditioning that will enable the soldier to live in the simplest types of bivouac structures and improvised shelters of his own construction instead of permanent shelters.

c. Mobility—training in skiing; conversion of wheeled vehicles into sleds (winter mobility of antitank guns is especially important); clearing existing roads or building winter roads, and making ice crossings; movements in winter terrain on foot, skis, and sleds, and in motor vehicles.

d. Construction of positions and obstacles in frozen ground and snow.

e. Firing and combat in severe cold and deep snow, combat on skis, scouting, patrolling, and camouflage.

There are no special "winter tactics." The hampering effect of deep snow, however, greatly influences the combat methods of normally organized and equipped troops. Ski troops and troops equipped with light sleds take over the missions assigned in temperate seasons to mobile troops (motorized, mounted, and bicycle troops). (The special characteristics of combat in winter are discussed in par. **5, "Winter Combat Methods,"** p. 7.)

The clothing and equipment intended for winter warfare must afford not only comfort but freedom of movement for combat, and especially for attack in severe cold, deep snow, and strong wind. If supplies issued to the unit are not sufficient, they must be augmented by improvisations and substitutes of all kinds. The ingenuity of the individual soldier and of the leader in contriving makeshifts keeps the unit efficient and reduces casualties.

The following are basic requirements for clothing, equipment, and weapons in winter:

a. Clothing should not be too warm, but it must be windproof. It should permit quick movements (jumping, creeping, shooting). Extra underwear for changing after sweating, and additional warm clothing (such as a slipover sweater), should be carried for wear during rest periods and bivouacs.

b. Camouflage suits should be supplied at least to patrols and sentries. If such suits are not available they must be improvised.

c. Footgear is especially important. Felt boots are best, but they must be kept dry. Keep the uppers of leather boots from freezing hard by wearing overboots[1] or cloth covers over them. In addition, paper and foot cloths (see par. **40b**) should be wrapped on the feet in addition to socks. Footgear must be roomy enough to permit moving the toes.

d. Bivouac equipment makes one independent of permanent shelters. Cloth tents of the Finnish type (see par. **24**) are the best, but in emergencies, shelter halves (which may also be used as ground sheets) will do. The equipment should also include plywood shelters, portable stoves, and individual cooking utensils so that the men can cook their own food.

e. Skis should be provided for ski troops, scouts, messengers, and signal and medical personnel of all ranks. These classes of personnel should also be provided with felt boots and overboots if possible, otherwise with laced shoes. Snowshoes may be used as expedients.

f. Sleds must be substituted for most wheeled vehicles. The sleds must be light, and of standard width, and horses should be harnessed one behind

---

[1] Canvas covers which fit over German leather boots (see par. **64d**, p. 196). Oversized pairs are often worn so that straw can be packed in for added warmth.—EDITOR.

the other (tandem). Field kitchens and heavy weapons must be loaded on sleds or runners (see pars. **65** and **66**).

g. Snow-clearing equipment is needed to facilitate movement, especially off the roads. Snow plows should be provided or improvised.

h. Weapons must be mobile, and therefore their weight and caliber must be limited. They must be in condition to fire in any weather. For close combat, many automatic weapons are needed, but it is better to have an abundance of ammunition rather than a large number of weapons with only a limited supply of ammunition.

i. Individual motor vehicles, tanks, and assault guns are often valuable aids in winter combat, and must be ready for operation in any kind of weather. Snow must be cleared to facilitate their movement.

j. Medical equipment must be provided in greater quantities than in other seasons. Provision must be made for adequate transportation of the wounded, even in front lines, and for protecting them against cold.

5. WINTER COMBAT METHODS

Troops must not be deprived of their freedom of action in winter, no matter how inclement the weather. They must try in every possible manner to attack the enemy, to damage his installations, and to destroy him. Mobility on the battlefield and the ability to deceive and outwit the enemy give even a numerically weaker force a feeling of superiority.

The ability to carry out a march in winter may be the basis for the successful outcome of a battle. If possible, the enemy must be surprised, and surprise is more likely if the troops avoid highways and roads and move across terrain which is considered impassable. Experience has shown that enemy resistance is weakest in terrain that he considers inaccessible, and that cross-country marches frequently permit envelopment of his position.

The enemy is particularly susceptible to attack on his flanks and rear. A frontal attack is very difficult in deep snow, even when it is executed on skis.

In winter the systematic preparation and disposition of forces for combat are even more important than in summer, and require more than twice the time. All heavy-weapon vehicles and tanks must be employed to cut roads (see fig. 1). Probable weather conditions must be taken into consideration in preparing for these activities. Continuous attacks are a proved method of winter combat. They deprive the enemy of breathing spells, throttle his supply lines, prevent him from making fires to warm himself, and force him to

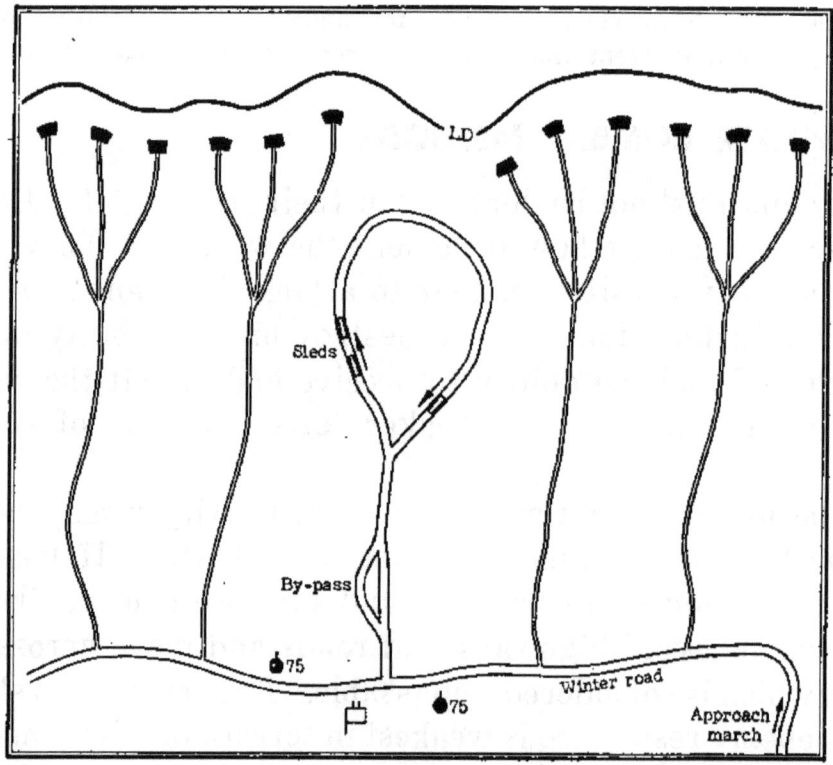

Figure 1.—Sleds cutting trails and roads in an assembly area. (Sequence of activities: (1) make trails and roads to positions at the line of departure (LD); (2) bring heavy weapons, including artillery, into position; (3) move up the infantry as far as possible on skis or on foot along the trails.)

make frequent counterthrusts. Thus the fighting strength of the enemy is sapped without appreciably weakening our own forces, and he will be incapable of employing his own numerical superiority.

For this purpose, even weak but mobile forces may be employed. They may be specially formed units, patrols, or raiding parties. It is their mission to attack the enemy on all sides and to harass him during the night and in misty weather, and in terrain in which observation is difficult, particularly in wooded areas.

As a breakthrough into enemy lines and close combat are very difficult and costly, especially in deep snow or in terrain which cannot be reconnoitered easily, it is advantageous to isolate enemy forces by cutting their external communications. The enemy then must attack in order to extricate himself, and this action compels him to move into deep snow from quarters which protect him from fire and cold.

Troops must frequently dig in rapidly, even in deep snow and hard ground, after they have advanced their attack to points within range for machine-gun and rifle fire. Thus they will have cover against fire and protection against cold and will be able to install themselves adequately for defensive action against counterthrusts. If they lie around unprotected in open terrain for long periods, they will suffer heavy casualties from enemy fire and the cold weather.

Organizing for defense in frozen ground or deep snow requires much time and labor in order to construct obstacles and prepare for the commitment of reserves along tracks leading into the probable operation areas (see fig. 2). Experience has proved that the main line of resistance must be held as an uninterrupted line, particularly at night and in hazy weather, in order to prevent infiltration by the Russians. It is necessary, however, to establish several strongpoints. Active reconnaissance and aggressive conduct of operations serve as protection against surprises. The enemy who has broken through is repulsed by counterattack before he can gain a foothold. The Russian is very fast at digging into the snow.

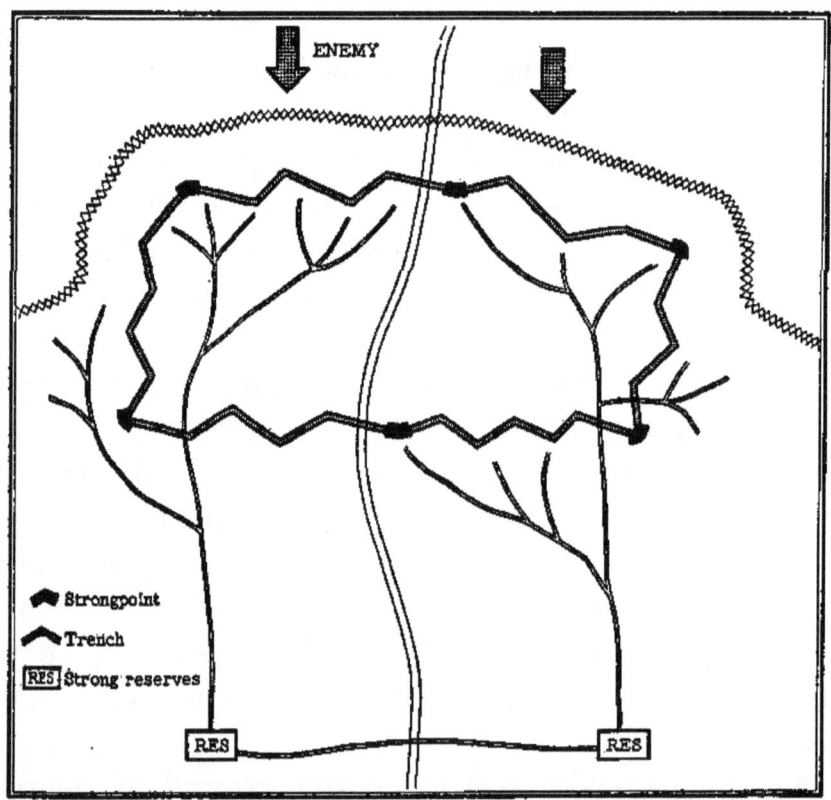

Figure 2.—Prepared trails in a defensive position. (The strongpoints are connected by communication trenches; strong reserves are held back for a thoroughly rehearsed counterattack on the prepared trails.)

Valleys and ravines, which the Russians favor as approaches, must be blocked with obstacles and must be secured by adequate forces. Steep slopes must be utilized as tank obstacles. Terrain which is impassable during the summer months, swampland, and bodies of water lose their effectiveness as obstacles in winter. This point must be especially considered in laying out defensive positions at the beginning of winter.

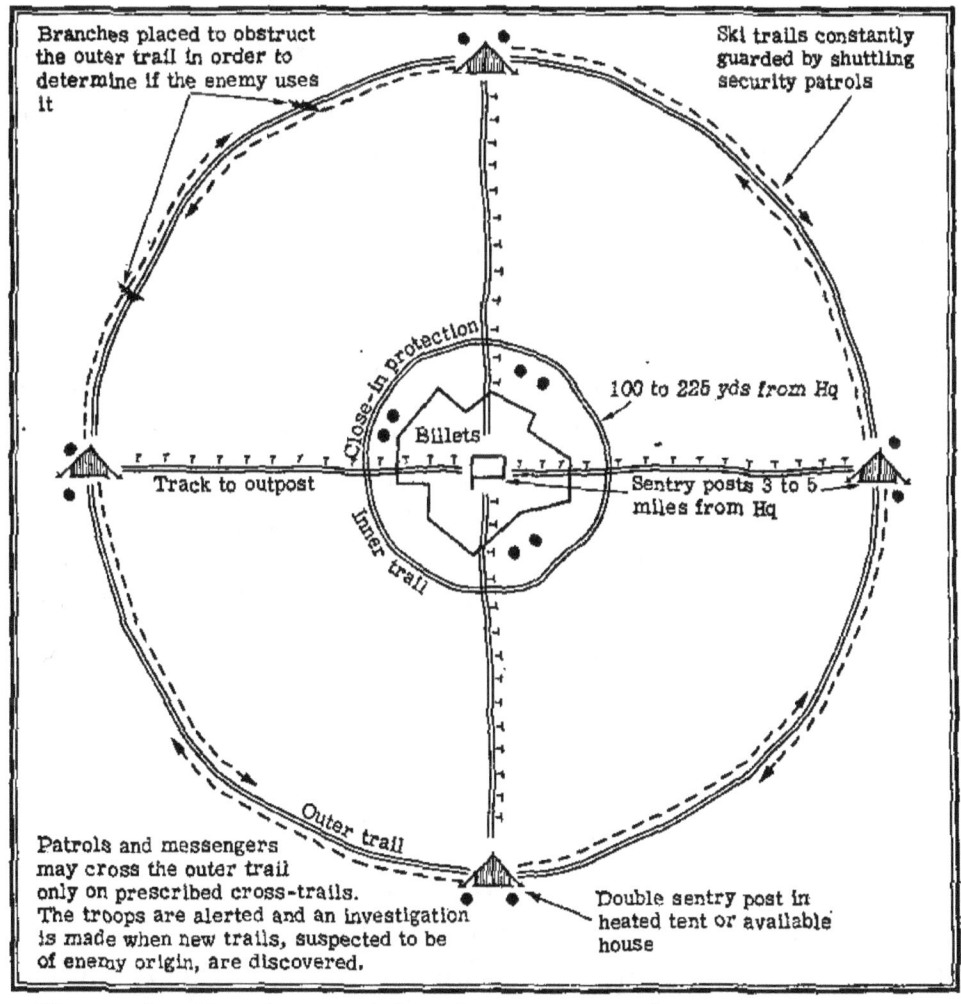

Figure 3.—Circular trail for the security of a winter position.

Wide fronts and troops in rest camps are protected by strongpoints or stationary patrols, as well as by a great number of light mobile patrols (if possible, on skis). Around billets and bivouacs a circular trail is the most effective security measure (fig. 3).

6. MORALE

a. General

The coming winter will again severely tax the spiritual stamina of the soldier. All suitable means commensurate with the situation and combat conditions will be employed to bolster his inner resilience. The example of the soldier, especially the officer who has proved himself in all situations, is a determining factor in maintaining the morale of the troops. Eagerness for action and good discipline must be maintained, especially behind the lines. Prerequisites in assuring morale are consideration for the welfare of troops, tolerable shelter, and adequate provisions. Winter equipment, lighting facilities, and fuel must be procured in advance or substitutes provided. Important! Stimulate the initiative of troops. Shows should be staged and soldiers encouraged to participate in them. Intelligent organization of spare time is the best means of preventing useless brooding, rumor-mongering, and disciplinary offenses.

The welfare of troops in the lines has priority. Morale-building supplies for the front must actually reach the front lines. There must be no pigeonholing in depots, railroad stations, headquarters, or orderly rooms. Checks against delay must be made continually. Commanders and headquarters must be in constant communication with field offices of the High Command of the Armed Forces.

b. Recreational Aids

(1) *Reading material.*—Do not leave newspapers lying around. Newspapers, bulletins, and magazines must reach the front fast. There the soldier is waiting for recent news. Papers of occupied territories should be sent forward because they do not have to be transported far. Front papers of field armies also serve the purpose of inculcating combat doctrine in troops.

Exchange of library kits between battalions and regiments should be encouraged. Field library kits of the Army Book Service (*Heeresbücherei*) are exclusively for frontline troops. Rear echelons and higher headquarters are normally equipped with Rosenberg libraries.

"Information for Troops" (*Mitteilungen für die Truppe*) continues to be distributed through the Army Postal Service (*Feldpost*) to divisions, two copies per unit. Report immediately any failure to receive copies. This also applies to "Information for the Officer Corps" (*Mitteilungen für das Offizierkorps*).

(2) *Lectures.*—Important lectures by speakers from the High Command of the Armed Forces are possible only under quiet conditions and after long preparation. Lectures by members of units on general cultural subjects (history, geography, travel, economics, engineering, fine arts) have been successful even in small units. The units themselves have good men for this purpose!

(3) *Radio.*—The Army radio receiving set has worked even in winter on the Eastern Front. The further issue of

sets and spare parts, on the basis of current production, is confined to front-line troops and is carried out only through higher signal officers of signal regiments. Production and distribution of additional sets and spare parts is being stressed. Rear installations and welfare organizations are equipped with commercial receivers.

(4) *Movies.*—Theaters are improvised behind the front lines on the basis of experience. The increase of available machines, especially of the projector unit with direct-current generator for localities without power supply, is desirable. Pictures shown are coordinated by the division G-2 (*Ic der Division*).

(5) *Employment of "Strength through Joy" groups.*—On the Eastern Front only tours by small acting troupes are ordinarily possible. Transportation and shelter must be considered. When constructing new motion-picture theaters, provide stage facilities for acting troupes. The stages will also be used for official business (lectures, instruction, briefing, schools, etc.).

It is important to employ "Strength through Joy" groups (*KdF.-Gruppen*) according to plan. Provide them with transportation facilities, cooperate with them, pay attention to their welfare, and provide for their security in guerrilla territory.

(6) *Competitions.*—Competitions are particularly valuable in all respects. New facilities have been provided for the winter of 1942–43. Important activities in this field are inventions and improvements of arms and equipments.

(7) *Improvement of quarters.*—The troops should be urged to improve their quarters by their own handiwork. Arts and crafts have a place in the construction of shelters. In view of the bare-minimum shelter conditions in the east,

this is particularly important. Encourage by competitions the improvement of quarters, moving-picture halls, theaters, kitchens, storerooms, stables, and gardens.

(8) *Organization of spare time.*—In organizing spare time, schools for choir leaders are particularly valuable. Train choir leaders for the units of divisions and regiments. Also encourage hobbies, crafts, and amateur theatrical performances by and for the troops. Occupational aid through correspondence courses and civilian work groups is also successful. This kind of instruction has practical value for the future of the soldier.

(9) *Service centers.*—Service centers should be especially promoted. Unattractive living conditions and the lack of "places to go" and restaurants on the Eastern Front must be remembered. The establishment of numerous service centers is necessary. At larger service centers a senior hostess and several junior hostesses of the German Red Cross (*DRK*) must be assigned.

(10) *Front convalescent camps.*—These are successful without exception. Convalescent camps behind front lines meet an urgent need of troops. In large areas and broad front sectors the establishment of small convalescent camps for regiments has been successful.

Section II. MARCHES AND ORIENTATION

7. MARCHES

a. Reconnaissance

For every winter march, early and thorough reconnaissance is required. Road reconnaissance should furnish the answers to the following questions:

(1) What is the depth and type of snow (wet, crusted, etc.)?

(2) How is the subsoil of the roadbed?

(3) How wide is the available road? Is it rutted? What is the condition of its shoulders? Is the construction of a new traffic lane more practical?

(4) Where are the gradients, curves, and narrow sections?

(5) Where is there danger of avalanches and of falling rocks?

(6) What sections are impassable owing to ice and snowdrifts? How can they be rendered passable? (Estimate the manpower, materials, and time required.)

(7) Is there material in the vicinity for strewing on icy roads to prevent skidding?

(8) What possibilities are there for detouring around obstacles and bad sections of road?

(9) Which sections permit two-way traffic? Where can by-passes be constructed?

(10) What is the carrying capacity of bridges (consider that they may have been weakened by drifting pack ice), and of the frozen surface of bodies of water?

(11) Are the roads easily found at night and in fog? Are markers necessary?

(12) Where are wind-protected resting places and facilities for shelter?

(13) Where are the watering points?

b. Preparation for Marches

Endurance in marching may be maintained and increased by intensive preparations. The clothing and equipment of each man must be examined so that ill effects from the cold during the marches may be avoided. Shaving in the morning must be prohibited in severe cold weather. Ointments for the prevention of frostbite must be issued. March rations must be ready for consumption, wrapped in paper and carried close to the body or in the trouser pockets. Warm rations in adequate quantities must be issued before marches. Warm drinks may be taken along for distribution en route. On marches through sparsely wooded terrain, it may become necessary to take along fuel for bivouac fires.

Weapons and weapon parts which are not to be used immediately (especially rifle bolts) must be protected with covers against snow and moisture.

Winter equipment of all vehicles must be examined. Towropes for hauling vehicles which bog down, as well as planks and material to provide traction on icy roads, must be kept within easy reach. A sufficient number of assistant drivers or escorts must be assigned to vehicles proceeding singly on missions. In deep snow it is advisable to load on sleds or other vehicles single motorcycles which are not equipped with snow runners.

Calks intended to prevent horses from slipping must be examined. Spare calks and calk wrenches must be kept in readiness.

All measures for clearing roads must be initiated well in advance so that advance detachments can maintain their distance ahead of the main body. Men assigned to haul vehicles, as well as special towing details with traction machinery or horses, must be incorporated in the march column or held in readiness at places where traction is difficult. (For instruction in making trails and clearing roads, see pars. **10** and **11**.) Reconnoitered roads must be marked for the troops which are to use them (for directions, see par. **9**). To regulate passing and two-way traffic, by-passes must be prepared.

c. March Discipline

Troops who are to be organized into a march column should be kept in motion during severe cold. Standing around, especially in a biting wind, must be avoided. Harnessing must be done at the last possible moment. On the other hand, the time allowed for the preparation of motor vehicles must be ample. Motors must be warmed up before the march is started.

At the beginning of the march the pace must be slow. In severe cold and strong wind it is advisable to cover long distances at a slow pace, interrupted only by short rest stops. It is recommended that short distances be covered entirely without halts. Existing trails must be utilized; if need be, even relatively large formations must be marched in file or in column of twos. In deep snow, severe cold, and strong wind, the front ranks or those marching against the wind must be relieved frequently. Horsemen usually must dismount and proceed on foot.

Regulations on wearing the uniform, or special measures for protection against cold, must be revised and adapted to fit local conditions. Rifles are carried slung so that the men may warm their hands in their pockets. The most effective measure against freezing is mutual observation for first signs of frostbite. Men riding in automobiles will be allowed approximately one brief stop every hour for the purpose of alighting and warming themselves. Drivers of open cars must be relieved frequently.

In case of interruptions, the march column must halt at wide intervals. Special pushing details from all halted vehicles must be sent forward to deal with cases of difficult traction, if hauling details have not already been assigned along the road. Special detachments equipped with vehicles must be assigned to the rear of the column to pick up exhausted men and horses, and motor vehicles that break down.

d. Halts and Rest Periods

Short halts of 5 to 10 minutes are the most effective. They afford the men necessary rest without exposing them too long to the cold. Squads must be sent ahead to reconnoiter and prepare rest areas. Their tasks are essentially the following:

(1) Arrangement of facilities for arrival and departure.
(2) Preparations for sheltering men, horses, vehicles, weapons, equipment, and skis.
(3) Cleaning and warming existing shelter facilities.
(4) Preparation of hot drinks if field kitchens are not available.
(5) Arrangements for medical-treatment areas and for repair of automobiles, skis, and other equipment.

Areas protected from the wind are the most suitable for resting places. Protection against the wind may be increased rapidly by constructing windbreaks made of branches or snow. Whether fires may be started for warming the men depends upon the situation. For extended rest periods, simple tents must be pitched or snow caves dug.

Guards must be detailed to wake up all the men, individually, at specified intervals to prevent them from freezing. (For details of tent pitching and the construction of snow houses, see sec. **V**, "Winter Bivouacs and Shelter," p. 57.)

Troops need warmer clothing while resting than while marching. Overcoats must be put on. Men should also drape themselves with shelter halves or blankets. During longer rest periods the changing of sweaty underwear must be enforced by specific orders and must be supervised. If possible, warm rations and, above all, hot beverages must be issued. Alcoholic drinks are prohibited.

Horses must be sheltered from the wind and placed close together for warmth. They must be warmly covered, their blankets strapped to their bodies, and they should be bedded down on fir boughs for protracted rests. Precautions must be taken when the horses are watered. The water should be warmed, or hay should be placed in it to prevent the horses from drinking too fast.

The proper temperature of motors and the water in their cooling systems must be maintained by all means. If the rest is a long one, motors must be started several times to keep them warm.

8. ORIENTATION IN SNOW-COVERED TERRAIN

a. General

The appearance of a landscape is changed considerably when it is under a cover of snow. In the east the broad plains appear even more monotonous in winter than in summer. Outstanding orientation points often are completely lacking. The nature of the terrain is also changed by snow and cold. New roads frequently come into existence, while others which are passable in summer become useless or vanish under snowdrifts. Road designations on maps are therefore not dependable reference points in snow-covered terrain. On the other hand, ridges, gorges, woods, inhabited localities, structures, and telephone lines become more prominent.

Orientation in snow-covered terrain is made more difficult by unusual climatic conditions. Extreme cold, for example, affects the accuracy of the lensatic compass. Fog and snowstorms may make visibility negligible, even over short distances, hence it is all the more important that the soldier maintain his energy and attentiveness in order to be able to exploit all means of orientation. Experience and training play a determining role. Theoretical instruction may supplement field training, but will never replace it.

The use of existing trails must be undertaken with great care because they often lead in the wrong direction. They may have been made by the enemy for purposes of deception and may lead into an ambush. Snowstorms and snowdrifts quickly obliterate trails. On skis, bearings are very easily lost at the start of a march. Therefore, in terrain where observation is difficult, and in hazy weather, only one man should start while the others observe his route.

b. Fundamentals of Orientation

A fundamental principle for determining direction and location is the knowledge of one's own position. It is important to check one's location repeatedly, even while marching. In fog or snowstorm, when the danger of losing one's direction is greatest, this may become necessary every 100 meters (328 feet). A complete picture of the vicinity should be obtained, after one's own position has been fixed, by comparing the terrain with the map. The orientation of the map is accomplished by means of a lensatic type of compass, the stars, or conspicuous terrain features. Methods of determining cardinal directions, the time of day, and time factors for the distance to be covered are also necessary for orientation in the field.

In place of a map, a road sketch may be employed as an auxiliary means of orientation. It should contain data on cardinal directions, distances, azimuths, and special terrain features. Elevations and natural obstacles must be indicated. The drawing of road sketches and their use on marches must be thoroughly practiced.

The most important means of orientation is the lensatic compass. Every unit marching independently and every reconnaissance squad must, if possible, have several compasses of this type.

c. Methods of Orientation

The method selected for getting oriented depends on visibility. By day, of course, the most favorable conditions usually prevail. The cardinal directions may be determined by the position of the sun. It indicates due east at 0600, due south at 1200, and due west at 1800 (valid for the armies of the Eastern Front).

If the sun is not visible, an idea of the cardinal directions may be deduced from the fact that in snow-covered terrain the lee side of trees, poles, and sheds is grown over with moss and lichen. In European countries the weather side usually is toward the west, but in Russia it may also be in other directions. (Do not rely entirely on this phenomenon, but orient yourself as soon as possible by means of a compass.) In winter there generally is more snow on the weather side. However, if the weather side does not indicate a cardinal point of the compass beyond doubt, it nevertheless is useful for reference in relationship to the direction of march. Similarly the parallel formation of snowdrifts on great plains, and of the courses of ridges and streams, is also useful. In taking bearings, note the angle which the line of march makes with the general trend of these terrain features. Then, during the march, maintain direction by keeping the features always in the same relative position.

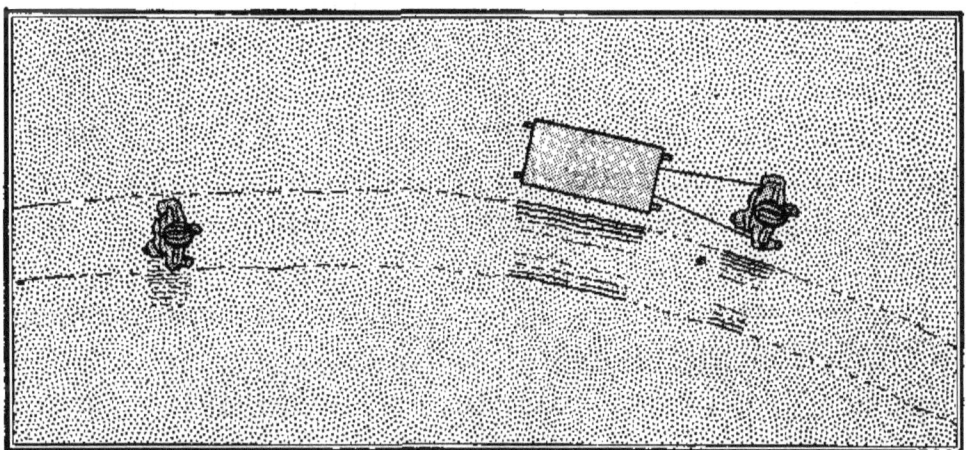

Figure 4.—Shadow-casting as an aid in following a weak trail.

Direction may also be determined by one's own shadow, but the changing position of the sun must be taken into consideration. In diffused light, shadows are weak and it is advisable to observe them closely. In such light a poorly defined snow trail will be difficult to follow but it can be made easier by casting a shadow on it constantly. One man, pulling a small sled, walks on the edge of the trail, on the side from which shadows fall. His shadow, weak though it may be, will bring out in relief the slight depression in the snow on the trail. It is necessary for another man to walk on the trail about 6 feet behind the shadow. This man will keep watching for the outline of the track and will give directions which will keep the shadow of the first man constantly on it (see fig. 4).

A cloudy sky, during periods of clear visibility, reflects the color of the terrain over considerable distances. The clouds over snow-covered ground are bright; over a pine forest or open water they are dark.

By night in clear weather, cardinal and march directions are fixed by the North Star and by a knowledge of the position of the moon and such a prominent constellation as Orion.

At night, also, ground lights are perceptible over considerable distances and may be useful for orientation (automobile headlights, burning villages, muzzle flashes, flashlights, etc.).

Fog reduces visibility. Therefore, the other senses must be applied all the more intensely, especially the sense of hearing. Sound travels very far over snow-covered terrain, frozen ground, and vast lonely areas. For better hearing, it is advisable to halt frequently and listen, to wear the field cap instead of the steel helmet, and (if the temperature permits) to uncover the ears temporarily. The terrain must be studied carefully when relying on sound for orientation in order to determine whether the sound is heard directly or is an echo from the edge of a forest, slope, or wall of a house.

The sense of smell serves as an additional aid in case of fog. The wind disperses odors over large areas. Thus, for example, newly cut timber, a factory, or a stable may be identified by their characteristic odors at a considerable distance. A dog's sense of smell may be successfully used (to stay on trails and to detect habitations and fires). A snowstorm almost completely eliminates perception by smell. The lensatic type of compass, therefore, must always be used in fogs and snowstorms. The wind sometimes furnishes assistance. When there is a steady wind, its pressure on the face can be useful in following a prescribed direction.

d. Controlling March Direction

Experience proves that where observation is difficult (for instance, in extensive wooded areas), it is necessary to employ special measures for controlling the direction of march. The leader of the unit or patrol is responsible for orientation. Under difficult conditions he may require the help of several men. One man will make checks with a lensatic compass, another will use a map and watch, and two men will count paces. If additional men are detailed for marking the route, they may be organized to form a direction squad (Finnish method) under a special leader.

The length and time factors of the distance covered must be carefully checked. Guessing always results in errors. Exact knowledge of the length of one's own pace is necessary. At night and during snowstorms, measurements taken with a string or a length of old telephone wire are more accurate. The distance covered, the time required, azimuths, and similar data are best recorded on a road sketch, or in a march table as shown in figure 5. This procedure must be carefully practiced by patrols and raiding parties.

In case orientation is impossible as a result of an encounter with the enemy, it must be determined later by all available means. If this proves impossible because of

Route of march[1]	Azimuth (mils)	Meters (according to map)	Estimated paces	Actual distance in paces[2]	Time of departure	Estimated march time	Estimated time of arrival	Actual time of arrival	Remarks
1. Village A to Village B.	4,800	1,540	1,410	X	0815	46 min.	0900	X	X
2. Village B to hill, 2.2 km (1.4 miles) NE.	5,600	2,200	2,008	X	X	1 hr, 12 min	X	X	X
3. Hill 2.2 km NE of Village B, to Village C.		1,460	1,322	X	X	42 min	X	X	X
		5,200	4,750	X	X	2 hr, 40 min +16 min[3]	1200		
						2 hr, 56 min			

[1] Village A to Village C.
[2] Columns marked with "X" are to be filled in en route.
[3] Ten percent must be added to the time calculated from the map.

Figure 5.—Example of a march table.

nightfall, it may, in particularly uncertain situations, be necessary to stop marching and await daybreak. If the night must be spent alongside the road, the point last marked at nightfall must be noted so that it may be located with certainty in the morning. During a heavy fog, it may be avisable to wait on a known road until it lifts rather than to proceed into unknown terrain. An effort should be made, so far as the situation and terrain permit, to maintain the straightest possible direction. After detouring around obstacles, the original direction must be resumed.

e. Conduct When Lost

When one is lost, calm and composure are necessary above all. Hasty and ill-considered searches generally lead to no result and increase the possibility of accidents and exhaustion. It is therefore best to think over the situation calmly, to retrace mentally the route already covered, and to recall occurrences during the march. Men already exhausted must be left behind under guard in a protected spot while the leader and selected men search for the right way. Anyone who is not participating in the search is not permitted to leave his place.

If the way back cannot be found, it must be decided whether a continuation of the march will serve any purpose—whether, within a reasonable distance, it will lead to identifiable terrain such as roads, railroads, or a river valley, which will further aid orientation. If, however, even such an effort proves futile, it is advisable to await a change of weather which will make orientation possible. Cover against the wind must then be sought, and steps taken to ensure security and protection against freezing.

Section III. ROADS

9. ROAD MARKING

In winter, snowfalls and snowdrifts frequently make roads unrecognizable. Therefore, careful road marking is essential. If possible, through roads must be uniformly marked prior to the first snowfall. Road designations must be known to troops who will use the routes. The removal of markers and the use of them as firewood is sabotage. Permanent routes should be designated by durable markers. In open country, poles, about 8 feet high, with direction markers, "snow men" (*Schneemänner*), wisps of straw, brushwood, cairns, and flags serve the purpose best. Snow markers may be rendered even more visible by staining them (for instance, with urine or coffee grounds; yellow is the most conspicuous color).

In areas where heavy snowfalls, fog, and other conditions make it difficult to recognize terrain features, numer-

Figure 6.—Snow-man type of road marker.

ous road markers are necessary. Orientation is facilitated if the markers are numbered in the direction of march, and if they are placed at equal distances from each other. "Snow men" have proved to be especially effective. They are constructed of small blocks of snow, 39 to 47 inches tall, with an opening at a height of about 31 inches in the direction of march. In the opening is placed a very thin pane of ice, through which refracted rays of light can be seen over relatively great distances even when visibility is poor (see fig. 6).

Road markers must be erected at least 3 feet off the trail in order to avoid damage to them by traffic. In wooded terrain, tree trunks are marked with placards or paint; branches are bent; boards, paper, or cloth remnants are fastened to trees. If complete road marking is impossible, arrow signposts must be erected at prominent points to indicate the direction of march and distance to the objective. For shorter distances, direction arrows will be sufficient.

Road markers which have been in use for long periods must be watched, because the enemy may move them. If routes are changed, the distances indicated on the markers must be revised.

Simple marks in the snow (for instance, three impressions made close to each other with the ring of a ski pole), snow men, and similar signs are adequate for the marking of temporary roads, such as those used by patrols. If strange trails cross the route, they must be obliterated within the immediate vicinity of our own tracks so that the troops will not go astray. It is frequently advisable to leave guards at such points in order to keep units on the proper route.

10. ROAD MAKING

a. General

The construction of roads in winter is not the special task of the engineers but is the duty of all troops and arms of the service. In snowy terrain it is frequently easier to construct new roads at favorable locations (for instance, to by-pass defiles) and to maintain them than to clear existing roads. It also will be necessary to cut new cross-country roads frequently (for evading marches, bringing heavy weapons into position, etc.). Roads in snow-covered, pathless terrain are cut by small trail details which speed ahead on skis to mark the route and by larger road-construction detachments on foot. In winter warfare the formation, equipment, and training of trail details and road-construction detachments are indispensable in all units.

In establishing routes for tactical and technical purposes the following types of terrain and approaches are most suitable: flat country, plateaus, sparsely wooded land, forest paths protected from the wind, frozen rivers, lakes, swamps, and existing field paths. Across open country, trails should be laid preferably along telegraph lines, fences, and similar installations. Terrain which is exposed to snowdrifts is less suitable. Therefore, routes should be established from 100 to 150 meters (328 to 492 feet) from the edges of woods, and in clearings at the narrowest points. Heavily wooded terrain is difficult and should be by-passed whenever possible. This also applies to insufficiently frozen swamps, patches of melting ice, snow-filled hollows, deep ravines, gorges, defiles, and steep slopes.

Obstacles around which snowdrifts may form (for instance, farm buildings, piles of stones, and brushwood) must be removed or by-passed at a distance equal to 10 times their height. On inclines steeper than 10 percent it is necessary to cut the trail in serpentine fashion, oblique to the slope. Curves must be made as wide as possible, because sharp curves are more difficult for sleds than for wheeled vehicles.

When trails are being reconnoitered and plotted, the question whether the roadway is to be a one-lane or a two-lane artery must be considered. At first only a one-lane section is constructed. (The standard width of sleds is approximately 9 feet 10 inches.) By-passes wide enough for two sleds are later added; they should be at least 15 meters (about 49 feet) long. Finally the road may be enlarged to make a two-lane artery. A double lane is preferable to two separate lanes because the latter are less efficient in case of traffic jams and snowdrifts.

b. Methods

The method of making roads depends upon the type of traffic the roads will have to bear, upon the depth of the snow, and the equipment available. Ski trails cut by a trail detail will suffice for small ski detachments which use only man-hauled sleds. Larger units with animal-drawn sleds and wheeled vehicles will require a road-construction detachment. Trail details must start about 1 hour ahead of a marching column. Road-construction detachments need a start of several hours, depending upon the length of the road to be cut.

A trail detail usually is composed of one noncommissioned officer and 6 to 12 men on skis. Several trail details form a trail troop. It is advisable to attach rulers to ski poles for measuring the depth of snow. The trail detail lays several ski trails to facilitate the movement of the following unit. If possible, it removes minor obstacles and erects simple road markers. In case the unit uses man-hauled sleds, two men of the trail detail ski behind each other in such a manner that the rear man uses only one ski track of the front man in order to cut a third track, thus making a trail for the sleds (see fig. 7).

Light sleds loaded only with shovels and picks travel at the head of the column. They are followed by others which drag coniferous trees or logs. Next in the column come

Figure 7.—Functions of the trail detail. ((1) The leading pair cuts the first track; (2) the second pair clears the curves; (3) the squad leader maintains the direction of march; (4) this pair removes obstacles; (5) these men cut a third track (triple ski trail) for light sleds; (6) this pair levels the trail; (7) these men post road signs and improve the sled trail.)

Designation	Strength	Mission	Equipment
Trail-blazing detail on skis	1 O, 6 EM	Under command of an experienced officer, the detail plots the trail, straightens curves and grades rough spots, removes small obstacles such as branches, and marks the route.	Compass, wire-cutters, ice-drill, crowbar, ice measuring stick, 2 axes, marking equipment, skis.
Trail-blazing group without skis	2 NCO's, 18 EM	Packs down snow on trail, removes obstacles and cuts away obstructing brushwood and trees, strengthens weak sections of trail, relieves trail-blazing detail.	1 or 2 LMG's, and portable entrenching tools. Other equipment is loaded on sleds.
Lightly loaded sled	2 EM, 2 horses	Cuts the first sled track.	4 shovels, 2 axes, 4 pickaxes, 1 crowbar, 1 saw, demolitions material, 1 ice-drill, instruments for measuring ice capacity.
Heavily loaded sled	2 or 3 EM, 2 horses	Deepens and solidifies the sled track.	6 shovels, 8 axes, 6 pickaxes, 3 crowbars, 3 saws, 1 pair of wire-cutters, 4 Finnish hoes, 1 hammer, 1 pair of pliers, demolitions material, construction material, wire.
Sled with tree trunks	1 NCO, 1 EM, 2 horses	Clears snow from foot and vehicular trails.	1 axe, 1 pickaxe, 1 snow shovel, 5 tree hooks or chains.
Sled with fir tree	2 EM, 2 horses	Clears snow from foot and vehicular trails.	1 axe, 1 pickaxe, 1 snow shovel, 5 tree hooks or chains.

Figure 8.—Organization and disposition of a road-making detachment.

animal-drawn sleds to cut a roadway and pack it down. Supply sleds and wheeled vehicles form the rear. The effect of this sequence of sleds with varying loads is to produce a road for the main body of the unit. (For details, see fig. 8.) The men in the march column pack the snow solid and remove obstacles. If the snow is deep, skiers are sent ahead of foot troops. Men and draught animals at the head of the column must be relieved frequently.

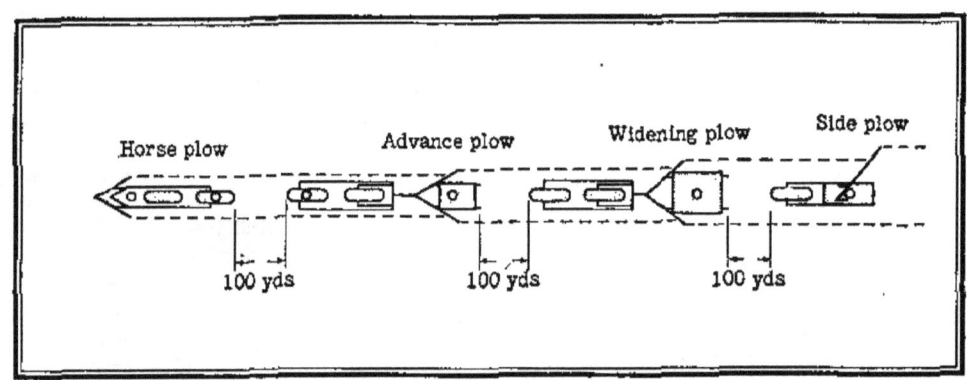

Figure 9.—Sequence of snow plows for clearing roads.

Since newly cut roads are soon damaged at many points by large bodies of marching men, it is advisable to assign a road-construction detachment to the head of each column for the purpose of making repairs. The detachment is generally composed of a reinforced platoon under the command of a commissioned officer.

Snow about 20 inches deep can be cleared with snow plows. For this purpose, the following types are used in sequence: horse plows, advance plows, widening plows, and side plows (fig. 9). The horse plow is not drawn but is pushed by horses. A strong detachment of men must always be allotted to each plow section. They must be

ROADS 35

equipped with shovels, axes, and pickaxes for the removal of obstacles. An improvised snow plow is shown in figure 10.

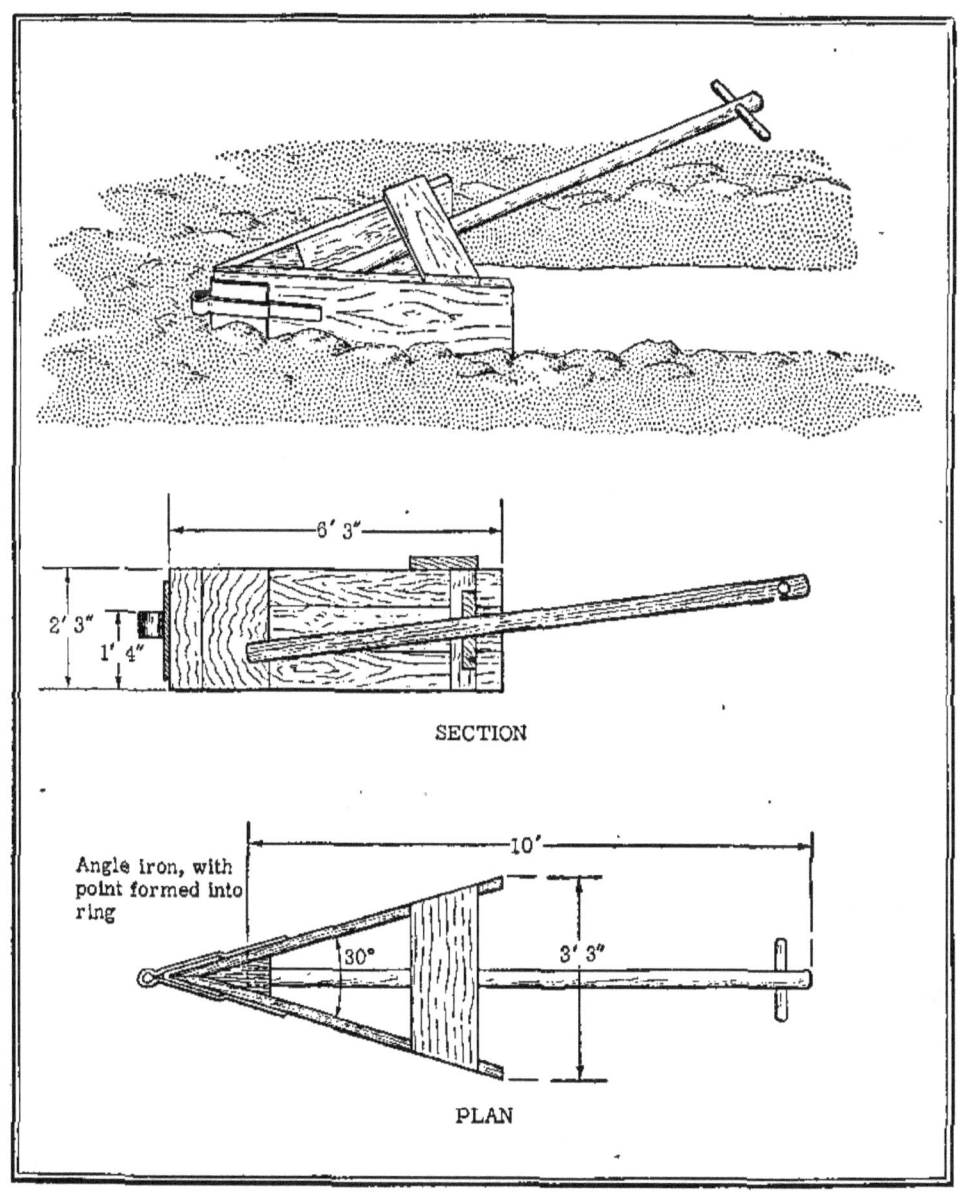

Figure 10.—Improvised snow plow.

Roads with 20 inches or more of snow which will be used by heavy traffic can be packed solid with snow-rollers. The rollers are preferable to snow plows because they do not create earth banks at the roadside. (Rollers are not included in tables of basic allowances. It is desirable to have them made by construction troops for issuance to combat troops. A suggested improvised type is shown in fig. 11.)

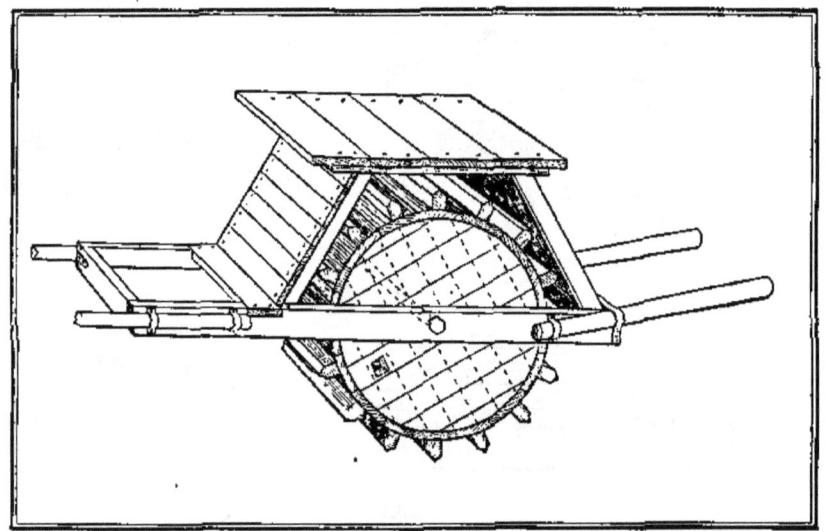

Figure 11.—Improvised snow roller.

Another method of hardening roads is to freeze them. This method was very successful in Finland and northern Russia and depends upon the availability of water. Only sleds with wooden water tanks are required. The tanks must have several openings on the bottom, at the rear, for spraying the water. To prevent the freezing of the water while it is being transported, the tanks must be heated with hot stones or by other means.

11. WINTER ROAD SERVICE

a. General

Continuous and safe travel on all thoroughfares of military importance must be assured in the winter as well as in other seasons.

Various types of vehicles can negotiate, on level ground, the depths of snow listed below:

```
Horse-drawn vehicles .................................................12 inches.
Commercial-type passenger cars ................................ 8 inches.
Commercial-type trucks ............................................12 inches.
Cross-country-type passenger cars with chains................14 inches.
Cross-country-type trucks with chains.......................16 inches.
Prime movers and tanks (for instance, an 8-ton prime mover
    with a trailed gun).........................................22 inches.
```

Icy roads, especially on grades, can hardly be used without special maintenance. Roads must be cleared after every snowfall, and icy surfaces must be sanded. This procedure requires special road service in winter, and such service is the duty of all troops. Natives with horse teams, prisoners of war, and, especially, municipal road services, will be used as auxiliary forces as much as possible. (For this reason, it is often advisable, in regions with many settlements like the Ukraine, to use roads which lead through the villages.) Regulating and supervising traffic is an essential part of the winter road service, which should be linked with the existing communication net. In case of a block system of traffic, communications must be installed between block points. Every individual using the road, especially the drivers of motor vehicles, must, for the common good, adhere to strict road discipline, observe all traffic signs, obey all orders which may be issued, and help in a comradely manner in case of traffic jams and accidents.

b. Preparations

With the beginning of cold weather, a winter road service must be started on all important roads and paths. Posts for road guards must be established along the road, and communication between the posts and headquarters must be provided.

The road guards reconnoiter certain sections of the road before the first snowfall, and after the beginning of freezing weather and snow, they travel over these sections and check their condition. They report immediately the depth of snowfalls, snowdrifts, and icy surfaces.

A simplified system for reporting road conditions, which was used successfully by an army group in the east during the winter of 1941–42, is given below:

(1) *Weather conditions on the road.—*

Free of snow and ice	0
Muddy	1
Slush of snow or ice	2
Slippery	3
Hard snow crust	4
Soft during the day, frozen at night	5
In the process of drying	6
Dry	7
Snowdrifts	8

(2) *State of repair.—*

No repairs in progress at the moment	0
Work in progress on road	1
Single-lane road	2
Single-lane road with by-passes	3
Double-lane road	4

(3) *Capacity of roads.—*

For vehicles of all kinds	0
For trucks up to 3-ton capacity	1

For trucks up to 1½-ton capacity and for tanks............ 2
For tanks and animal-drawn vehicles only................. 3
For one-horse sleds only 4
For pack animals only 5
Closed to all vehicles and for all purposes............... 6

For example, if in a reconnaissance report the condition of the thoroughfare was reported as 433, it would be interpreted as follows: the street is covered with a hard snow crust, has a single lane with by-passes, and is suitable for tanks and animal-drawn vehicles.

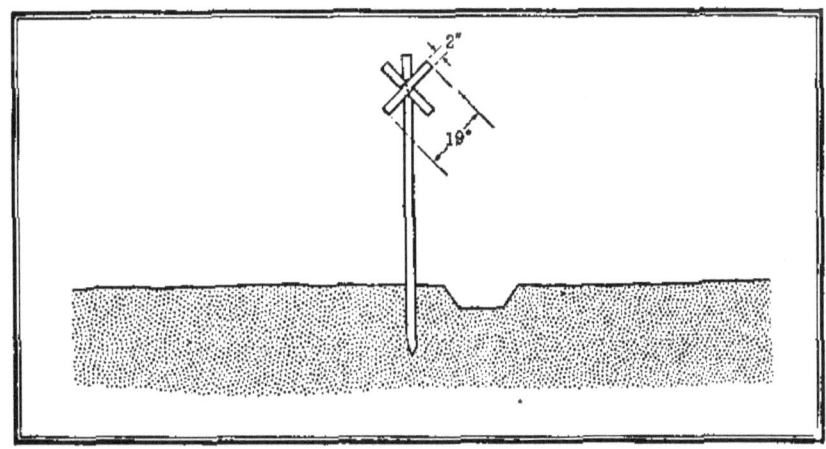

Figure 12.—St. Andrew's cross used to mark by-passes.

All personnel and auxiliary forces available in billets along the road, including reliefs and reserves, must be equipped and organized with foresight. Proper equipment must be furnished them. The equipment should consist of weatherproof clothing, good footgear, mittens, knitted wool caps, snow goggles, wide shovels, spades, pickaxes, and picks. The road must be cleared of everything that might impede traffic.

Shortly before the first frost sets in, the surface of soft roads is made even by the use of graders, agricultural equipment, and heavy harrows. Later snow-clearing work is considerably facilitated by these measures.

Markers are placed at the edge of the road, on both sides if possible. They are attached to milestones, to trees, and to fence rails at points where material for road construction is stocked, and are also put up at passages and obstacles of all kinds. By-passes are especially marked by St. Andrew's crosses (*schräge Kreuze*) (see fig. 12). Snow fences and antiskid material are stored alongside the road.

c. Clearing Roads

Troops will use all available equipment—shovels, rollers, and horse-drawn, motorized, and centrifugal plows—for clearing roads. (Motor-equipped snow-clearing troops are usually army troops.) After a heavy snowfall, a mass employment of manpower is always required. Clearing must be started immediately after the first snowfalls and must be repeated continually. Waiting makes the work more difficult.

If possible, the road must be cleared down to its surface. If some snow is to be left for sled traffic, only a depth of 1 to 4 inches is needed. It is desirable, for the protection of road surfaces, to retain a firm snow cover on the central and northern fronts until the end of freezing weather.

Snow cleared from roads must be widely scattered away from road ditches. It must not be piled up, as piling would cause new snowdrifts (heavy work done once is worthwhile). Deep-rutted snow which has been hardened by traffic or freezing and has an uneven surface can be leveled with agricultural plows and heavy harrows. Loose snow is packed into the ruts. Melting snow must be drained far off to the side, and mud must be removed. All traffic signs, especially warnings at railroad crossings, must be shoveled clear and checked continuously.

d. Snow Fences

Snow fences of two types have proved effective in preventing snowdrifts on roads. When an "accumulation fence" (*Ablagerungszaun*) is used, snow piles up on either side of it. "Guide fences" (*Leitzäune*) cause the snow to be swept by the wind at an oblique angle to the road and deposited at a distance from the thoroughfare where it will not interfere with traffic (see fig. 13).

Snow-fence protection where the prevailing wind blows approximately parallel to the axis of the road is shown in figure 13 (7) and (8). All fences must be set at an angle of 25 to 30 degrees to the axis of the prevailing wind, and they must be erected 65 to 80 feet from the edges of the road. Additional fences must be erected 100 to 130 feet from the edges.

Snow fences are made of poles and slats in sections 3 to 7 feet square. Rigid or flexible sections may be made and erected (fig. 14). They must be prepared in advance and erected before the first snowfall (often even before the frosts begin). Fences must be used where the natural contours of the terrain may cause snowdrifts. They should be erected at a distance from the edge of the road which is 10 to 20 times the height of the fence. They must be vertical and, if possible, at right angles to the prevailing direction of wind. Natives must be asked for information on wind conditions and drift spots. If wood is lacking, timber fences may be replaced by snow walls made of snow blocks. These require constant repair, but they have proved their usefulness in sparsely wooded regions, such as the Ukraine.

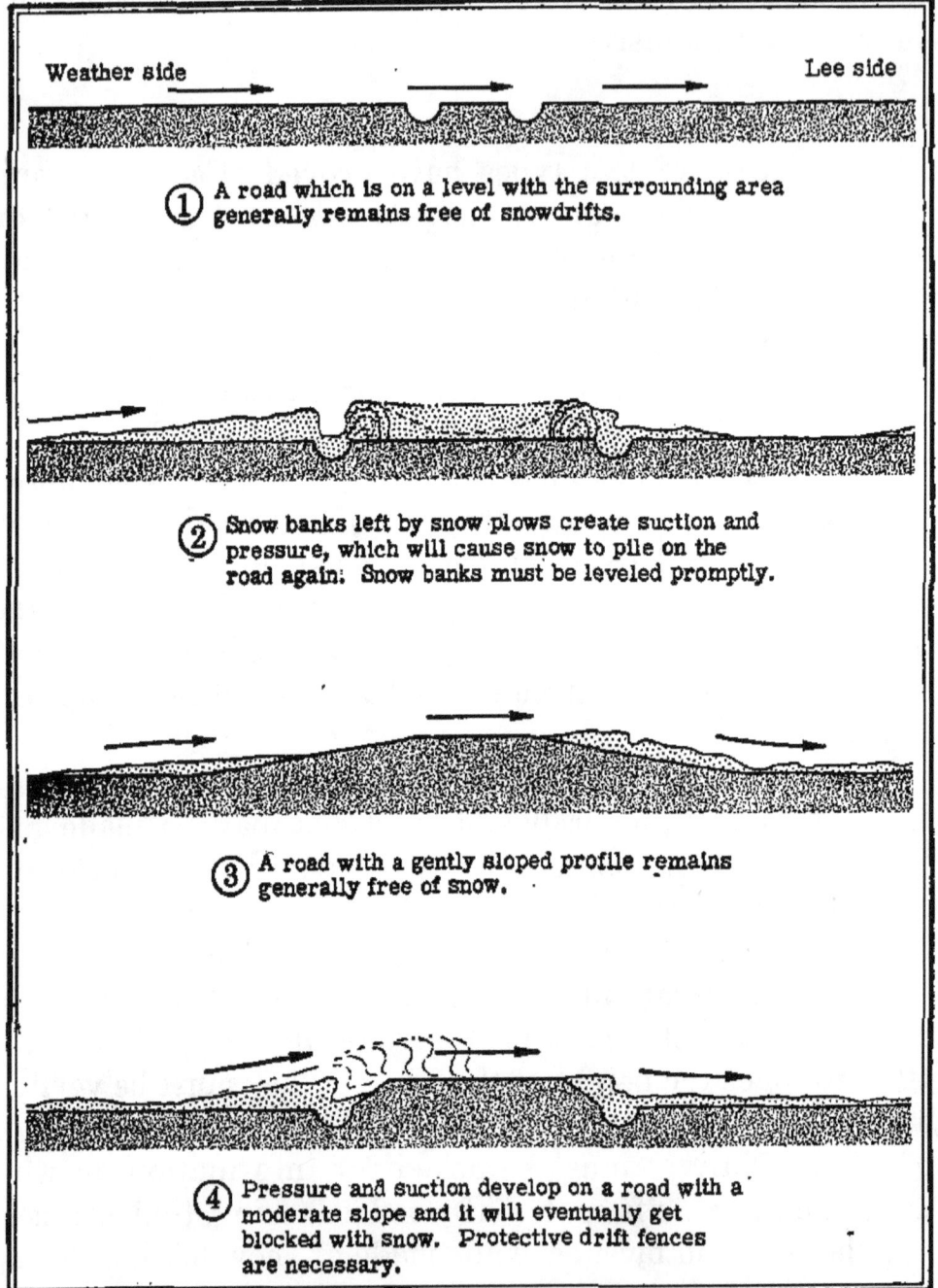

Figure 13.—Snowdrift factors affecting roads.

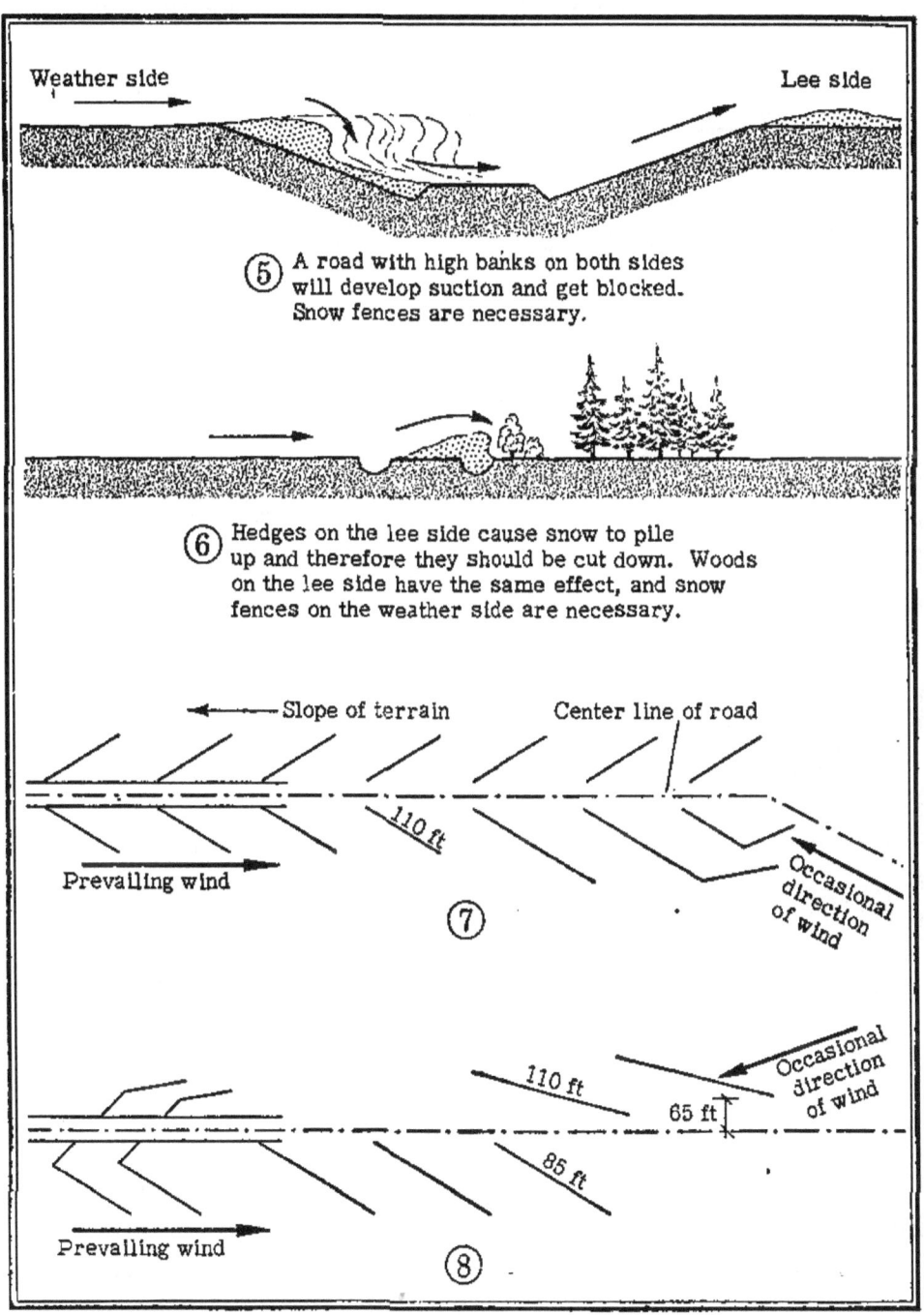

Figure 13 (continued).—Snowdrift factors affecting roads.

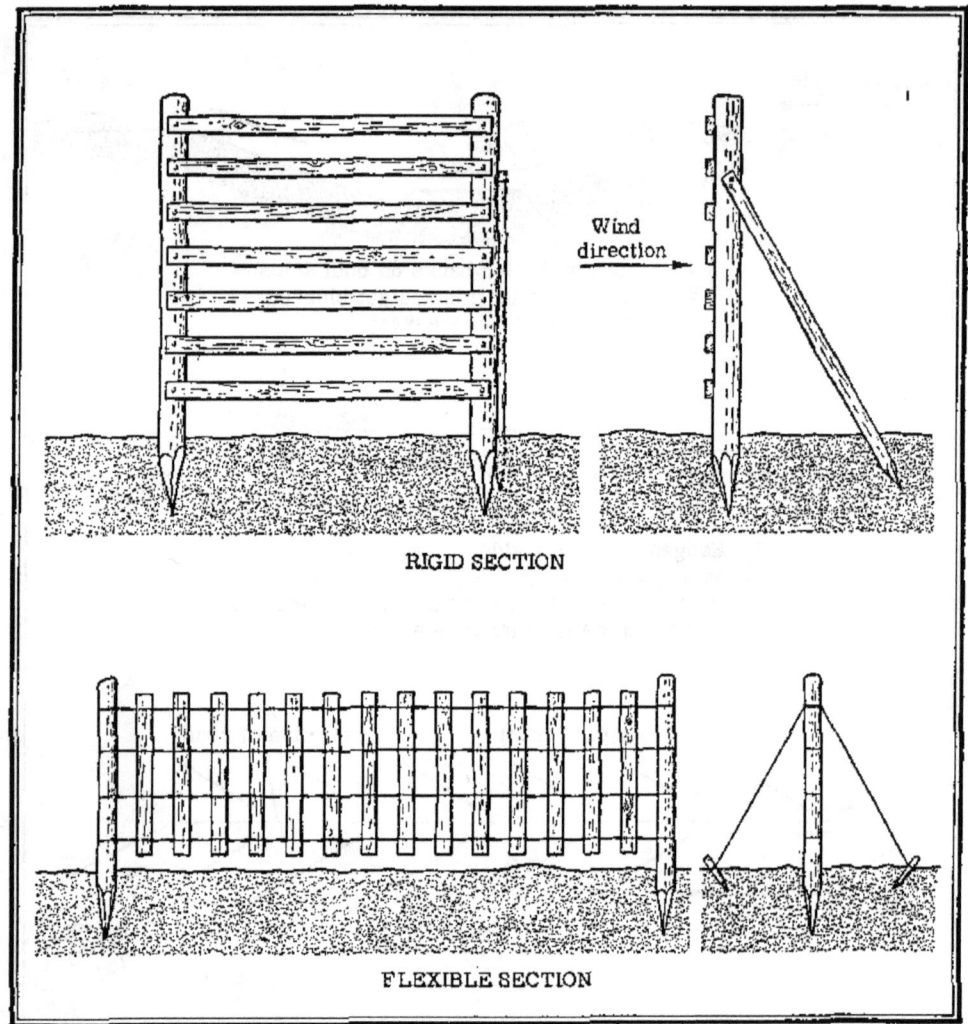

Figure 14.—Types of snow fences.

e. Treatment of Slippery Surfaces

Slippery snow and ice surfaces should be sprinkled with small-grained sand, gravel, or crushed rock. For slippery snow surfaces, a coarser type of antiskid material can be used than for ice because it is pressed into the snow. The antiskid material must be piled in advance along the roadside. It should contain no earth. The piles must be marked so that they may be found after they are covered with snow. The material is spread immediately after the surface becomes slippery. If sprinkling is done from trucks, the shovelers must be tied to the trucks with ropes. When the ice crust is chopped or removed, the surface of the road must not be damaged.

f. Transition from Snow to Mud

When, during the transition period from winter to spring, temperatures are above freezing in daytime and below at night, roads are dry and hard only at night and in the morning. Vehicular traffic, therefore, must be limited to these hours. Men whose duty it is to dispatch vehicles must see to it that advantage is taken of the most favorable hours. All drivers, and especially drivers of motor vehicles, must strictly observe traffic discipline.

Besides the measures mentioned under the heading "Seasons of Mud and Thaw" (par. **3**, p. 3), the following points are important in maintaining roads:

(1) Water must be drained off the roads. Roads, therefore, must be cleared of snow before the thaw period so that ditches and culverts can function properly.

(2) Driving on dirt roads must be absolutely avoided unless such roads are completely dry. Cart traffic during the mud period must be directed to tracks on the left and right of the road.

(3) The drying of dirt roads can be expedited by grading the surfaces with emergency leveling plows. The mud thus removed must not interfere with drainage. Ditches and culverts must be kept open.

(4) In inhabited localities, roads can be graveled by the demolition of stone buildings. Large stones make the road worse; only an even layer, improvised from bricks, will serve the purpose. Sticks and planks for the construction of corduroy roads must be prepared during the frost period in the combat zone and on all indispensable supply roads. This applies

especially to those sections of road which lead through depressions or valleys and thus dry later than roads on high ground.

(5) Sources of sand should be located. The sand should be piled in readiness wherever it may be needed for spreading on wet sections of roads.

(6) Lumber for the construction of small bridges should be available at the lowest points of roads and paths.

12. ICE CROSSINGS

a. Capacity of Ice

The thickness of ice crusts may vary in every body of water. Over river currents, near the banks, and under snow, the ice crust is generally thin. This also applies to swampy ground and warm springs. An ice crust under which the water level has fallen breaks more easily than one resting on the surface of the water. Large blocks of ice

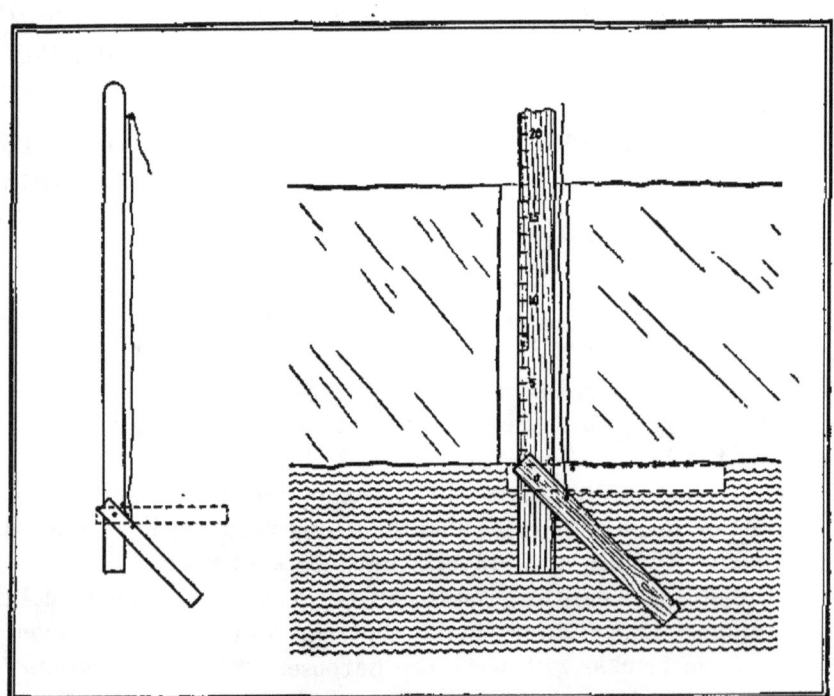

Figure 15.—Ice-measuring stick.

can serve as a raft for several persons. Caution! During the thaw period ice becomes dull and brittle, and loses its carrying capacity, and heavy traffic wears through very quickly. In determining the carrying capacity of ice crusts, not only the thickness but also the nature of the ice is a factor. Only light, clear ice is a reliable carrier. The familiar dull upper and lower layers must not be considered in estimating its strength. Before venturing on large-scale ice crossings, sample blocks must be cut out and checked for firmness. Measurements are taken with a centimeter rule equipped with a movable angle arm (see the "ice stick," fig. 15).

The load capacity of ice is shown in figure 16. These factors are dependable only when the proper march intervals are observed, and they give only a general idea of the weight which can be sustained by ice surfaces.

b. Preparations and Safety Measures

A crossing must be made on an ice crust of uniform thickness and, if possible, one without holes. Approach and departure roads and some by-passes must also be available.

For measuring the thickness of the ice along the crossing, holes are cut at distances of about 10 to 16 feet from the center of the route, and spaced from 33 to 65 feet apart. The crossing and a strip about 20 feet wide on both sides of it are cleared of snow so that the condition of the ice may be watched during the march. Crossings for motor vehicles and foot troops are sprinkled with sand. For sleds, a thin layer of snow should be spread on the ice. The various crossings, roads of approach and departure, and holes will be marked by small snow walls, railings, or poles. The carrying capacity of the ice and the intervals to be maintained will be clearly shown on posters.

Ice thickness (inches)[1]	Type of march column	Minimum interval (feet)[1]
1.5	Single riflemen on skis	16
1.9	Infantry in extended order	16
2.7	Infantry in file with double intervals	23
3.9	Infantry in march column; single horses; sleds without loads; motorcycles.	33
5.9	March column of infantry and cavalry; single sleds with up to 2,000-kg (4,410-lb) loads; gun and limber of light gun-howitzer, separated.	49
7.8	Light artillery (up to and including light gun-howitzer, horse-drawn); medium passenger cars; 1½-ton trucks with a total load of 3½ tons.	65
9.8	2-ton trucks with a total load of 4 tons.	82
11.8	Closed column of all arms; 3-ton trucks with a total load of 6 tons.	98
13.7	7-ton trucks with a total load of 13 tons; 10-ton trucks with two rear axles; armored scout cars; Mk II tanks.	115
15.7	20-ton vehicles; Mk III and IV tanks	131
23.6	45-ton vehicles	164

[1] The explanation for the odd figures is that they were converted from centimeters and meters.—EDITOR.

Figure 16.—Load capacity of ice surfaces.

Surveillance for cracks must be maintained by bridge guards. Cracks can be frozen solid by filling them with snow or water. Single cracks oblique to the crossing do not essentially decrease the carrying capacity of the ice, but large parallel cracks are indications of exhausted carrying capacity, and when they occur, a new crossing must be sought.

Traffic across ice, like traffic across a bridge, must be strictly controlled. Traffic guards must be stationed on both banks and on the ice. Rescue services and salvage parties must be kept on the alert near the crossing to act

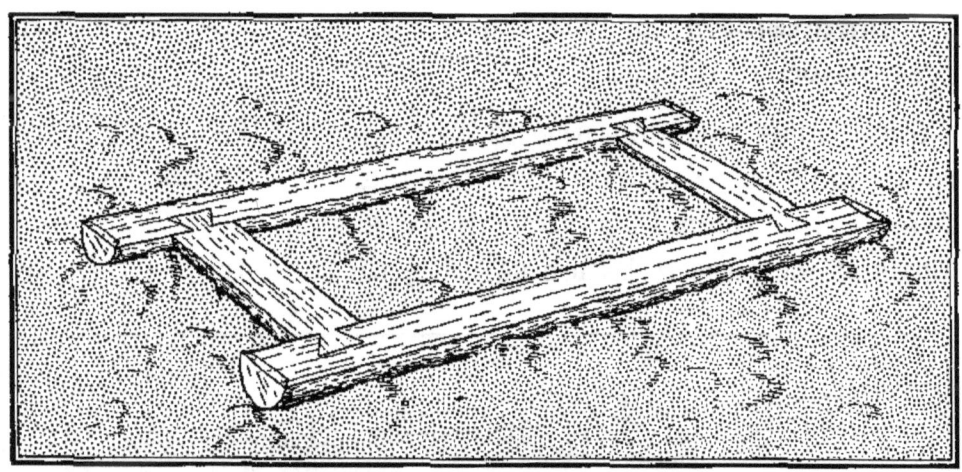

Figure 17.—Ice-crossing frame for guns and heavy vehicles.

in case of accidents. They must have proper equipment, such as planks, trees, ropes, tripods, and block-and-pulley arrangements.

c. Crossing

The crossing must proceed continuously. Do not halt on the ice! Mounted personnel and drivers of horse-drawn vehicles will dismount and lead the horses (screw in the calks). Motor vehicles and tanks must drive slowly. They are not allowed to turn or to pass other vehicles while on the ice.

The assistant drivers of heavy vehicles must observe carefully the vehicles ahead of them. For the crossing, guns and heavy wheeled vehicles can be mounted on sled-like wooden frames; this procedure will make traction easier, distribute the weight, and prevent the wheels from cutting into the ice (see fig. 17).

d. Reinforcement of Ice Surfaces and Ice-Bridge Construction

Weak crusts which are to be used for the crossing of troops may be reinforced by freezing. The simplest method of ice reinforcement is to put layers of snow and small lumps of ice (about 1 inch square) on the surface and pour

Figure 18.—Ice reinforced with layers of twigs and straw.

water on to freeze them. Three of these layers, each frozen separately before the next is added, increase the carrying capacity by about one-fifth.

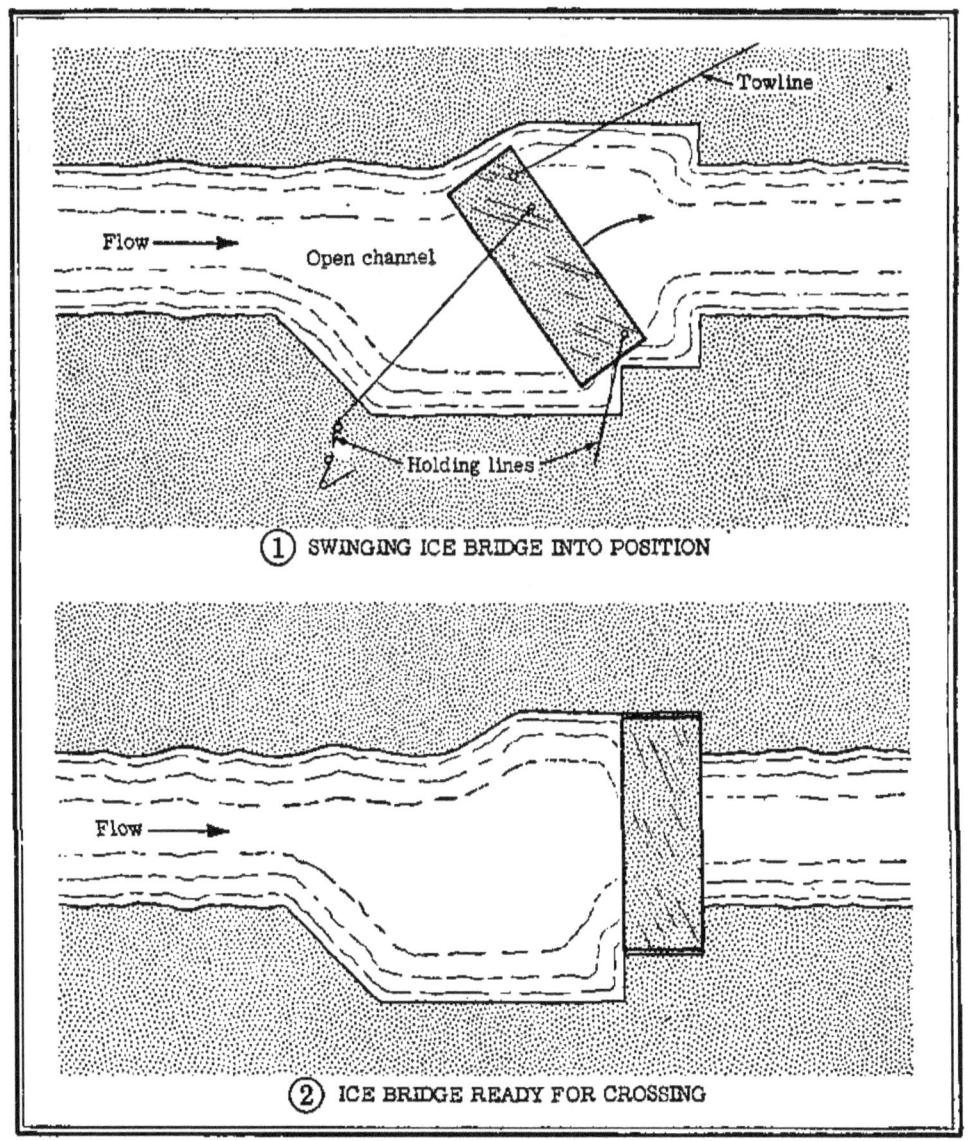

Figure 19.—Ice bridge for crossing open channels in partially frozen bodies of water.

The carrying capacity of the ice crust is increased by about one-fourth by adding and freezing to it several layers of twigs or straw, each 2 to 4 inches thick (fig. 18). Likewise boards, planks, or round lumber can considerably reinforce the crust if they are added and frozen in a similar manner. (Be careful: sunshine causes the ice to melt.)

It is also possible to traverse open sections of partially frozen bodies by means of an ice bridge if the water is still or flows slowly. For this purpose, a long block of ice is sawed out near the bank and swung across the opening (fig. 19). This method proved very effective in Finland.

Frozen swamps can be crossed easily, though the thickness of the snow and ice must be checked prior to the crossing. Most swamps freeze rapidly and the ice remains as a solid crust on top. Mossy swamps (tundras) freeze slowly and the ice bursts open quickly when the thaw begins. Mossy swamps covered with brushwood are easier to cross. Swamps covered with the first growth of willows and elder trees do not freeze adequately.

Section IV. RAILROAD MOVEMENTS

13. GENERAL

The passenger cars which are available are not adequate for the movement of troops. Therefore, freight cars are being used as troop carriers even in winter, and it must be realized that not all freight cars are equipped with stoves. Even in passenger cars heating cannot always be expected, because of technical difficulties. This is especially true of foreign cars, railroad lines which are electrically operated, and small troop trains which are attached to freight trains. Consequently, before the start of any movement, troops must take all possible measures to protect themselves and their own equipment against extreme cold; the transportation authorities may be consulted for advice.

14. PREPARATIONS FOR A TRAIN MOVEMENT

The movement of groups larger than 30 men should be planned at least 4 days in advance so that the most suitable cars may be prepared and the heating installations checked. For the comfort of troops or horses, the floors of freight cars should be abundantly covered with straw. Walls which are not air-tight should be sealed with paper and straw. If possible, additional blankets should be issued.

Wooden compartments should be constructed as protection against the weather for antiaircraft crews, and also for field-kitchen crews if the field kitchens have not been placed in freight cars constructed for this purpose. If compartments are made, however, care must be taken that the cars are neither damaged nor overloaded. Planks should not project. The antiaircraft crews, as well as the field kitchen crews, should be equipped with antifrostbite salve (*Frostschutzsalbe*), protective goggles, guard-duty surcoats, and overboots.

In snow or in slippery weather motor vehicles and tanks should be loaded and unloaded only if railroad cars, portable loading platforms, and loading bridges have been cleared of snow, and sand has been strewn on the floor. Motor vehicles and tanks should be wedged in especially tight and lashed down with cables in order to prevent them from sliding. Storage batteries should be removed from vehicles and transported in heated passenger cars. In extreme cold the radiators of motor vehicles should be covered to prevent freezing. If necessary, pack them completely in straw, straw mats, or blankets. Water containing only a small amount of antifreeze solution should be drained out of radiators and kept in receptacles, if they are available. When chemical stoves are used as protection against the cold on trains which are transporting tanks, the stoves should be refilled at the scheduled fuel stops.

In slippery weather, horses should be loaded and unloaded only when portable loading platforms and loading bridges have been strewn with sand. Horses must be well covered.

All measures should be taken to insure adherence to the time limit fixed for loading. For this purpose, prompt contact with the loading station is important. If the time limit for loading and unloading is not observed, there might be serious disruption of the train schedule.

15. PROTECTIVE MEASURES EN ROUTE

The passenger cars should be arranged behind the locomotive in such a way that the heating of all cars will be assured. German freight cars are, with a few exceptions, equipped with stoves which are the property of the railroads. These are installed by the railroad authorities, who also provide each car with a supply of fuel. In order to obtain new supplies of fuel, the transport officer must communicate with the railroad station provost or the station master.

In an emergency, fuel may be taken from the fuel supply for the engine. In the Russian broad-gauge freight cars issue stoves should be installed, but the stove must not be permitted to come in contact with the wood. The smoke should have a free outlet. Fire extinguishers must always be in readiness. The use of car furniture, snow fences, or equipment from railroad stations as fuel would be very much to the disadvantage of the units which follow and must absolutely be avoided. This also applies to the stealing of heating hoses, stoves, pipes, coal boxes, sitting and sleeping facilities, and door panels. Heating installations should be handled with great care. The misappropriation of stoves upon detraining is forbidden. The railroad authorities are responsible for the illumination of the cars, but the failure of lighting facilities in Russia must be reckoned with. Emergency illumination with the unit's own materials should therefore be prepared. Lights should always be covered.

If units are transported without their own field kitchens, a request for supplementary rations must be made at the same time that the movement is arranged. During the trip continuous contact with the transportation authorities must be maintained. A request for warm drinks from the food distributing points of the German Red Cross should be made in advance through the transportation authorities.

If a movement is made in unheated cars, the troops should be permitted to stay in heated waiting rooms during comparatively long train stops. For this purpose, contact with the transportation authorities should be established and maintained en route in order that arrangements may be made.

At every stop the field kitchen should dispense hot drinks. Frequent relief of the antiaircraft crews and train guards should be arranged. At fuel stops, troops in heated cars will regularly change places with those in unheated cars (never while the train is in motion).

During long stops, the men should detrain and engage in calisthenics, but they may detrain or entrain only upon command. Guards should be posted to prevent soldiers from crossing the rails. Doors and windows should not be left open unnecessarily; otherwise, the train will become cold. A guard should be posted at each stove, especially during the night.

Section V. WINTER BIVOUACS AND SHELTER

16. BIVOUACS

a. General

Combat requirements and the dearth of settlements, which often are useless anyway for the quartering of troops, frequently make it necessary to be completely independent of permanent billets. On the other hand, frequent bivouacking may impair the combat efficiency of the unit.

Especially careful security measures are required when in bivouac. The site of a bivouac should be camouflaged as much as possible, and should be difficult to approach by the enemy. Nearness to protecting sectors is therefore generally advisable. In addition to aggressive reconnaissance and security measures, the construction of field fortifications (and, above all, of obstacles) guarantees the safety and unmolested quartering of the unit. Small units, especially patrols, can best provide security for themselves in terrain which cannot be reconnoitered easily.

Sentries must be well camouflaged to avoid revealing the bivouac. Low temperatures or biting wind will make it necessary to relieve them frequently, but care must be taken to maintain continuity of observation and to prevent the enemy from drawing definite conclusions concerning the posting of security forces. Weapons and skis must be kept within easy reach.

Aside from tactical requirements, the selection of the bivouac site must depend on protection against dampness, wind, and cold; and nearness to a supply of wood and lumber is desirable. Low ground, depressions, and valleys usually have lower temperatures than their surroundings. Snowdrifts around hollows and accumulations on the lee side of elevations may be used in the construction of snow caves. Areas free of snow are exposed to the wind and are not suitable for bivouacs. Wooded areas are warmer than open fields and conceal the glow of fires. Fir trees which are not too high, with branches that extend down to the snow, afford good shelter possibilities for smaller units which are heavily snowed in.

Work on the bivouac must begin immediately after the halt so that the men may stay warm. Extra time spent on construction shortens the time available for rest but ensures greater relaxation and warmth later.

Beds of foliage, moss, straw, boards, skis, furs, and shelter halves may be used as protection against dampness and low ground temperatures. Clothing and equipment must be cleaned of snow before they are brought into the bivouac. It may be necessary to have this measure enforced by sentries. Since wind diminishes warmth and affects the heating of the shelter, the entrance must be placed on the side that is least exposed to the wind. It should, if possible, be close to the ground and is best if it leads upward. The shelter itself should be as low as possible, while bedding facilities should be as high as possible. The sources of heat must be placed low in fire holes and cooking pits. Special protective walls and plastering with earth and snow minimize the effect of wind.

The types of bivouac construction depend upon the situation and upon the material and equipment which is available. Experience teaches that even bivouac conditions which in the past have been considered unsuitable, or practical only in an emergency, are completely suitable for German soldiers.

After adequate training and experience, living in winter bivouac is not injurious to health, even in very cold weather. Preliminary acclimatization is necessary. Extra underwear and an under jacket should be worn as protection against the cold. Blankets warm the body better than overcoats. If the underwear is wet and there is no chance to dry it, it must be worn over the dry extra underwear and the under jacket. Otherwise, if the wet underwear is taken off, it freezes stiff. The changing of underwear must be enforced. Several light layers of clothing keep a man warmer than one thick garment. All tight-fitting articles of clothing must be loosened. Rags and newspapers pushed in several layers into the trousers and under the jacket (especially near the chest, abdomen, and kidneys) are good protection. Ear muffs, knitted wool caps, mufflers, wristlets, and gloves complete the bivouac uniform. Shoes must be put on again after socks are changed in extremely cold weather in order to prevent the leather from freezing stiff. During the night, the haversack may be used as a footsack to warm the feet.

Prior to sleeping in a cold bivouac, the body must be warmed by vigorous movements such as calisthenics and long-distance running. If several men sleep alongside one another, it is advisable that they do not wear too many garments, but use some of their garments as ground sheets and some as blankets. If possible, the bivouac must be heated. It is especially important to heat a tent bivouac. If tents are pitched on bare frozen ground, it is advisable to warm the ground beforehand by means of well-distributed fires. (For further measures pertaining to life in winter bivouac, see sec. **IX**, "Protection against Cold, Snow, and Thaw," p. 127.)

b. Snow Shelters

The basic types of shelters are snow huts, canvas tents, branch tents, and earth huts. Practice in the construction of the shelters described below is indispensable for winter warfare in Russia, and a prerequisite is to conquer the great aversion to snow as such. Only thorough training and adaptation will help.

Snow is windproof and retains warmth (three times the warmth retained by wood). It is merely necessary to place a layer of some insulating material between the body and the snow to keep the snow from melting. This layer may be bedding made with thick underwear, the uniform, camouflage dress, the overcoat, a shelter half, or a blanket.

Where the situation permitted and the depth and consistency of the snow was suitable, types of snow shelters that proved effective were the snow hole, the snow cave, the snow pit, the snow house, and the Eskimo-type igloo.

17. SNOW HOLE

The snow hole is an emergency shelter for protection against freezing in a snowstorm, or in case an attack is stopped in open, snow-covered terrain. It is simple and can be made rapidly. Spades, skis, and bayonets may be used for digging it. Even when no tools are available, the soldier can lie on his back on top of snow 20 inches deep and create a hole in a few minutes (fig. 20). He pushes with his feet, digs with his hands, and repeatedly turns over, thereby fashioning a hole the length of his body and the

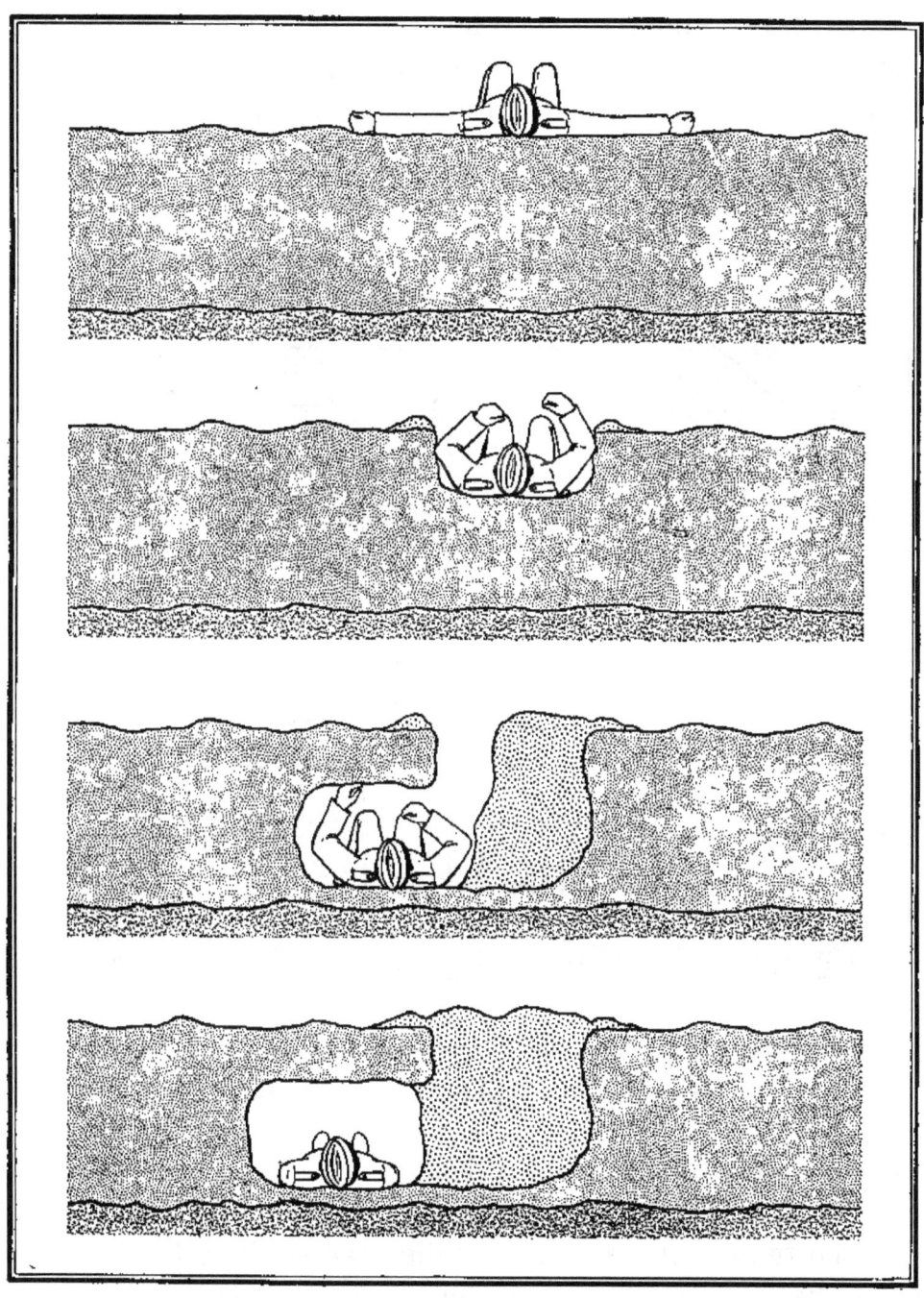

Figure 20.—Making a snow hole without tools.

width of his shoulders. When he has reached a 20-inch depth, he digs himself in sideways below the surface, and then fills in the original ditch with the snow he has ex-

Figure 21.—Types of snow holes.

cavated until only a small opening remains. This opening may be entirely closed, depending upon the enemy situation and the temperature. The smaller the shelter, the warmer it will be. In snow of lesser depth an open snow hole is dug and covered with snow blocks (fig. 21).

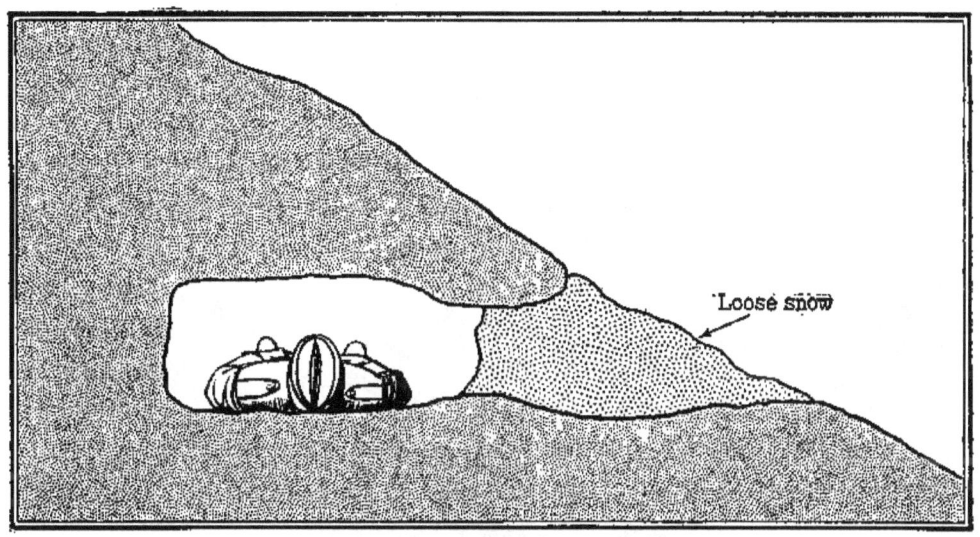

Figure 22.—Cave in snowdrift.

18. SNOW CAVE

One may dig a cave still more rapidly in a snowdrift. If the entrance is made to slope upward, the cave will be especially well protected against the penetration of cold air (fig. 22.) Snow caves may be built for several men if the

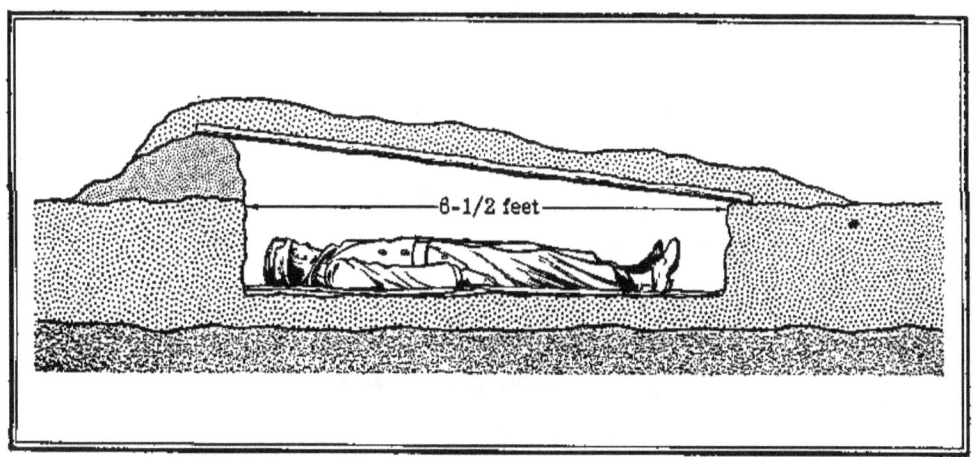

Figure 23.—Snow pit for several men.

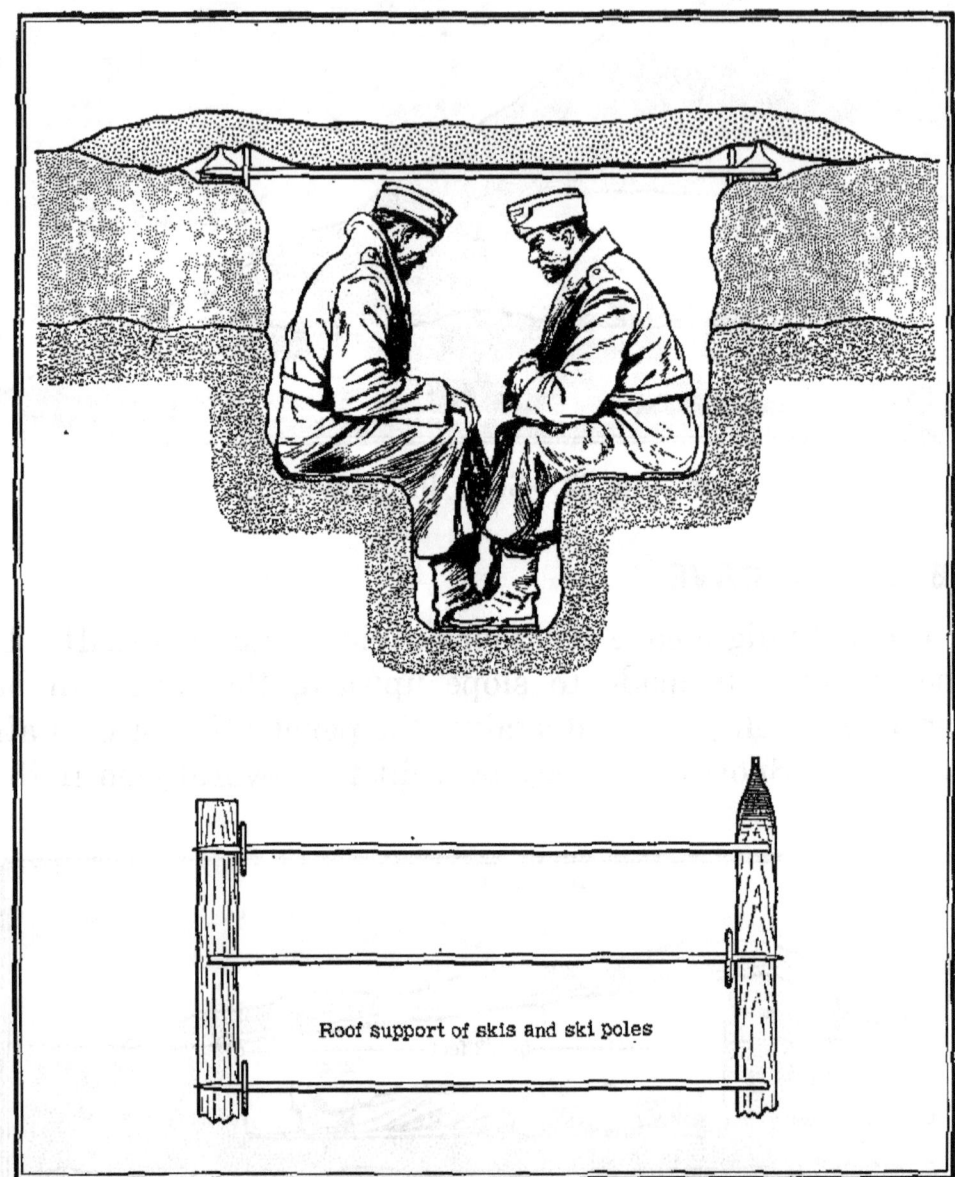

Figure 24.—Snow pit in deep snow.

consistency of the snow is such that it will not cave in. To expedite construction, the work is started from two entrances. One entrance is sealed after completion of the cave.

19. SNOW PIT

The snow pit is dug vertically into the snow in the same fashion as the snow hole, but it is larger and rectangular. Skis, sticks, poles, branches, shelter halves, and snow are used as roofing. The pit affords shelter for several men in a prone position. It is advisable to slope the roof down toward the foot end (see fig. 23). In very deep snow, the snow pit may be sunk deep enough to accommodate two men sitting or standing (fig. 24). If the snow is not deep enough, the sides of the pit are made higher by adding snow walls upon which are laid skis or similar supports for a roof (fig. 25).

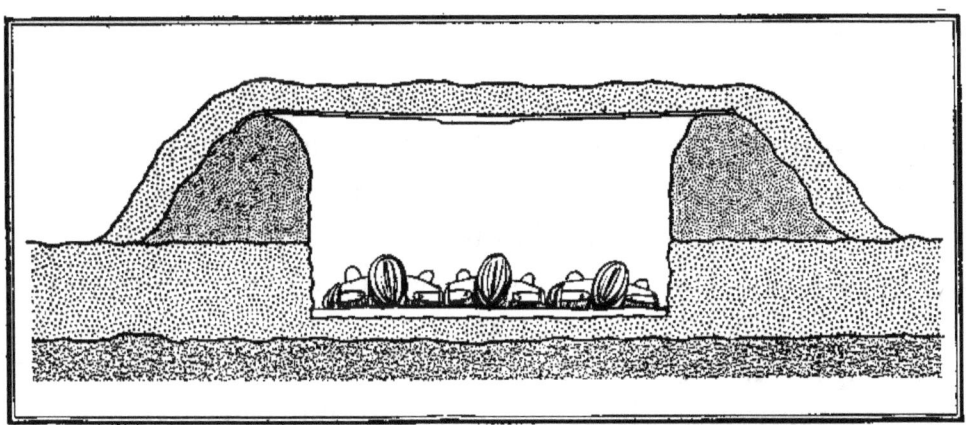

Figure 25.—Snow pit in shallow snow.

20. SNOW HOUSE

The size and the roof of snow houses are similar to those of snow pits. The side walls, however, consist of snow blocks and may be built, even in case of a light snow, up to the height of a man. Snow piled on the outside seals the cracks and camouflages the building (fig. 26).

Figure 26.—Snow house with walls of ice blocks.

21. IGLOO, ESKIMO TYPE

a. General

The Eskimo type of igloo (*Iglu nach Eskimoart*) is a very useful shelter and can be built easily if the snow is deep enough and of the right consistency. It is especially valuable in treeless, uninhabited areas, or when tents are not available. Its construction requires practice and familiarity with snow as a material.

The igloo is a domed house made of snow blocks. It offers protection against wind, cold, rifle and machine-gun fire, and shell fragments. It can be used in many ways—as a shelter, sentry box, firing position, pillbox, dressing station, refrigerator for foods, and shelter for horses and motor vehicles. It can be occupied throughout the winter. The colder it is outside, the more comfortable the igloo will be. Outside temperatures of about −58 degrees F. are not felt within the building.

The igloo can hold from 4 to 50 men, depending on its size (6½ to 26 feet interior diameter). For a short stay, a small igloo is preferable; for a long stay, a large one. If the snow is of poor quality, several small igloos can be built more quickly than one large one.

The standard igloo has a diameter of 16 feet, measured through the thickness of the snow blocks, and an interior diameter of 13 feet. It is 6½ feet high inside, and its walls are 19 inches thick, not including the snow piled around the outside. It has proved to be especially practical as a shelter for 12 men. Skilled troops can build it in 1½ hours; unskilled men require 2 to 3 hours.

b. Building Equipment

The equipment necessary for constructing igloos consists of the following:

3 whipsaws or fretsaws (length of blades, 16 to 20 inches) for cutting and trimming snow blocks.
4 long-handled shovels with cross grips for lifting snow blocks.
2 hatchets for cutting ice.
1 hand sled for carrying snow blocks.
1 wooden form (trapezoid shape) for measuring snow blocks.
4 field spades for carving snow blocks.
1 piece of string, 10 feet long, for use as a ground compass and plumb-line during construction.

c. Condition of Snow

Dry, hard snow, from which snow blocks can be cut quickly, is best suited for building an igloo. Frozen snow is less suitable; fresh powdery snow is useless. The thickness and solidity of the snow are tested by probing with the saw. The snow should be at least 12 inches thick. The lower layers under powdery snow may be cut into blocks after the loose snow is removed. Thawing snow can always be used for building an igloo. If the snow is not deep, large snowballs can be made by rolling; then blocks are cut out. The thicker the blocks, the more quickly the building will be finished.

Figure 27.—Cutting snow blocks.

d. Preparation for Building

To construct a standard igloo, a center point for it is fixed by driving a field spade or a wooden peg into the ground. The measuring line is tied to the space or peg at snow level. Distances of 6 feet 5 inches and 8 feet from the spade are marked by knots in the line, and circles are drawn around the spade at these distances. Between the two circles is laid the foundation for the igloo wall. The building site must be leveled, and soft snow must be packed down or removed. In deep snow the lower part of the igloo can be dug out and a dome built over it.

e. Cutting the Blocks

The snow blocks are cut out of a pit with vertical walls 12 to 20 inches deep. Standing in the pit, a man cuts out

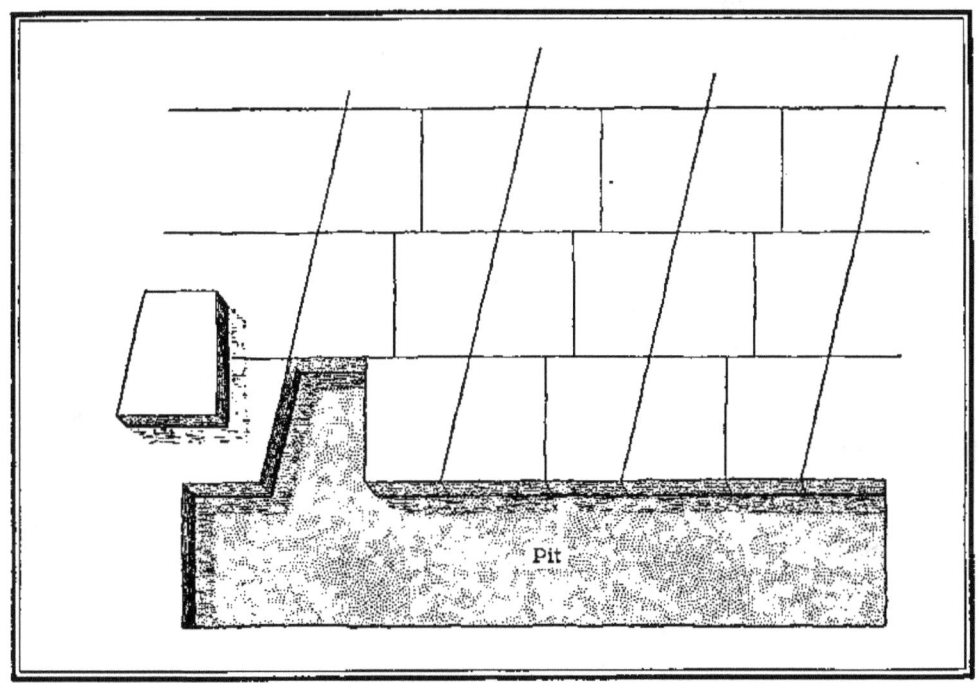

Figure 28.—Pattern formed in cutting snow blocks.

blocks along the edge of the pit in order to obtain perpendicular (not slanting) surfaces (fig. 27 (1)). It is advisable, especially for beginners, to use a wooden form of the trapezoid shape (fig. 27 (2)) which all the blocks must have. In cutting the blocks, the long and the short parallel sides are alternately placed on the edge of the pit. The resulting pattern is shown in figure 28.

The blocks should be lifted out carefully with one or two shovels in order to avoid damaging their surfaces.

The speed of building depends essentially on the speed with which the blocks can be cut. Therefore, the men charged with this task must be relieved frequently. The blocks are brought to the building site on a hand sled. If skis are available and the ground slopes to the building site, the skis are placed in pairs to form a continuous track, with the waxed surfaces turned up, and the blocks are slid to the building site. This method of moving the blocks is best.

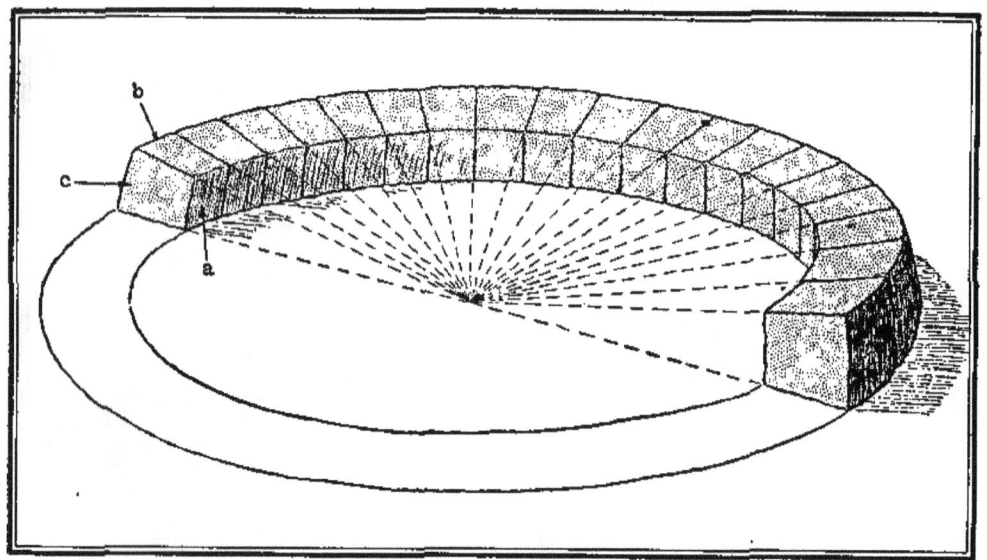

Figure 29.—Part of the first tier of the igloo. (Four edges and four planes of the blocks slant toward the igloo floor.)

f. Building the First Four Tiers

The blocks are fitted together within the double lines of the circle marked out in the snow. In figure 29 the surfaces marked "a," which are 13 inches long, face inside, and the surfaces marked "b," which are 16 inches long, face outside. The thickness of the wall (marked "c") is

20 inches. (See also fig. 27 (2).) A space in the circle, about 24 inches wide, is left open as an entrance on the side away from the enemy. The top surface of the blocks is slanted slightly inward with the saw. The degree of slanting can be determined by using the measuring string and extending it from the center of the igloo to make a straight line to the outer edge of the blocks. In this way each block is given its final shape and position. (See fig. 30.)

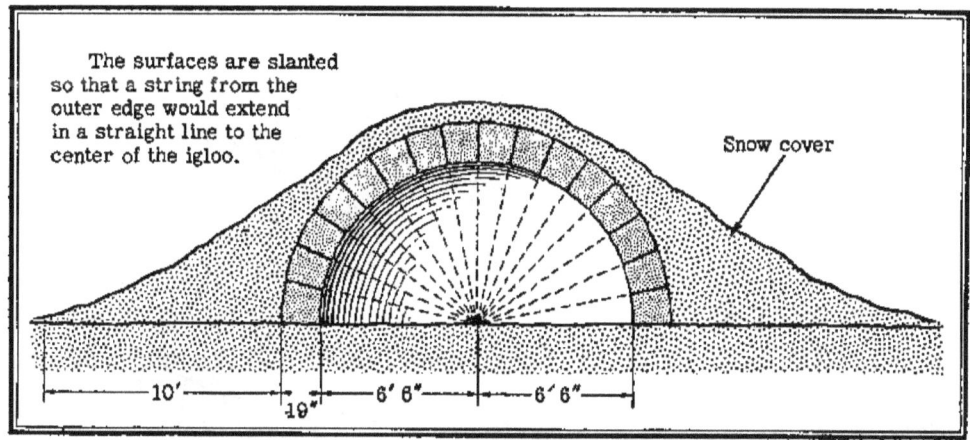

Figure 30.—Cross section of the igloo, with snow cover, showing lines radiating to the center.

The blocks of the second tier are placed on the first tier in the same manner, beginning at the entrance gap, and the third tier is also added in the same fashion. In order to speed up construction, the first three tiers need be cut only roughly. It is important, however, that they form a solid foundation for the upper tiers. Remnants of snow blocks are left inside the igloo during construction, so that the building detail later can stand on the pile to reach the ceiling. The measuring line is used constantly to test the circular form of the building and the slant of the top surface of the tier. When the wall is 3 or 4 tiers, or about 50 inches high, the entrance gap is bridged by a long block.

g. Completing the Dome

As the structure grows higher, the diameter of the tier diminishes sharply and the blocks slant more toward the

Figure 31.—Installing support blocks. (The entrance gap is bridged by a long block.)

center of the circle. All blocks at this stage must be cut especially clean and even so that a good fit and adhesion may be obtained. Up to about two-thirds of the height of the igloo construction difficulties increase; then they decrease because the tiers become almost self-supporting as they grow smaller.

If newly placed blocks will not adhere, support blocks 4 to 8 inches longer than the others are inserted in at least four places in each tier (fig. 31). Blocks of normal size are joined to them. Thus a vertical adhering surface is provided in addition to the bottom, slanted surface. At this stage of construction two men should hold the blocks in place from the inside with their shoulders and arms, and they should continue this support until the last block is wedged in at the center of the roof. As each tier is completed, the individual blocks should be tapped with the fists from the outside until they fit very tightly. If it is necessary to get a tighter fit, space for contracting a tier may be made with the saw by cutting along the vertical seams. The mutual wedging in of the blocks, the contraction of each tier, and the installation of support blocks are the main feature in building the curved structure without scaffolding. It is important to cut the last block carefully, as the tight fit of this block keeps the others from falling out.

An **S**-shaped tunnel, 10 to 13 feet long, about 2 feet wide, and 48 inches high, may be added to the entrance. The side walls consist of rectangular blocks. The ceiling consists of snow blocks placed either horizontally or in an inverted **V** shape. The **S** form of the tunnel provides protection against wind and enfilading fire and prevents light from showing outside. At the point where the tunnel joins the igloo, it can be enlarged sufficiently to form a little anteroom (a small igloo, about 6 feet in diameter). The anteroom serves as a storeroom and as a place for removing the snow from the clothing before entering the igloo (see fig. 32). In order to admit light, four holes may be cut into the walls at shoulder height, and panes of ice fitted in. These windows may be used as loopholes by breaking the ice panes.

h. Finishing Touches

Blocks protruding on the inside are smoothed down. The igloo can be frozen and strengthened by sprinkling it with water up to a height of 4½ feet. The top of the dome,

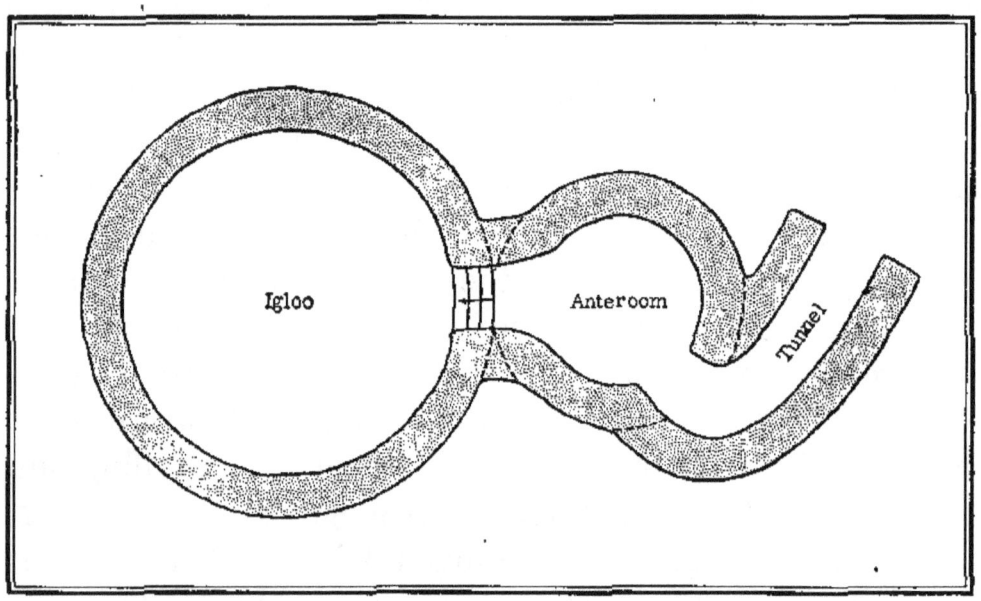

Figure 32.—Tunnel entrance and anteroom of the igloo.

however, should consist only of dry snow, which is best for ventilation and for protection against cold. The outside of the igloo is left rough to provide a holding surface for a cover of snow which will fill in the cracks and further strengthen the structure. The snow cover is made to serve a double purpose around the lower part of the igloo. Banked to a thickness of 10 feet or more, the snow provides protection against rifle fire and shell fragments. It also camouflages the igloo to make it appear like a snowdrift.

i. Furnishings

The snow floor of an igloo is covered with insulating materials. Branches of birch, willow, larch, fir, Scotch pine, dry leaves, underbrush, boards, heather, dry moss, hay, straw, paper, cardboard, animal skins, shelter halves, woolen blankets, sleds, and skis are suitable. Layers with plenty of air space between them are excellent (for instance, alternate layers of shelter halves and brushwood).

The igloo can easily be heated to more than 68 degrees F. with cooking apparatus, kerosene lamps, or candles. It is better, however, not to increase the air temperature at head level to more than 41 degrees F. The igloo should be heated sparingly in order to keep the snow dry and retain air for a long time. The dome above the lamps must be protected against rising heat. When the interior of the dome becomes glazed with ice, it must be scraped off and more snow should be added on the top outside. If the igloo is smooth inside and nothing protrudes from the walls, melting snow will not drip but will run along the walls. Before retiring at night the occupants of the igloo must close the entrance at the outer end with snow blocks.

j. Building of Large Igloos

Since construction difficulties increase with size, it is advisable first to build an igloo 6½ to 10 feet in diameter for practice. Measurements of the wooden forms for making snow blocks of varying sizes are given in figure 33.

22. PLYWOOD SHELTERS

Plywood shelters (*Sperrholzzelte* or *Finnenzelte*) are intended as substitutes for cloth tents. The general-issue

Diameter of igloo		Dimensions of wooden forms			Personnel capacity
Inside	Outside	Short parallel a^1	Long parallel b^1	Leg side (wall thickness) c^1	
6 feet 7 inches	9 feet 10 inches	12 or 16 inches	18 or 23½ inches	20 inches	2 to 3 men
9 feet 10 inches	13 feet 2 inches	12 or 18 inches	16 or 23½ inches	20 inches	5 men
13 feet 2 inches	16 feet 5 inches	13 or 16 inches	16 or 20 inches	20 inches	12 men
16 feet 5 inches	19 feet 8 inches	14 or 20 inches	16½ or 23½ inches	20 inches	18 men
19 feet 8 inches	23 feet	16½ or 19 inches	19 or 22 inches	20 inches	25 men

[1] See fig. 20.

Figure 33.—Measurements of wooden forms for making snow blocks.

prefabricated plywood shelter consists of the following parts:

    12 rectangular wall boards.
    12 triangular roof boards.
    1 support pole.
    1 box containing 72 bolts, wing nuts, and washers.
    1 mounting ring.
    1 ventilation hood in two parts, with 4 rods and 8 wedges.

[The German manual, though it gives instructions for assembling the shelter, gives neither its dimensions nor its

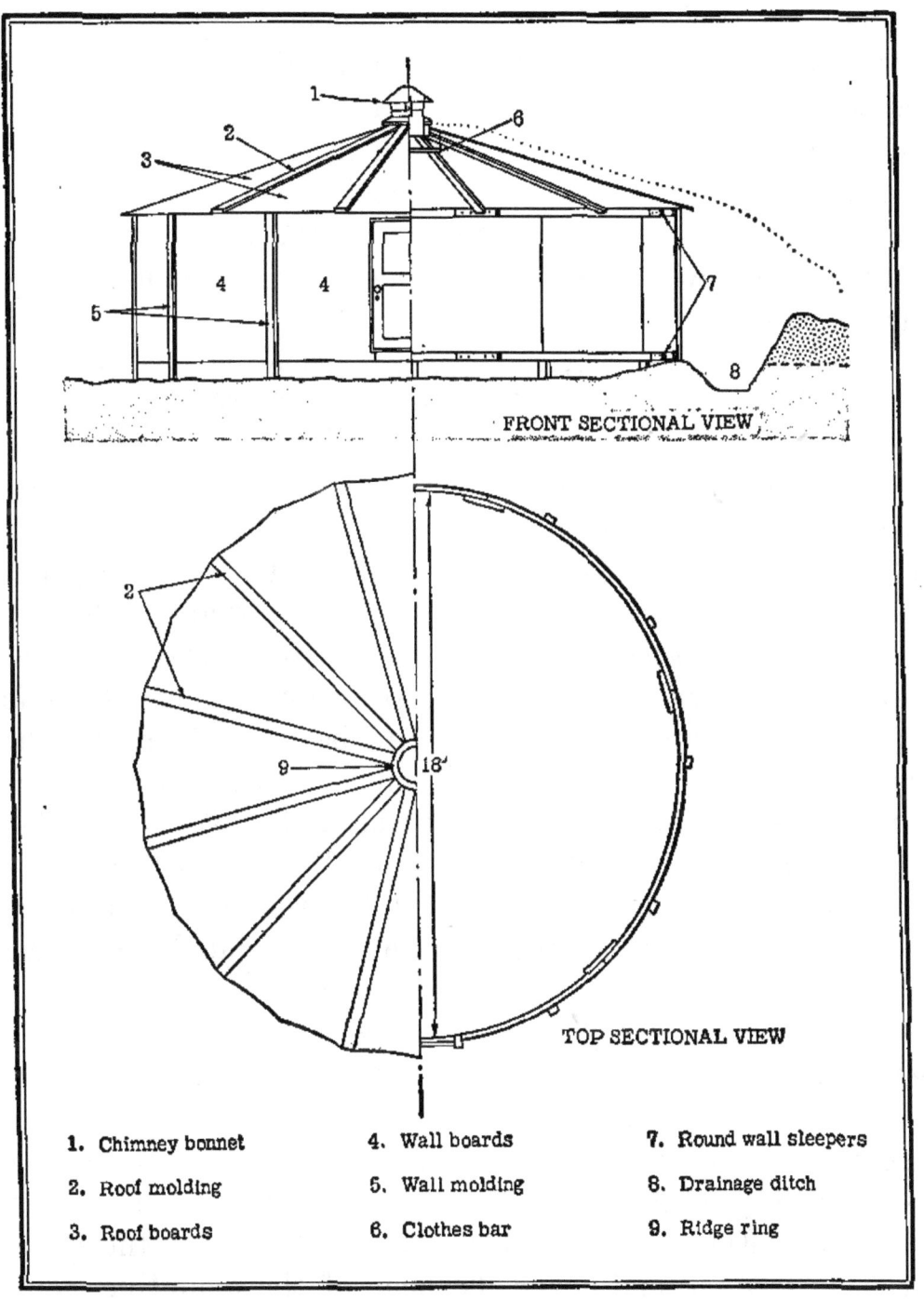

Figure 34.—Plywood shelter for 20 men.

capacity. However, in another German document entitled "Supplement 2, Enclosure to Army Regulation 319/1" appears a detailed description and drawings of a plywood shelter large enough for 20 men (fig. 34). It is either the shelter referred to in the "Handbook on Winter Warfare" or one of a very similar pattern, and therefore the dimensions and drawings are included here. The dimensions are as follows:

>   Inside diameter ....Approximately 18 feet.
>   Height of wall...............................Approximately 5 feet.
>   Height in center...........................Approximately 7 feet.

The document states that when several of the shelters are erected, they must be spaced at least 16 feet apart. It also recommends that the roof be treated with waterproof preparations, such as tar and bitumen, and that the shelters should be insulated against the cold with layers of leaves, branches, or packed snow. In situations where there is danger of enemy fire, earth should be banked around the shelters. The document recommends leaves or twigs as a substitute if lumber is not available for flooring. The shelters are heated with stoves placed on stone bases.]

At least two men are required to erect the shelter; if possible, four men should be used. The wall boards, the door and the window frames are laid out on the ground and arranged in proper order. The wall boards are then erected one at a time and screwed together. The bolts are inserted from the outside, and the wing nuts fastened from the inside. Do not forget the washers. The mounting ring is set on top of the support pole, which is held upright by one man. Four roof boards are put in by fitting the holes at their tapered ends over the pegs of the mounting ring. The crosspiece near the outer edge of each roof board is fitted against the inside of the corresponding wall board. The roof boards are screwed down with wing nuts which are inserted from the inside of the tent. When four roof boards have been installed, the man holding the support pole may let it go and assist with the rest of the work. When

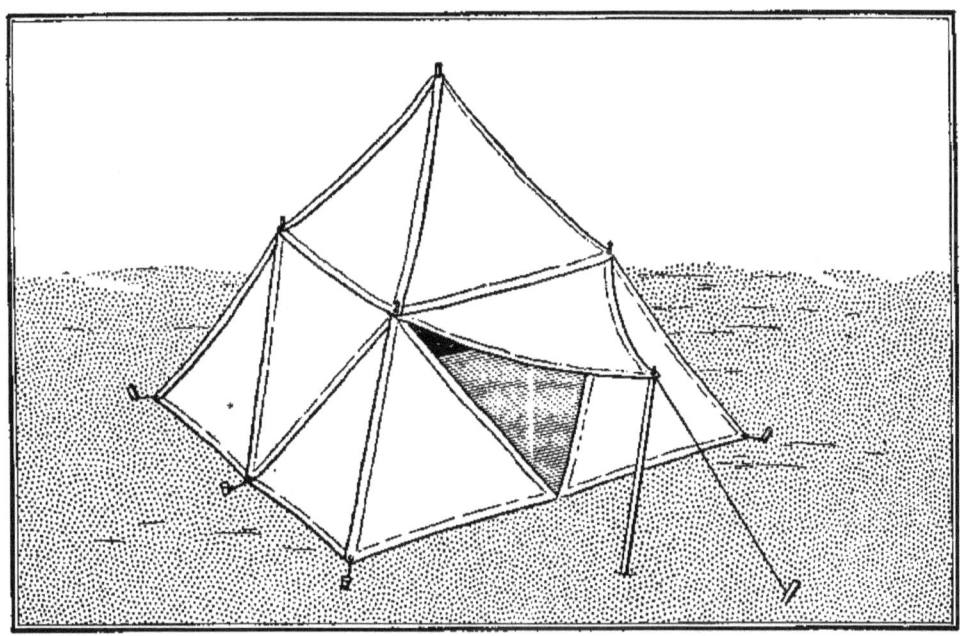

Figure 35.—The 16-man tent.

all the roof boards have been screwed tight, the support pole and the mounting ring are removed and the ventilation hood is installed. The shelter is taken down in exactly the reverse order.

23. TENTS

Tents are the bivouac shelters which can be erected most rapidly for protection against wind and cold. They are easily transported and therefore are especially suited for mobile winter forces. The types of tent shelters discussed here are those made with shelter halves, and circular tents of the Finnish type.

The 16-man tent made by buttoning together shelter halves, known as a "house tent" (*Hauszelt*), is suitable for use as an emergency winter tent because a warming fire or tent stove can be installed in it. (See fig. 35.) It covers an area of about 25 square meters (269 square feet) and is about 9 feet high. It affords shelter for at least 16 men. If the shelter halves are sewed together, the tent may be erected more rapidly and will provide a greater degree of

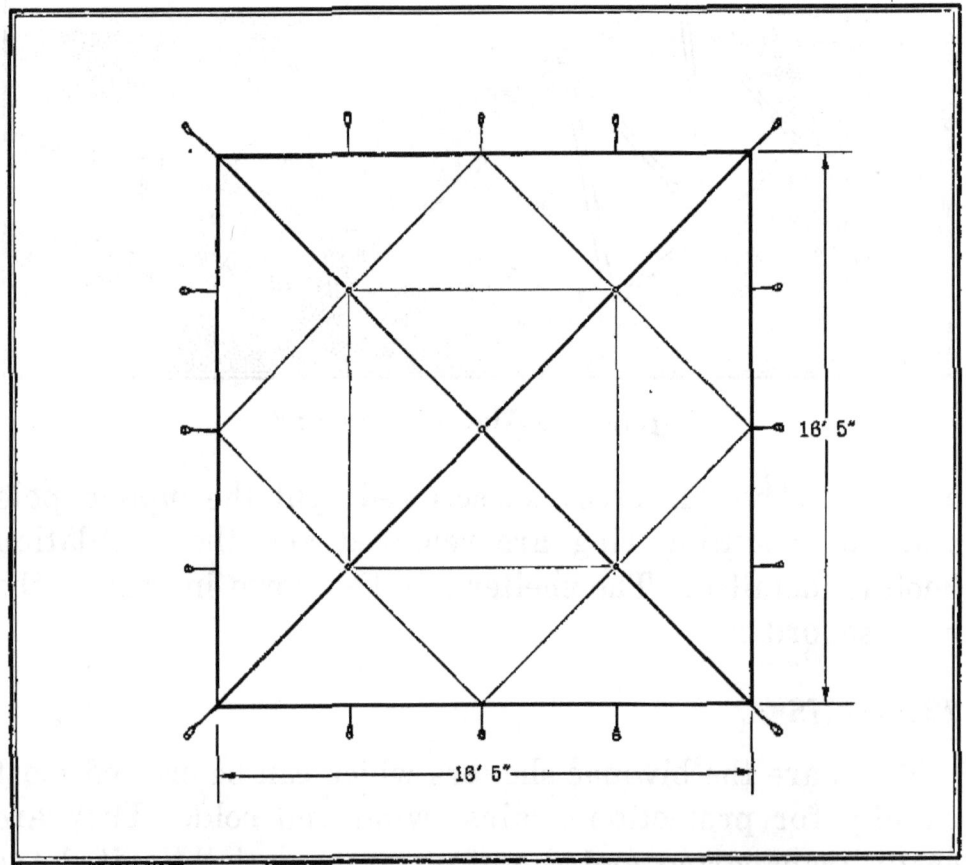

Figure 36.—Layout of the 16-man tent.

warmth and protection against the wind. Waterproof ground sheets or captured shelter halves should be furnished to men whose regular shelter halves are used in making the "house tent."

To pitch the tent, the four sides are prepared by joining three shelter halves for each side. They are buttoned to-

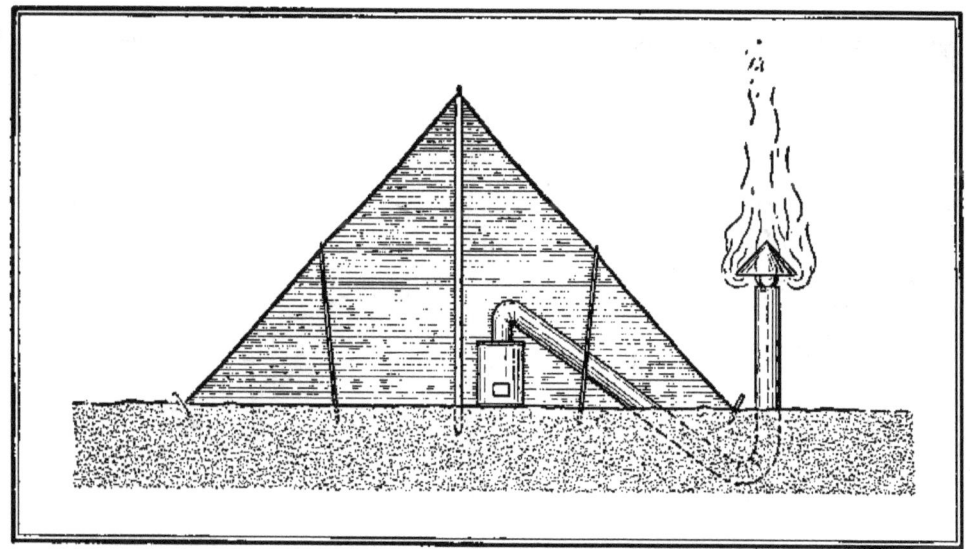

Figure 37.—Method of tubing a stove chimney underground.

gether to form a hollow square, as in figure 36, except that two oblique sides of one of the middle shelter halves are left unbuttoned in order to provide an entrance. The assembled canvas is then spread out and the edges are fastened to the ground with tent pegs. Next, the canvas is raised by inserting a tent pole at each corner of the open, center square. (Consider the weight of snow and employ poles of sufficient strength.) The tent is completed by buttoning a four-man tent (four shelter halves) in the hollow square. Finally a 10-foot pole is raised in the center of the tent to serve as the central support. An opening may be left at the top, when required, to serve as a smoke vent.

If a tent stove is available, the chimney is tubed through the ground into the open in order to retain as much heat as possible (fig. 37). If digging is impracticable because of frozen soil, the stovepipe is led out through the entrance.

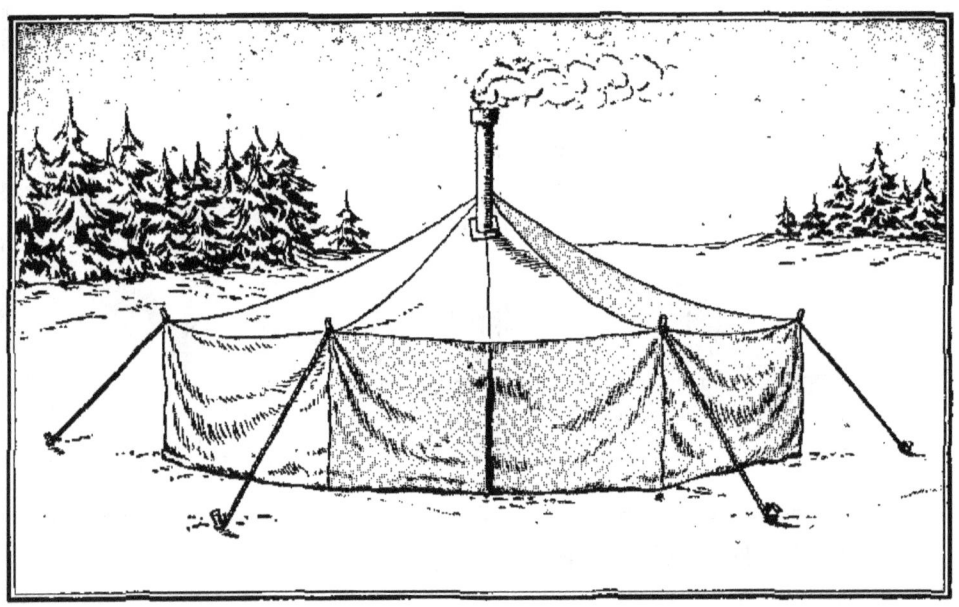

Figure 38.—Circular tent, Finnish type. (Notice the absence of pegs around the canvas: the canvas folds under to form a floor covering.)

The warmth of the tent may be increased by pegging it down in an excavation and covering it partially with trees, branches, earth, and a layer of snow. This method also provides some protection against shell fragments. During a thaw a drainage ditch must be dug around the tent. When house tents are not practicable, it is recommended that four- or six-man tents be pitched instead.

WINTER BIVOUACS AND SHELTER

24. CIRCULAR TENTS, FINNISH TYPE

The Finnish type of circular tent (*Rundzelt nach finnischer Art*) (fig. 38), together with the tent stove, is easy to transport (by man-drawn sled). The tent may be pitched in 15 to 20 minutes. It permits bivouacking in the open at temperatures of −40 degrees F. and below. Thus these tents are especially suitable for mobile winter forces, and it is desirable to issue them to troops.

25. LEAN-TOS AND OTHER IMPROVISED SHELTERS

In wooded areas lean-tos and branch huts may easily be constructed from logs and branches. The denser the walls

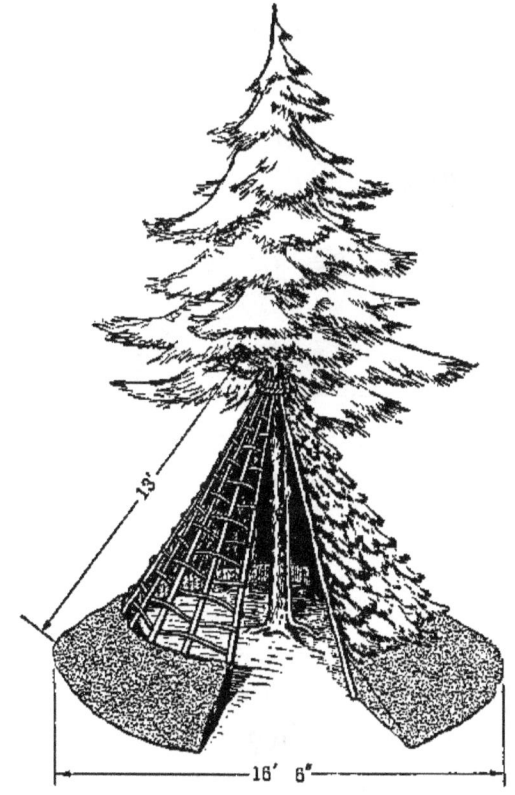

Figure 39.—Shelter built around a fir tree.

are woven and the tighter they are plastered with earth and snow, the warmer the huts will be. With heat furnished by log-fires or stoves, they may be suitable even for overnight stops in winter.

For just a few men the simplest structure is the circular shelter, built around trees (fig. 39), or the circular

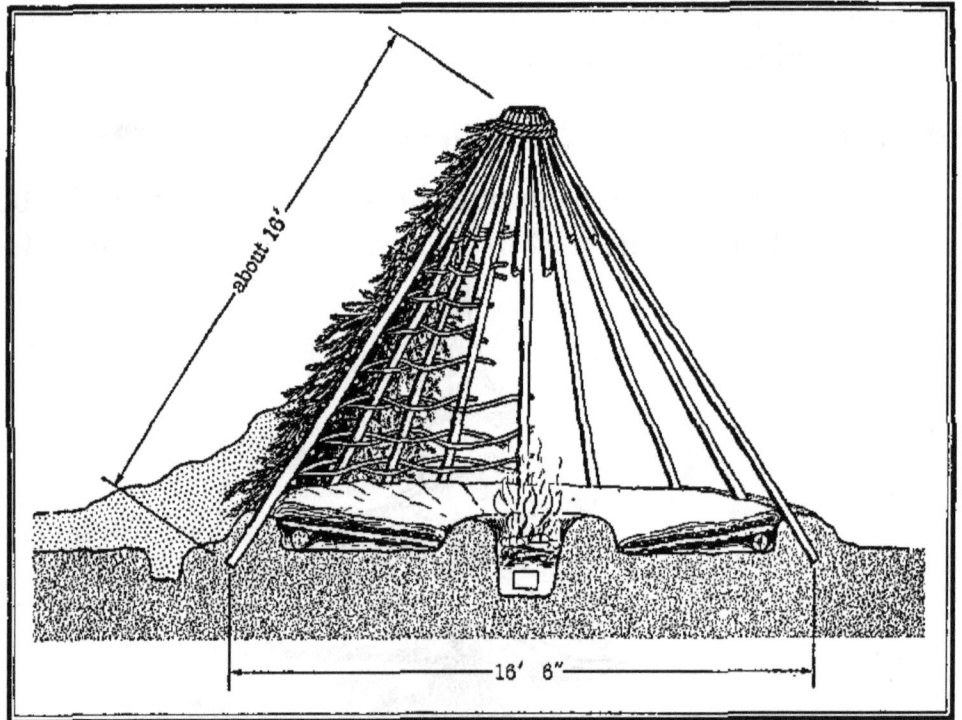

Figure 40.—Circular hut made of branches.

hut made of branches (fig. 40). Large huts are best if they are built on a square base.

The framework of the branch shelter consists of props and wickerwork made from long shrubbery switches. Fir branches, reeds, or bulrushes are placed upon or woven into the wickerwork in the manner of roof tiling. The gable must be covered with a double layer so that the branches from one side of the roof overlap on the other. The shrubbery roof is covered with a layer of earth up to 1 inch thick to render it windproof. Then a 4-inch layer of snow is laid over it.

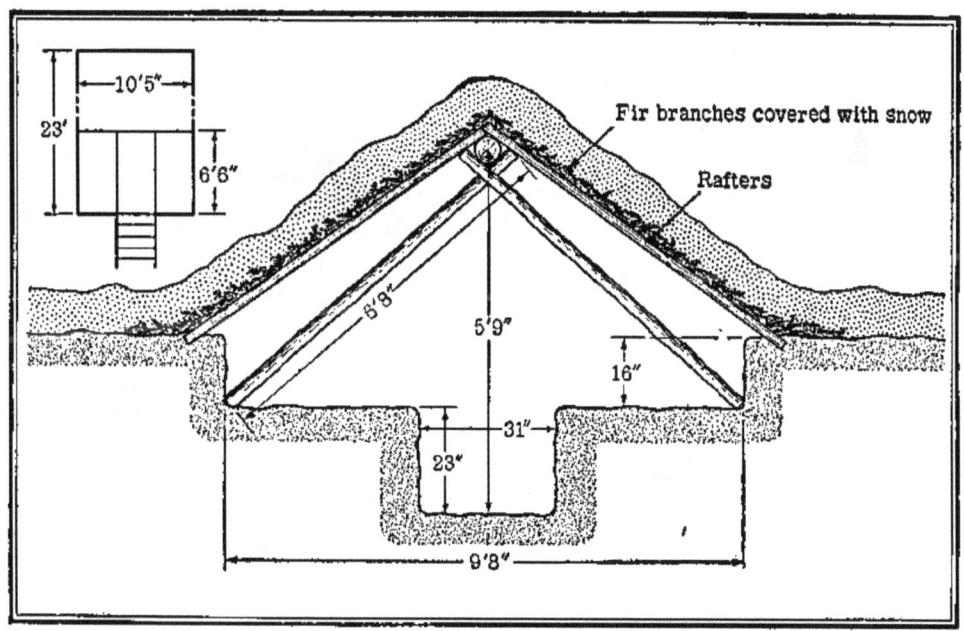

Figure 41.—Earth hut for 6 men.

In constructing the simple earth hut for 6 men (fig. 41) and the foliage shelter for 10 men (fig. 42) (approximately 12 by 16 feet),[1] the props must be bound to each other and to the rooftree by means of weaving (branches, inner bark, string, or wire). It is easiest to prefabricate the framework of the lean-to on the ground and then to erect it. A hut for about 7 men, erected against a slope, is shown in figure 43.

---

[1] The original text does not explain why the hut shown in figure 41 has less capacity than the shelter shown in figure 42, the dimensions of which are smaller.—EDITOR.

If these shelters are heated by means of stoves, a chimney leading into the open must be buried, as recommended for tents. It is advisable to provide a draught for the fire

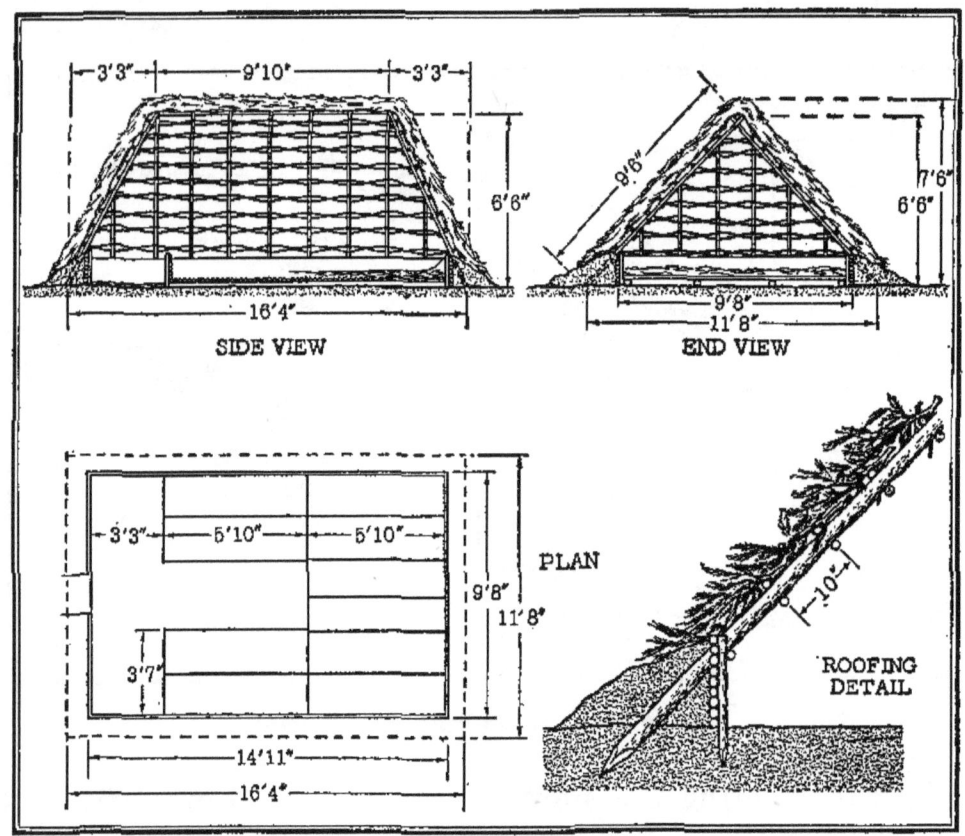

Figure 42.—Foliage shelter for 10 men.

by means of an air passage. (For further details, see sec. **VII**, "Heating Facilities," p. 105.)

26. SHELTERS FOR HORSES AND MOTOR VEHICLES

Horses and motor vehicles may be protected against cold and wind in the following types of shelters:

    a. Windbreaks for horses, heated with log fires (fig. 44 (1)).

    b. Enclosures for horses, constructed of snow blocks, with or without roofing (fig. 44 (2)).

WINTER BIVOUACS AND SHELTER 87

c. Shelters with special heating installations for motor vehicles (figs. 45 and 46).

27. PERMANENT BILLETS

a. General

Under the exigencies of winter warfare in hostile territory, even so-called "permanent billets" (*Dauerunter-*

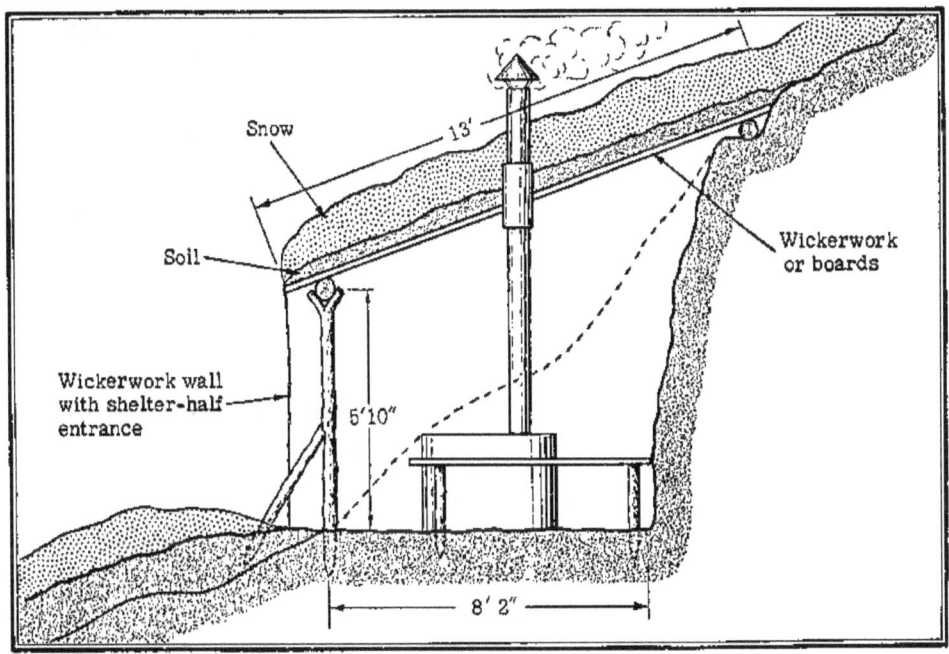

Figure 43.—Hut erected against a hillside.

künfte) may have to be improvised. The winter tactical mission of the unit, supply and sanitary facilities, security, and the resting and training of troops are determining factors in selecting a site and planning the type and size of the installation. Consideration for the homeland, the transportation situation, and the necessity for speed in constructing and furnishing quarters make it extremely imperative that units become self-reliant, reduce requirements to a minimum, and exploit the resources of occupied enemy territory.

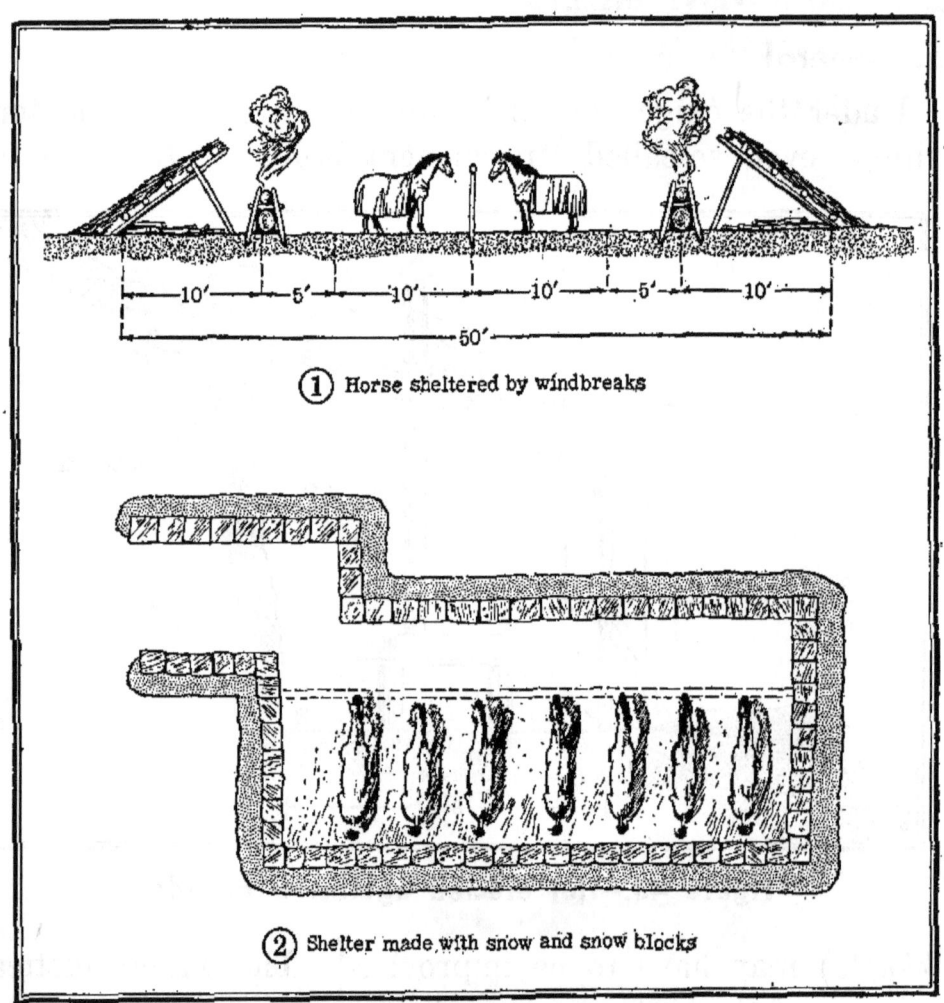

Figure 44.—Shelters for horses.

All large-scale construction of permanent billets for units of battalion strength and higher is done by the Army Construction Service (*Heeresbaudienst*) which is under the Quartermaster General (*IVa*) of the various army headquarters (*Armeeoberkommandos*), but with extensive help and cooperation from the troops. The units will provide labor details, engineer units, and vehicles. All construction of field-type shelters for smaller units is carried out by the troops themselves.

To guarantee shelter at the proper time, the Army Construction Service, the Army Billeting Administration, the

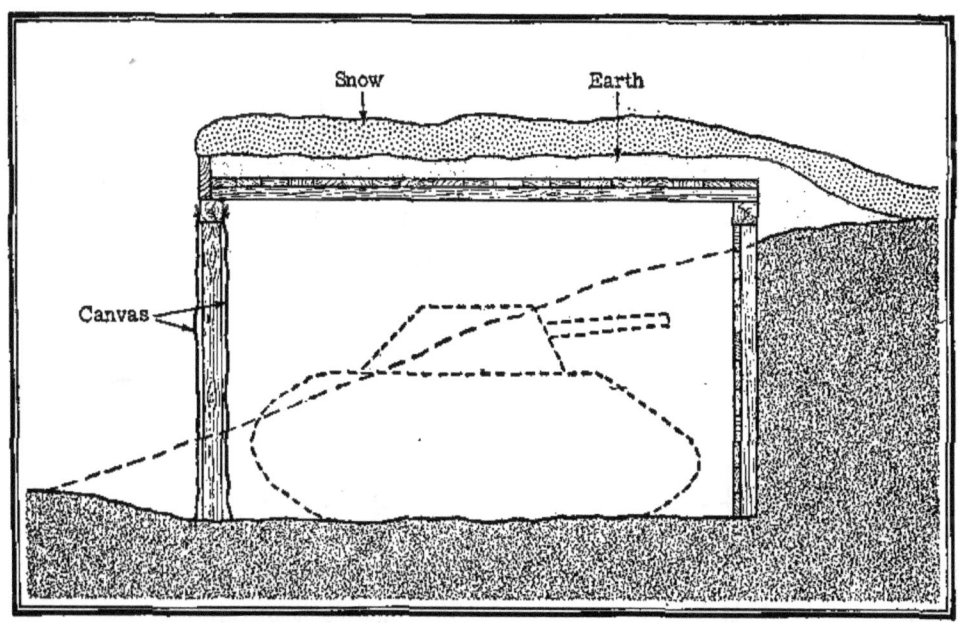

Figure 45.—Tank shelter built against a slope.

Military Building Site Troops, the Forest Protection Service Units, and the Civilian Construction Companies of the Army Construction Service are available. Building materials and ready-made parts such as doors and windows are prepared in the main construction-material warehouses. Sample blueprints and directions for construction of shelters for officers, enlisted men, and horses are available at the Army Construction Service.

90   GERMAN WINTER WARFARE

Command authorities (army, corps, or division headquarters) reconnoiter the winter position as soon as possible, select the sites for billets, and assign quarters to units. If the construction of permanent billets is necessary, the

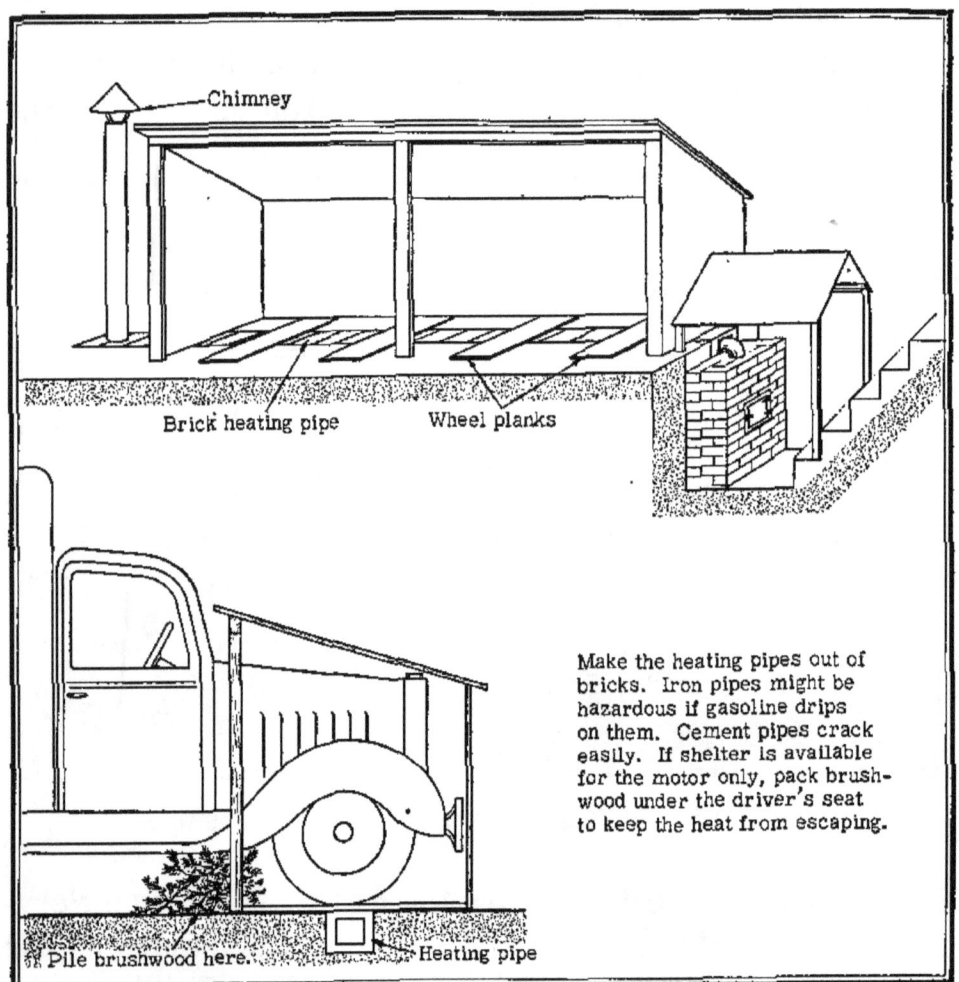

Figure 46.—Heated shelter for motor vehicles.

command authorities issue written orders to the Army Construction Service. The Army Construction Service determines whether the technical requirements for the building site can be met with available building materials, drafts the plan, and carries it out with its own forces and assigned Russian labor (prisoners of war or natives). These are augmented by labor details from the unit. The Forest Protection Service Units cut and prepare lumber with the assistance of the engineers.

From a tactical point of view, the factors which must be considered in selecting a site are accessibility, concealment from air and ground observation, and the possibilities for all-around defense and antiaircraft defense.

When existing buildings are adapted as quarters and the construction of simple field works and shelters is necessary, combat requirements and danger from the air must be taken into account. Consequently, billets and combat stations should be combined. Obstacles (on all sides), observation towers, machine-gun and other emplacements, and air-raid shelters must be installed.

Even when billets presumably will be used for but a short period, construction of sanitary installations, such as laundries, *sauna* (Finnish steam baths—see par. **47b**), and, above all, showers, must be undertaken with particular care.

b. Factors Governing Construction

(1) *Type of construction.*—The type of construction depends on the following factors:

(a) *Period of occupancy.*—The shorter the time of occupancy, the more primitive billets may be. (Caution! Keep improving them. Duration of use is often uncertain.) In case of extended use, adequate sanitary conditions and comfort must be assured.

(b) *Local construction material.*—The type of billets which will be constructed depends on the material available. In densely wooded areas log houses will be constructed; in regions poor in timber, turf houses; in mountainous terrain, stone huts; in the vicinity of sawmills or lumberyards, framework construction; near brickyards, brick construction.

(c) *Military construction material.*—Advance requisitioning of necessary quantities of military material, held down to a minimum, is desirable if materials are in stock at supply depots.

(d) *Investigation of site in detail.*—Ground consistency is important. If possible, select a dry site. Firm sand is most suitable. Less suitable are swampland, loamy soil, and humus (the latter may turn into a marsh).

(e) *Subsoil water.*—A source of water supply should be at least 6 feet below the surface. Several test holes should be drilled in the area. Data must be gathered on the rise of surface water during the rainy season.

(f) *Drinking water.*—Tests should be made by drilling to determine whether an adequate supply of drinking water is available. The water should be examined by the medical officer of the unit. If no water or only polluted water is available, or if clean water is too deep in the soil, the site must be selected near a stream or lake.

(g) *Waste-water drainage by means of open collecting trenches.*—For this method of drainage, an incline in the site is necessary—if possible, one that slopes toward a waterway with strong currents.

(h) *Proximity to roads.*—Avoid, if possible, the selection of a site with long approaches. This caution is especially important for motorized units.

(i) *Proximity to source of building materials.*—Short routes should be sought in order to economize on transportation.

(j) *Camouflage.*—If possible, construction should be undertaken in forests or close to existing buildings or inhabited localities.

(2) *Planning construction.*—When planning construction, the following factors must be considered:

(a) The participation of army construction authorities should begin with the reconnaissance for a site.

(b) At first, emergency construction should be provided to protect men from inclement weather. Construction of weatherproof and improved permanent billets should follow immediately.

(c) The buildings should be laid out in an irregular pattern, or they should be fitted into the layout of civilian structures in order to achieve camouflage of the position.

(d) Arrangements should be made for procuring locally in occupied territory material, shelter, and interior equipment (stoves, stables, roofing, doors, and floors).

(e) The skilled manpower of the unit and of the local population must be employed, as well as local vehicles of even the simplest type.

(f) The required building material and tools must be listed in advance.

c. Improvement of Existing Buildings

The improvement of existing buildings usually requires the following steps:

(1) Improvement of the heat-retaining qualities of floors, walls, and ceilings by using hay, straw, brushwood, and foliage; weatherproofing windows; construction of window shutters, storm windows, storm doors, and double floors; and construction of wind traps in front of entrances (the doors to open inward).

(2) Construction or improvement of stoves.

(3) Cleaning, covering, and protecting springs against freezing.

(4) Construction of latrines.

(5) Building of rat- and mouse-proof food cellars.

(6) Construction of furniture such as beds, tables, benches, and racks for weapons, equipment, and clothing.

d. Water Supply

An adequate water supply for a unit in permanent billets must be assured in the winter. To achieve this, supervision of the use of water by all commanders, with the cooperation of the medical officer, is required. The maximum daily requirement for one man is 5 to $7\frac{1}{2}$ gallons; and for one horse, 10 to 13 gallons.

The men themselves must make it their duty to protect all springs, pumps, and wells against freezing. For this purpose, a wooden frame should be built around them, and straw, hay, foliage, moss, and similar materials should be packed in. Roofs may be put over them to keep them from choking up with snow. Wooden containers are more suitable than metal containers for the transportation and storage of water in winter. The use of melted snow for drinking and cooking requires medical supervision.

Section VI. CONSTRUCTION OF WINTER POSITIONS

28. GENERAL

Many difficulties are experienced in the construction of positions in winter. Some of the main problems are reduced working capacity, owing to low temperatures; frozen ground, which requires increased energy and strong tools for excavating; and the hampering effect of snow on positions and material. Snow, however, may be utilized as a universally available, valuable building and camouflage material. (Ten feet of snow affords protection against rifle fire.)

The spring thaw period must be taken into consideration at the time the site is selected and during construction of the position. Drainage ditches must be provided. Communication trenches, tunnels, and dugouts must be sloped, and at the lowest points holes should be dug for drainage of water. The water may be bailed out when the holes fill up. If this is neglected, the installations will become inundated, and then soften up and disintegrate. Camouflage against aerial and ground observation must be given particular attention in snow-covered terrain (see sec. **VIII**, "Camouflage, Concealment, and Identification," p. 115). Sentry boxes must always be built for two men so that paired sentries can benefit from body heat and guard one another against freezing.

29. CONSTRUCTION OF SIMPLE POSITIONS

If it is impossible to dig in because of frozen ground, deep snow, or lack of time, cover above ground level must be provided by stacking sandbags to form walls which may be hardened by pouring water over them. Sandbags of cloth soak up water more readily than paper bags. The outside of the walls must be plastered with snow. Trampling increases the hardness of the snow. On top of the trampled snow, loose clean snow must be scattered for camouflage. The floor of rifle pits must be padded with a layer of foliage or fir branches. Such positions afford practical cover and are not easily detected by the enemy (see fig. 47). Positions for one or two riflemen or for one machine gun may also be built rapidly of logs or square timber (see fig. 48). The logs are stacked to form an open square, and are joined together by means of bolts or T hooks. The firing slit, just above the surface of the snow, is produced by a space left between the logs in the direction of the enemy. Such positions are surrounded by a thick wall of snow, or they are built into the snow. Camouflage may be provided by roof coverings of white cloths, or shelter halves covered with snow. The coverings also protect the infantryman against the weather. Firing slits are closed by means of pieces of wood painted white.

Positions for machine guns and mortars may be constructed in a similar manner, but it is advisable to roof over the rear portion with boards. The front portion remains open on top in order that the men may be able to defend themselves with hand grenades. (Protection against the weather is provided by a rapidly removable shelter half.)

Figure 47.—Sandbag position (rear view).

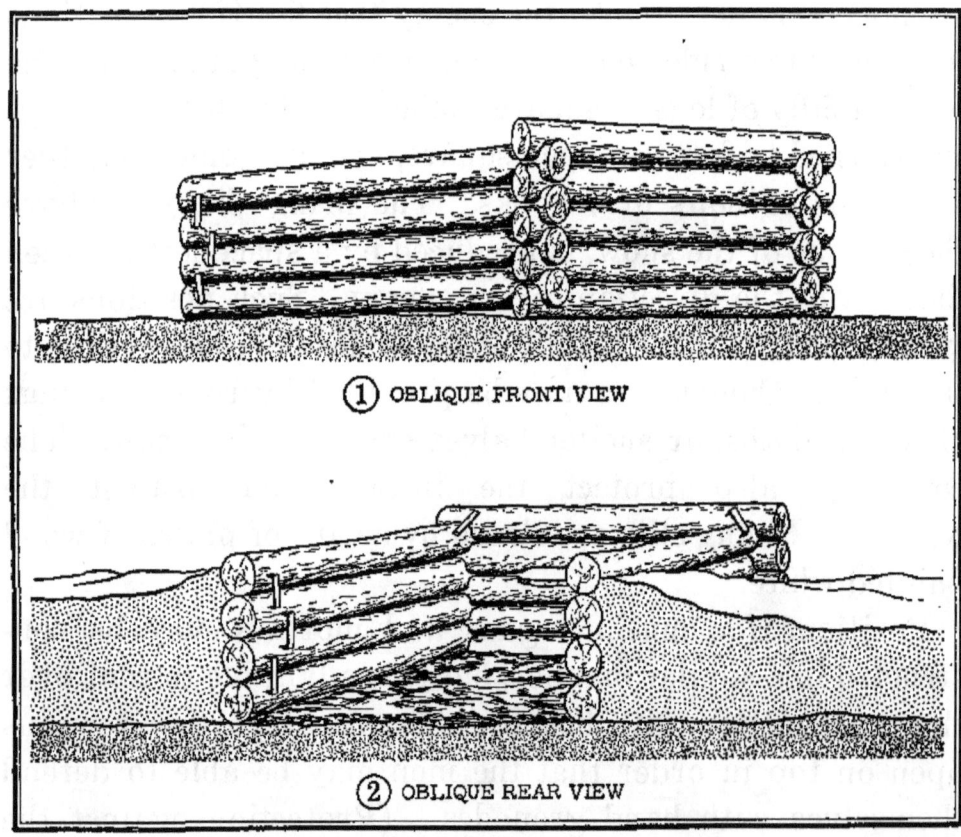

Figure 48.—Log position in snow.

CONSTRUCTION OF WINTER POSITIONS

When the ground is frozen too hard for the digging of trenches, snow walls may be used for cover instead. These walls afford protection against rifle bullets and shell splinters from small-caliber guns as follows:

Newly fallen snow	At least 13 feet.
Firmly frozen snow	At least 8 to 10 feet.
Packed snow	At least 6½ feet.
Ice	At least 39 inches.

Such walls may be used for constructing covered snow trenches (fig. 49). The inner walls should be lined, the lining

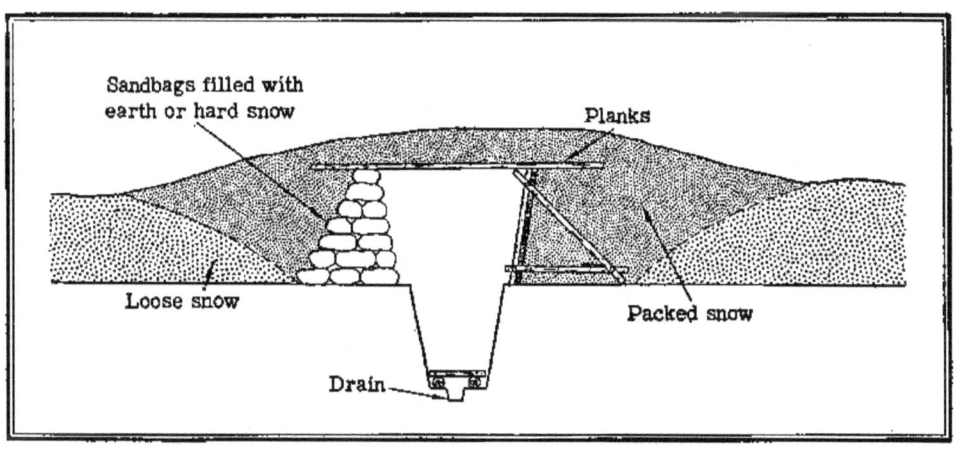

Figure 49.—Cross section of covered snow trench.

being nailed to simple triangular racks. The trench may be deepened later. It is then covered with snow as heavily as possible. A communication trench may also be built in this way and it would offer good concealment and protection from shell splinters. The roofing prevents the trench from filling up with drifting snow.

30. IMPROVED POSITIONS

In deep snow, simple caves and dugouts may be dug quickly. They afford protection against inclement weather and small shell splinters and have the advantage of complete camouflage. Such shelters are most substantial when they are vaulted and lined with boards, or they should be reinforced with wooden frames. In long caves, tubes or wooden boxes must be inserted in the ceiling at intervals to provide lighting and ventilation (fig. 50).

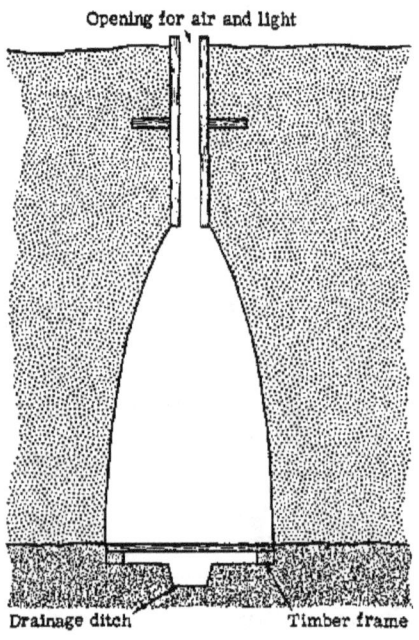

Figure 50.—Cross section of vaulted dugout.

When the situation permits, it is more desirable to dig positions in the ground. Such positions are safer, and they are constructed exactly as prescribed for normal terrain, except that there must be better provision for retaining heat. This is also true of sentry boxes, observation posts, machine-gun and mortar emplacements, infantry positions, shelters for antitank guns and infantry howitzers, supply and munitions depots, shelters, and dugouts.

Wherever the situation permits unhampered construction of trenches and dugouts, the frozen ground must be marked out and the positions excavated one at a time. If the soil is frozen deeply, holes of the required depth are made at intervals and then connected by tunnels. Holes for blasting charges may be made with sharp red-hot iron rods which are driven into the ground. The frozen upper layer is then destroyed by explosive charges.

Thorough weatherproofing of dugouts is especially necessary. The ground is covered with tar paper, and boards are laid on it. Brushwood or straw is spread over the boards. Sawdust may also be used, either by itself or mixed with straw or brushwood. A second layer of boards is laid on top of the insulating material. The framework of the dugout is constructed of logs. Like the floor, the walls are made with boards, lined with tar paper, and are hollow so that they can be filled with straw or brushwood. The ceiling is made of two layers of logs, covered with tar paper, earth, and snow. The stovepipe is equipped with a shield against falling snow and is later camouflaged. The furniture consists of the required bunks, benches, and folding tables. If field stoves are not available, the dugouts may be heated with hot stones, which are dropped into holes and covered with wooden or iron grates. (For details, see sec. **VII**, "Heating Facilities," p. 105.)

"Ice-concrete" (*Sandeis*) is an easily prepared, effective reinforcement for shelters and emplacements (fig. 51). It consists of a solid, frozen mixture of sand and water, or sand, gravel, and water, and is stronger than ordinary ice. A layer of earth over "ice-concrete" prevents the latter from thawing. "Ice-concrete" is made by slowly mixing water and sand in a trough or tub. The mixture is slowly

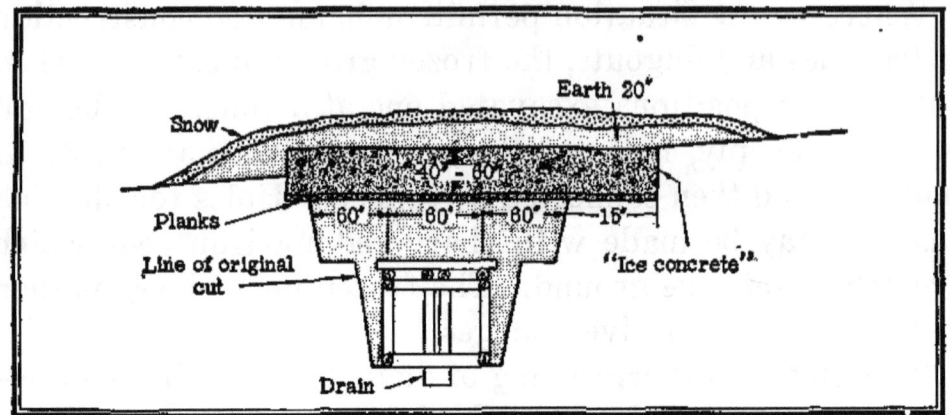

Figure 51.—Shelter made of "ice-concrete."

applied in layers and packed firm. A layer must not be applied until the preceding one has completely frozen. Thaw impairs its firmness; therefore, dugouts constructed of "ice-concrete" should be especially marked.

31. OBSTACLES

Winter influences to a large degree the construction and effectiveness of obstacles. Deep, loose snow is a natural obstacle. Russian tanks are able to traverse loose snow up to a depth of 1 meter (39 inches) but their climbing ability is reduced. Parallel snow walls, as shown in figure 52,

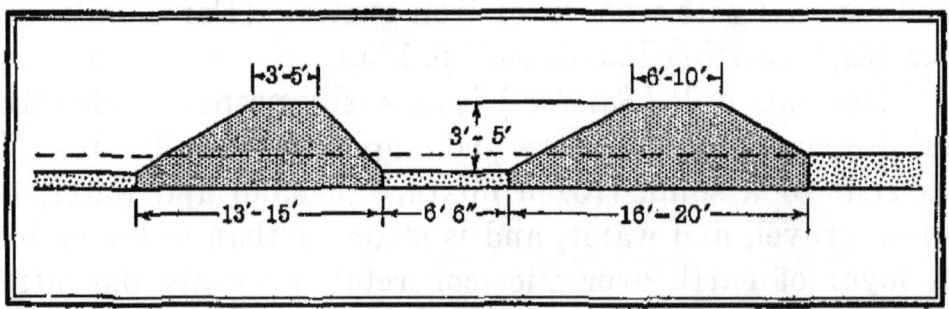

Figure 52.—Antitank obstacle of packed snow.

constitute an effective tank obstacle. The snow must be packed hard.

The effect of steep inclines and gullies is heightened by deep snow and ice. Deep snow-bound road ditches can become tank traps. Movements in deep snow are usually possible only on roads and then only after trails have been

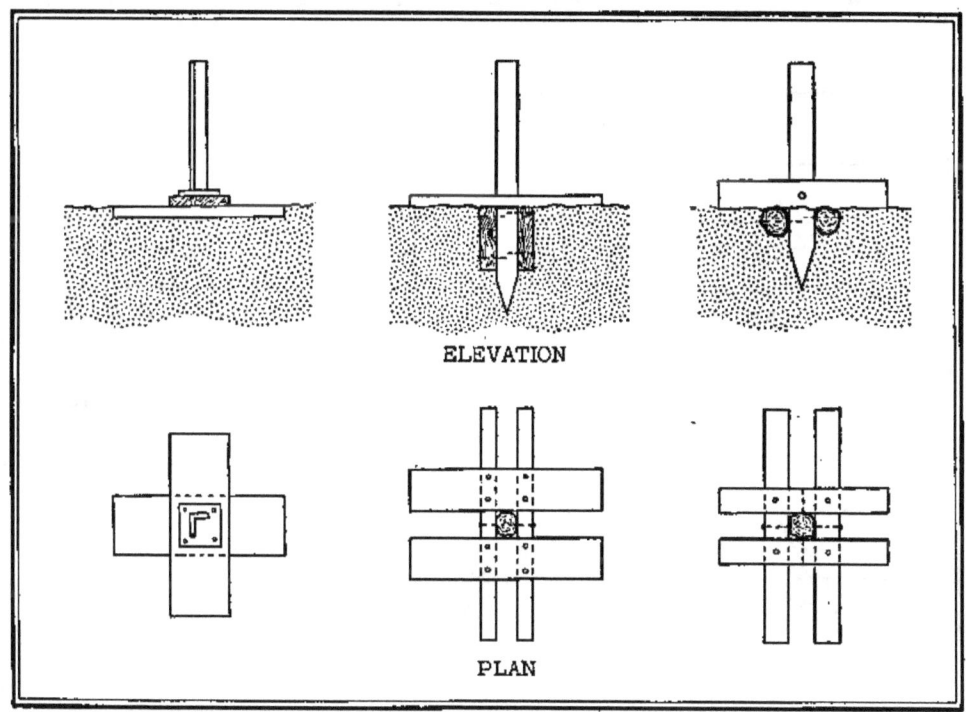

Figure 53.—Barbed-wire fence pickets in snow.

cut or snow has been cleared. Road obstacles are therefore especially important in winter.

The installation of wire obstacles in winter is made difficult by frozen ground and snow, which make it necessary to build obstacles considerably higher than usual (up to 4 meters, or 13 feet). If frozen ground must be blasted for the stakes, holes for the charges are made with strong pickaxes or red-hot iron rods. The narrow holes are then enlarged by means of blasting cartridges or other explosive charges until heavy stakes up to a length of 4 meters (13 feet) may be placed in them. Water is poured around the stakes in order to freeze them firmly. In deep snow, barbed-wire stakes should be erected with broad bases. Logs or

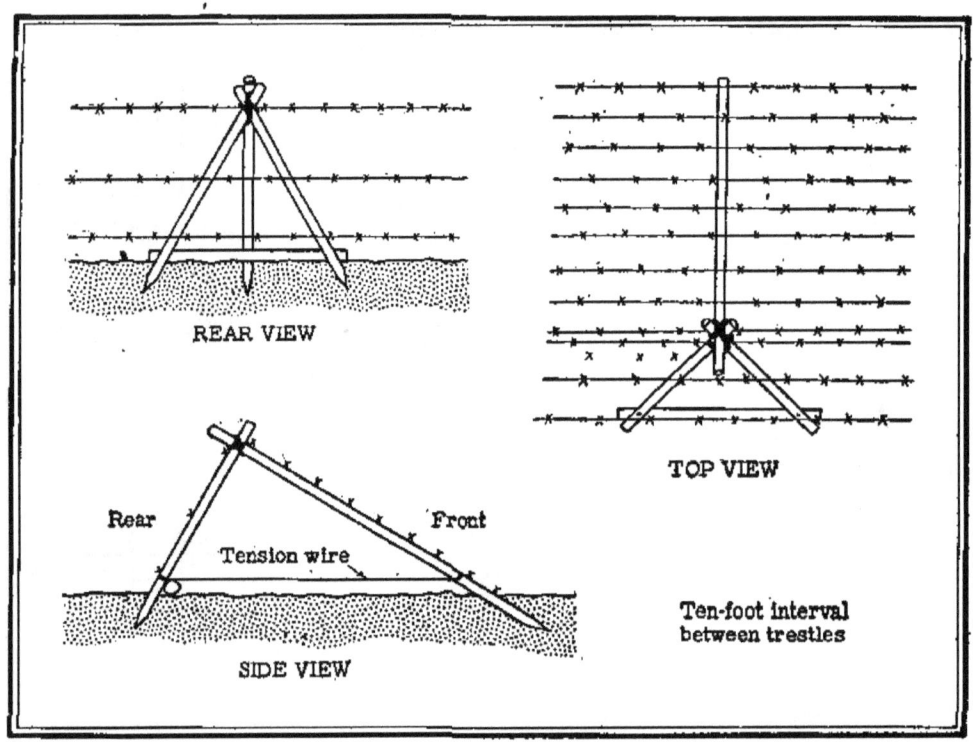

Figure 54.—Tripod trestle for barbed-wire fence.

squared timber and planks, 2 meters (6½ feet) in length, are used to make the pole and base (fig. 53). When obstacles of this sort are erected in several rows, wooden rods may be placed between them as braces. (Do not obstruct fields of fire!)

Another proved support for wire obstacles is the tripod trestle (fig. 54). It is manufactured in large numbers behind the front and then brought forward. The trestles for a whole section of fence are placed flat on the ground and barbed wire is nailed to them. Then the section is erected as a unit.

Barbed-wire rolls (S rolls) are used to better advantage than *chevaux-de-frise* in snow. Because of their broad surface, they sink only slightly into the snow. They are easily

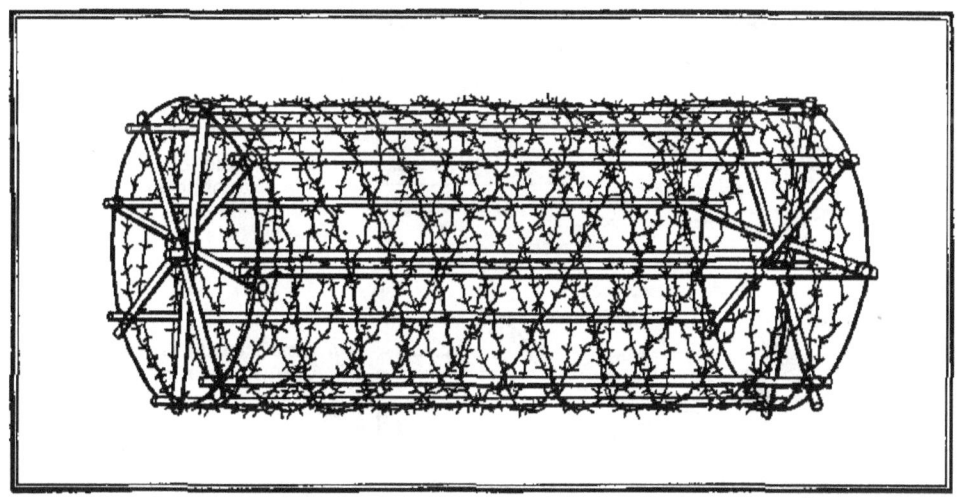

Figure 55.—Barbed-wire roll for use in snow.

constructed (fig. 55). But a disadvantage in building wire entanglements on snow is that the enemy is able to crawl under them. For this reason, alarm devices, such as cans filled with nails, must be affixed to the wires at various heights. (The effectiveness of such devices must be tested frequently, as they are unreliable.)

Antitank obstacles in frozen bodies of water may be constructed in the following manner. An opening about 4 meters (13 feet) wide is cut into the ice and covered with snow or other material which will prevent the water from freezing. The enemy, and especially his tanks, will usually fail to recognize the location of these obstacles before traversing them. The effectiveness of such obstacles depends on the absolute reliability of the covering material which keeps the water from freezing. The snow cover must

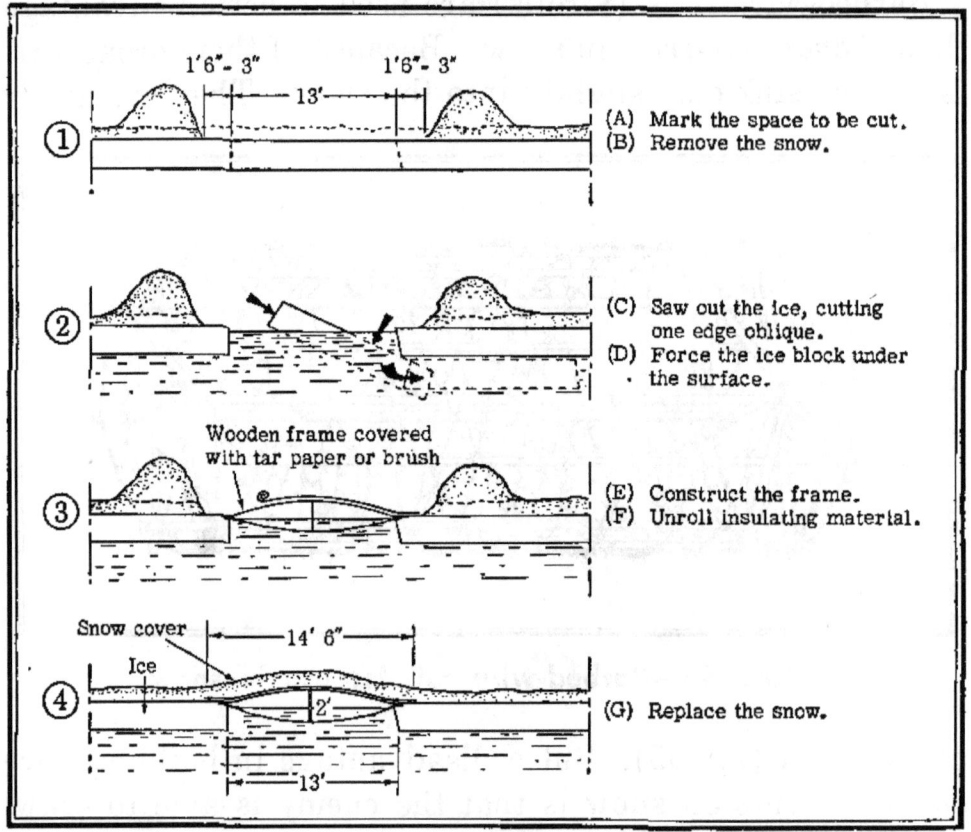

Figure 56.—Antitank trap in frozen body of water.

not be less than 4 inches; otherwise the water will freeze through again. A well-made trap remains effective from 1½ to 2½ months in temperatures of from 5 to −13 degrees F., provided it is continually inspected and maintained.

In winter, regular and makeshift mines of all kinds (even when laid in ice) are effective obstacles. In the snow they are laid on special supports to prevent them from sinking.

Section VII. HEATING FACILITIES

32. GENERAL

A soldier's power of resistance against the cold increases considerably if he is provided with maximum heating facilities. However, even slight heating is better than none at all. Combat positions, bivouacs, and temporary billets can be adequately heated with simple equipment or improvised devices.

The following can be used for heating purposes: candles, lamps, fuels (denatured alcohol, gasoline, kerosene), hot stones, and issue and improvised brick stoves. They should be covered to prevent snow from melting over them. Tents and snow bivouacs can be heated by candles, lamps, and cooking equipment to a fairly tolerable temperature. Care must be taken, however, that the heating facilities do not generate poisonous gases in confined shelters. (Follow instructions exactly!)

33. FIRES

There are various kinds of warming fires. That fire is best which gives heat for a long time but does not generate much smoke (concealment!). The log fire has proved very effective, and the wood of dead fir trees is most useful for this purpose. The sides of the logs facing each other should be notched, and chips and shavings or charcoal should be ignited between them. The fire burns slowly with a low flame and gives warmth for many hours without making much smoke (see fig. 57). The fire shown in figure 58 (1) gives warmth and also furnishes charcoal. Stand the wood in the pit; not much is needed.

To make the hunter's fire shown in figure 58 (2), place logs in a fan formation on top of two other logs. Light the fire where the logs cross each other, and keep pushing the logs into the fire as the ends burn away. This fire burns slowly

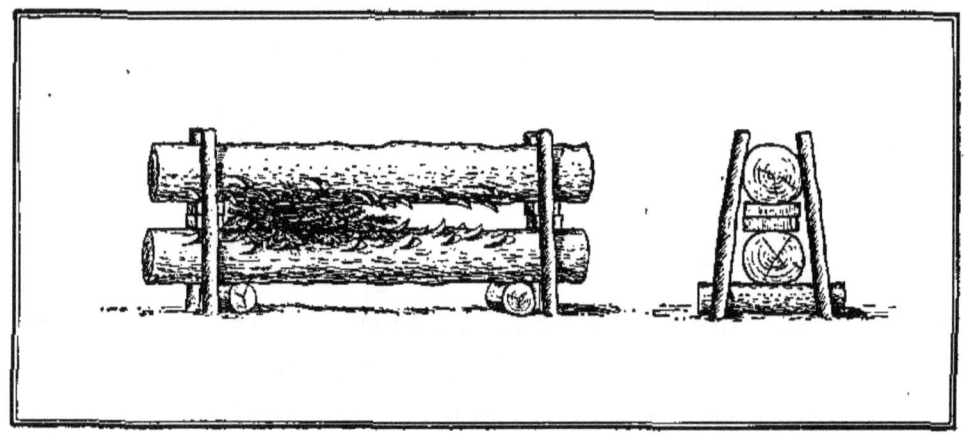

Figure 57.—Long-burning fir-log fire.

and warms well. Figure 58 (3) shows a star-shaped fire. Shove the logs forward as they burn.

The "invisible fire" (*unsichtbares Feuer*) shown in figure 58 (4) is made in a deep pit. Then place a piece of bark or wood over the fire with one end bent and projecting flat over the edge of the pit. The smoke will be led off horizontally and dissipated without betraying the fire.

Starting a fire with wet wood is often difficult. For this purpose, kindling wood should be used. A candle stump is also very useful. (One should always be carried.) Birch bark burns even when wet; dry pine, fir twigs, and dry tree moss also make good kindling. If matches are not available, prepare a tinder of dry bark or paper. Pour some powder from a few cartridges over the tinder; then load and fire the empty cartridge just over the tinder. The flame from the primer will ignite the powder and tinder. In emplacements, caves, and dugouts, fires like the one in figure 59 have proved effective.

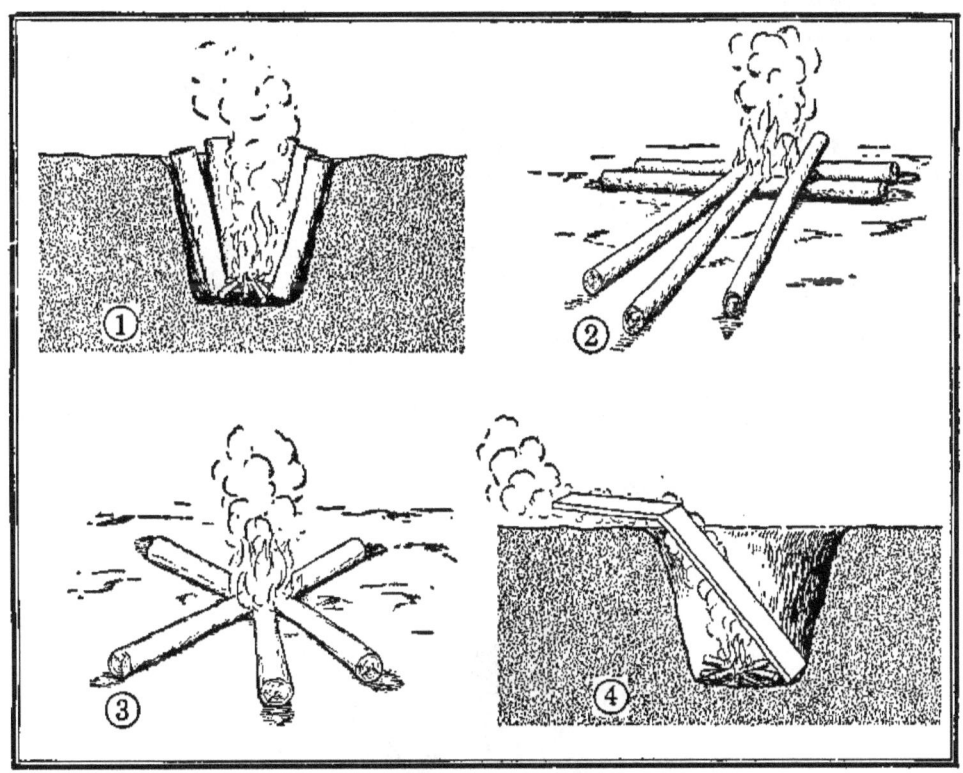

Figure 58.—Various types of fires, showing (1) pit fire; (2) hunter's fire; (3) star-shaped fire; (4) "invisible fire."

Hot stones contained in a grate or a box filled with paper or straw are useful for heating small shelters, such as sentry boxes. Similar expedients are especially suitable for warming the wounded while they are being evacuated; in addition to hot stones, warming bottles filled with hot water or hot sand, paper, cloth and fur wrappings, and blankets may be used. (See sec. **XII**, "Evacuation of Wounded," p. 149.)

Figure 59.—Fireplace for emplacements and caves.

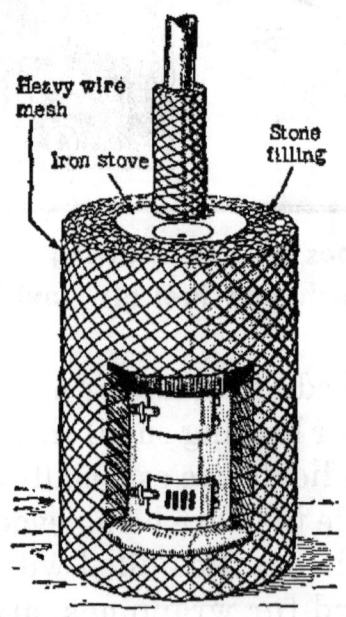

Figure 60.—Insulated trench stove.

HEATING FACILITIES

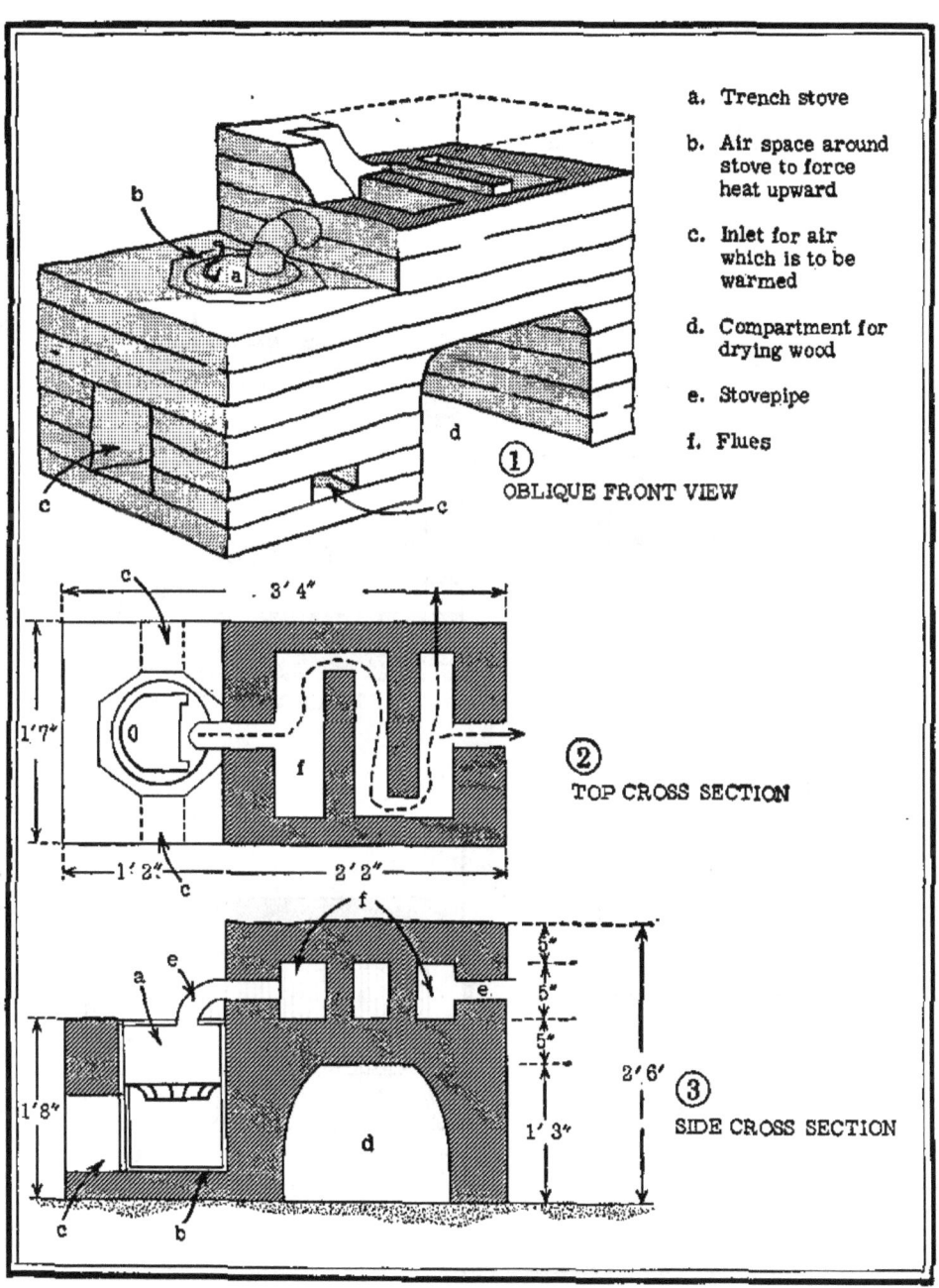

Figure 61.—Bricked-in stove.

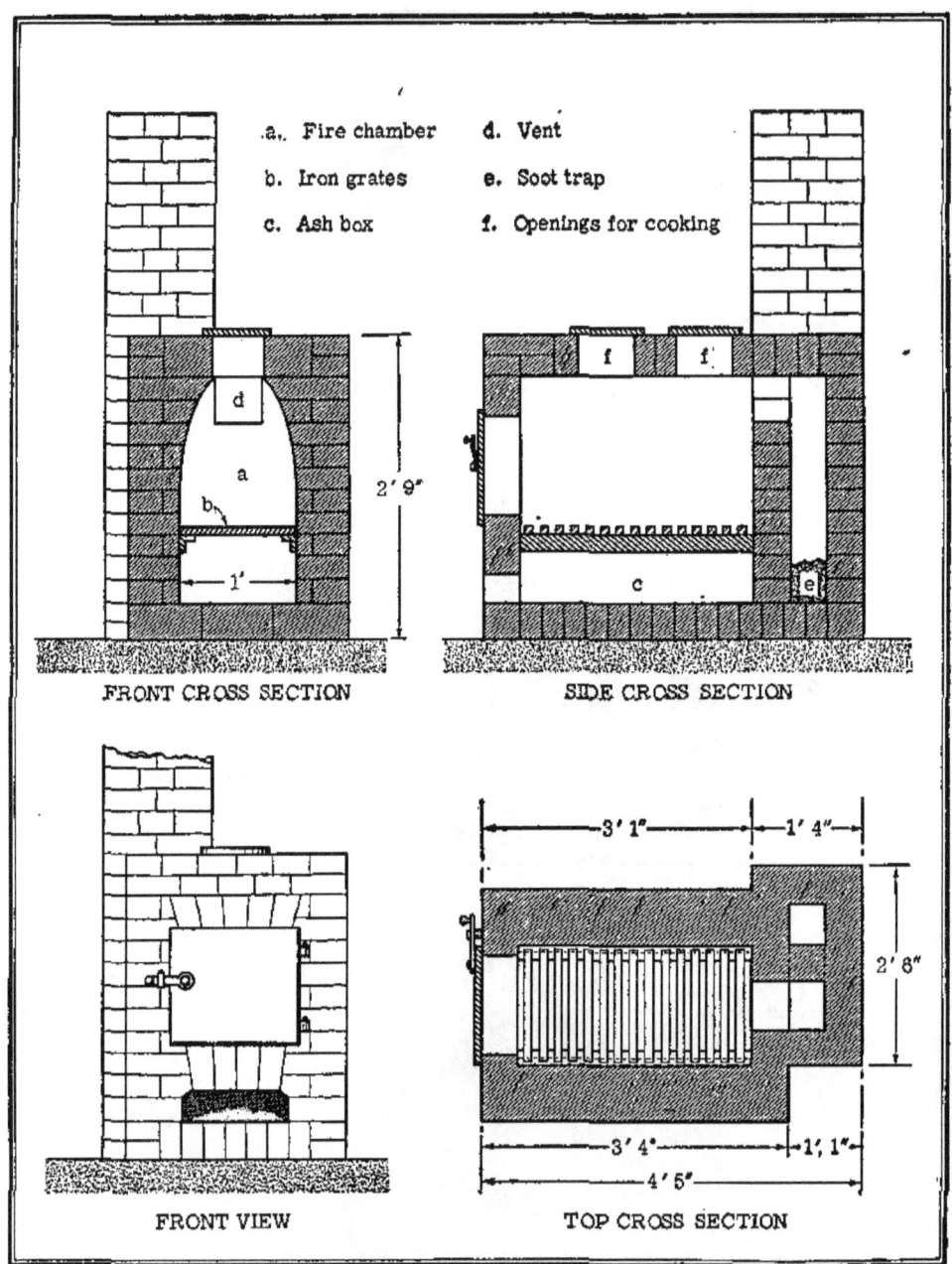

Figure 62.—Brick stove with two ovens.

Various types of field stoves are being issued, and can be insulated with stones to retain the heat (fig. 60). Instructions for their use should be followed precisely. In the front lines only charcoal should be used (fire without smoke). More heat can be radiated by field stoves if they are bricked-in (fig. 61). Brick stoves should be constructed in permanent billets (fig. 62). If possible, employ prisoners and natives to construct them.

34. MAKING CHARCOAL

Wood from deciduous and coniferous trees, 3 to 10 inches in diameter, is suitable for making charcoal. Larger logs must be split to facilitate charring. Wood must be cut in pieces 39 inches long and branches trimmed off. Dry wood is more suitable than green wood. Charcoal is produced in piles of one, two, or three layers. Piles of three layers of wood are most productive. Piles of one layer produce the least quantity for the effort involved, and piles of two layers are used only when little time is available. The duration of the charring process for two layers is 3 days. The pile should contain 10 to 15 cubic meters (353 to 530 cubic feet). The three-layer pile should contain approximately 100 cubic meters (3,531 cubic feet) of piled wood. The duration of the charring process is 10 to 12 days. One cubic meter (about 35 cubic feet) of piled wood produces 110 to 165 pounds of charcoal.

It is advisable to make several piles at one time, in a place where it is easy for the troops to watch them from their shelters. The best place is in the woods in a spot which is protected from the wind. If possible, select a site near water, which will be necessary for extinguishing the fire, and near moss or sod, which will be used for covering the pile. Protection from the wind is very important for uniform and thorough charring. Therefore, if necessary, a protective wall should be built of brushwood and filled in with moss. It should be as high as the pile and about 7 feet away from it.

To erect a two-layer pile, a space about 20 feet in diameter is required. Then a quadrangular shaft of sticks (the chimney) must be erected in the center (see fig. 63). The shaft

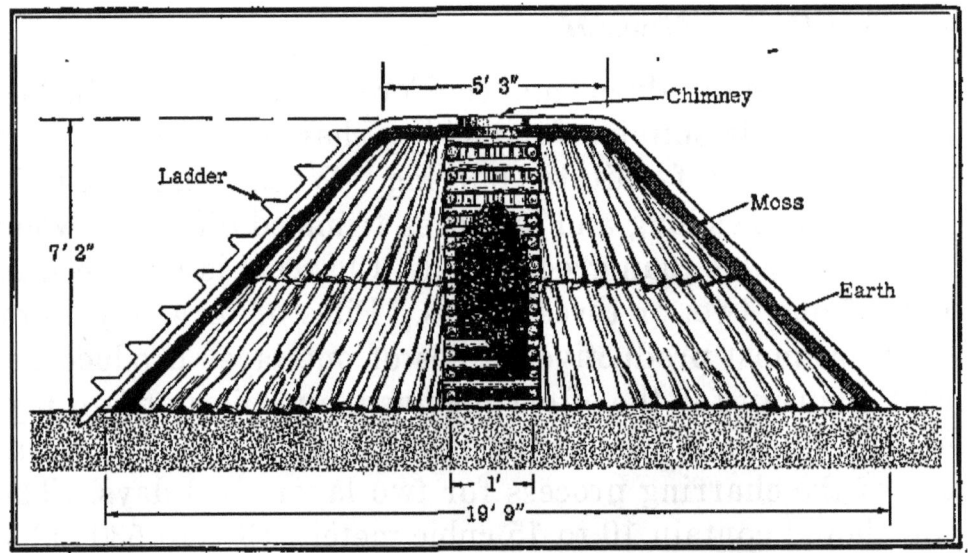

Figure 63.—Cross section of two-layer charcoal pile.

opening should be 12 inches square and as high as the pile. Then the wood should be piled vertically and rather tight around the shaft. The pile must then be covered with a layer of moss tightly packed down, and this in turn must be covered with a layer of sand or soil (not too dry) 4 to 6 inches thick. Only the upper part of the shaft is left open.

The shaft should be half-filled with kindling wood or charcoal, and air holes should be made by pushing a pointed pole as deeply as possible into the pile from the sides. The holes should be close to the ground and spaced 20 inches apart.

The process of charring is begun by igniting the kindling wood in the shaft from above. The shaft fire should be kept burning until the pile itself begins to burn. Then the shaft must be completely filled with fuel and covered with moss and sand. If the pile does not burn uniformly (which is indicated when the cover of the pile sinks in unevenly), more air holes must be made higher up in the pile. When the fire has burned down, the air holes must be closed either completely or partially. Likewise, all parts of the cover which have burned through must be replaced. Places which have sunk in deeply must be filled with fresh wood driven in with a mallet and covered up again; otherwise the pile will burn through and yield mostly ashes. Correct placing of the air holes and closing them at the proper time are especially important in producing a rich yield of charcoal. When blue smoke comes from the lower air holes and the pile cover close to the ground has burned through, the process is ended. Now the pile must once again be completely covered with soil and left untouched for a day to cool off. The finished charcoal must be taken out with hooks and cooled off with water. It is then ready for use.

35. DANGER OF CARBON-MONOXIDE POISONING

The danger of carbon-monoxide poisoning is greater when improvised quarters and stoves are used. Therefore fire guards should be posted. Exhaust gases from combustion engines can also cause carbon-monoxide poisoning. Therefore, doors of sheds where motor vehicles or motor machinery are stored should have large openings for ventilation. These openings should never be closed when a motor is running. A motor vehicle should not be started in an enclosed place or, if it is covered with canvas, even in the open air. Exhaust gases from machinery must be piped into the open air. The heating pipes of vehicles which are heated by means of exhaust gases must be well insulated. Have the unit medical officer speak regularly to the troops about the danger of carbon-monoxide poisoning.

Carbon monoxide is odorless, and therefore it is detectable only when mixed with other gases, such as illuminating gas and "smoldering gas" (*Schwelgas*) from stoves. Carbon-monoxide poisoning is first perceptible only through the behavior of an affected person. Change of mood and irrational laughter or singing may be warning symptoms. The poisoning develops quickly and the person becomes unconscious. A fresh complexion on a person who has fainted confirms the suspicion of poisoning. The fresh complexion remains for a long time after death. If it is suspected that a closed room contains carbon monoxide, it should be entered only by some one wearing the army respirator; gas masks will not afford protection against carbon monoxide. If a respirator is not available, one should smash the windows from the outside before entering, or open them from the inside while holding the breath. An afflicted person should be carried immediately into the fresh air and artificial respiration applied until the patient revives or dies. It may be necessary to continue artificial respiration for hours.

Section VIII. CAMOUFLAGE, CONCEALMENT, AND IDENTIFICATION

36. GENERAL

Proper exploitation of available and improvised camouflage facilities and materials may be of decisive importance. Snow completely changes the landscape and conceals details of the terrain and military installations from enemy air and ground observation. On the other hand, troops, vehicles, and trails of all types are particularly discernible. The deep shadows cast by prominent terrain features upon snow fields are so distinct to the aerial observer that they are not so reliable as in summer for concealment.

During the thaw period the terrain presents a mottled pattern of dark and bright patches which favors camouflage. Camouflage is futile if the conduct of the men is careless. Officers of all ranks must supervise camouflage discipline continually and must set a good example in observing such discipline themselves.

37. CAMOUFLAGE MATERIALS

a. Prepared Camouflage Materials

For camouflage in snow, extensive use must be made of white clothing. For this purpose white camouflage cloaks and two-piece white uniforms are available. If the supply is insufficient for all combat troops, priority must be given to ski patrols, raiding parties on skis, sentries, and similar detachments. Camouflage is improved if the face is covered with a mask of transparent gauze fastened to the parka hood. White gloves, if available, are the best camouflage for the hands. The belt and equipage should be worn under the white cloak. The most effective camouflage for weapons, equipment, material, motor and other vehicles, tanks, sleds, and skis is white oil paint or whitewash, which is issued. To make improvised paints durable, the admixture of glue is recommended. If there is a shortage of paints, use chalk or lime dissolved in water.

b. Improvised Camouflage Materials

Good camouflage may also be effected with improvised materials. The steel helmet may be painted white or pasted over with white paper. The edges of the paper must reach down to the shoulders and must cover the face. Slits are made for the eyes. The simplest way of camouflaging the head and shoulders is to fasten one end of a towel to the center of the headgear and to let it drape over the shoulders, to which the other end is pinned. The face is covered with a handkerchief, which is drawn back and pinned to the towel.

Camouflage cloaks can be made from old underwear, sheets, and other old garments, and they are worn like a cape. It is recommended that remnants of old garments be sewed to the lining so that the camouflage drapes may also be used in terrain of a broken color pattern. Horses may be camouflaged with white blankets which cover the upper part and sides of their heads and bodies, without interfering with their vision and breathing.

38. UTILIZATION OF CAMOUFLAGE

a. Individual Camouflage

Complete camouflage in white permits the soldier to move freely in snow-covered terrain. Even under favorable conditions he can hardly be seen at a distance of 500 yards when standing. In a prone position, he cannot be seen beyond a few paces. While in motion he must constantly utilize a white background and must select his position accordingly. When leaving woods, for example, he must creep until he is beyond the dark background of the woods. If he takes a position close to a tree or a stone, he must choose the snow-covered side; if he climbs a tree, it must be one which is covered with snow. Moreover, he must select a tree which is not too conspicuous. The snow must not be shaken off when the soldier climbs the tree.

In newly fallen snow, white camouflage clothing must be kept clean if it is to remain effective. It must, therefore, be taken off upon entering quarters or dugouts. Terrain with bare earth showing in patches through the snow and dark trees do not make an effective background for white camouflage clothing. In such terrain clothing smeared with earth should be worn.

An infantryman digging a foxhole in open, snow-covered country offers a good target if the pile of excavated snow is too high, or if earth is mingled with the snow. Excavated earth must be integrated into the surrounding ground features and covered with snow. When observing or firing from a parapet, the snow must be scooped out to keep the soldier's silhouette low and to avoid showing his head in relief.

b. Means of Identification

(1) *Brassards.*—Winter conditions often make it very hard to distinguish between friend and foe even at short distances. Therefore, the use of certain distinguishing marks is necessary, and the troops must be advised in orders of their meaning. For individual identification, brassards in two colors (black and red), about 3 inches wide, are worn. They can be buttoned either on the right or left sleeve. To avoid imitation by the enemy, they can be changed periodically, just like passwords. Eight different ways of wearing the brassards are possible, as follows:

- (a) Black brassard on left upper arm.
- (b) Black brassard on right upper arm.
- (c) Black brassard on both upper arms.
- (d) Red brassard on left upper arm.
- (e) Red brassard on right upper arm.
- (f) Red brassard on both upper arms.
- (g) Black brassard on left upper arm and red brassard on right upper arm.
- (h) Black brassard on right upper arm and red brassard on left upper arm.

(2) *Manner of wearing belt.*—The manner of wearing the belt depends on the style used by the enemy, and should be changed accordingly. If, for example, the enemy does not wear belts, German troops should wear belts over the outer clothing. Another method of identification is to wear a certain number of cartridge pouches, or to wear the bread bag [similar to the U. S. field bag] in a certain manner. The prescribed method should be announced in each new tactical order.

(3) *Ground flags and signals.*—The flag is spread out on the snow to identify the unit as a friendly one. It is especially important to know the use of ground panels for com-

munication purposes between the ground units and air units. Special prearranged signals between air and ground units fighting in close support have proved to be very effective. In improvising flags, only dark conspicuous colors should be used (red, black, blue, green).

The following can be used as auxiliary means of air-ground identification: arranging branches, tools, or equipment on the snow in the shape of a swastika; trampling of a swastika pattern in the snow; or shoveling snow away to expose the soil in a swastika pattern.

Ski poles and rifles may be used as follows as a means of identification. Raise the right or left ski pole up to shoulder height; move a ski pole in circles over the head, in front or to one side. Carry the rifle slung over the right or the left shoulder, or around the neck. Since these methods of identification can easily be imitated by the enemy, daily changes are necessary.

(4) *Passwords and blinker signals.*—Familiar names should be used as passwords. An example follows: challenge, "Garmisch"; countersign, "Partenkirchen."[1] This method of identification can be used by day as well as by night and can be imitated by the enemy only with difficulty. It is advisable to choose as passwords the names of rivers, towns, or mountains from the home region of the unit.

Blinker signals with flashlights are to be used primarily in darkness or fog. The sequence of colors must be prearranged. For example, in challenging with a red blinker signal, the reply should be given with a green one.

---

[1] Garmisch-Partenkirchen are twin towns in Bavaria, and are usually mentioned together.—EDITOR.

c. Camouflage of Field Positions

Camouflage must be considered immediately when a field position is selected, in order to take advantage of natural contours and features. This also applies to the construction of communication and approach trenches.

Figure 64.—Camouflaging trenches with willow frames.

Trenches must be camouflaged by covering them as thoroughly as possible within the available time. Mats and wooden frames woven with wire or willow branches may serve as a covering (fig. 64). They must be 5 or 6 feet wide, and long enough to span the trench. The frames are covered with brushwood and weatherproofed with straw or paper which has been previously wet and frozen. After

Figure 65.—Concealment of installations in a trench system.

the trench has been covered, camouflage is completed by adding a thin layer of snow. A cover of this type may be raised on supports on the side facing the enemy so that observation and firing are possible.

If there is insufficient time for complete camouflage, only important sections of the fortification system, such as

Figure 66.—Antitank ditch camouflaged to resemble an ordinary trench.

machine-gun emplacements and observation posts, should be covered. Thus the system will appear to an enemy observer to be merely a communication trench (see fig. 65).

Antitank ditches, because of their width, can rarely be camouflaged completely, but they may be covered partially to make them appear like ordinary, narrow trenches (see

Figure 67.—Tank concealed under snow-covered canvas.

fig. 66). The enemy may be misled into employing his tanks over these deceptively narrow points.

If positions are constructed of snow or snow blocks, their top edges must be rounded off in order to avoid strong reflections of light and marked shadows. When rifles and machine guns are fired, steps must be taken, especially in dry snow, to prevent disclosure of the position by snow clouds blown up by muzzle blast. Trampling the snow into a firmly packed mass in front of the muzzle, or covering the snow unobtrusively with fir branches, planks, or cloth are preventive measures. Dark spots from the muzzle flashes must be covered with camouflage materials or snow during lulls in firing. If a position is occupied for a long period, it is advisable to lay a board, painted white, under the weapon. Motor and other vehicles and tanks in open terrain can be camouflaged by stretching canvas covered with snow over them.

Figure 68.—Flat-top camouflage of tank in gully.

Digging shelters for vehicles in the snow is also feasible. They may be concealed under snow-covered canvas (see fig. 67). If a pit is dug for the vehicles, they will usually require a ramp to get in and out. Vehicles may also be concealed in gullies, under flat-tops (see fig. 68).

d. Camouflage of Trails

Tracks of any description are especially noticeable in fresh snow. From their appearance it is easy to deduce the types of units, strength, and other valuable information concerning the troops who used them. The use of existing roads is therefore even more important than in summer. To prevent detection of new trails, they must be made along natural terrain contours, gorges, knolls, ditches, and hedges, or through woods. They must always link with the existing road net and must never terminate at a camouflaged object. This applies especially to firing positions. In order to confuse the enemy concerning our own strength, when established roads are not used, it may be necessary for foot troops, skiers, sleds, vehicles, and tanks to march on a single trail. Sharp turns by tracked vehicles must be avoided because they produce easily recognizable snow banks.

The obliteration of tracks will frequently be necessary. This may be accomplished by lightly dragging branches, trees, or barbed-wire rolls across them. Inhabited localities conceal troops from aerial and ground observation. Artillery pieces, vehicles of every kind, and equipment depots must be housed under a roof. If this is impossible, they must be disposed in an irregular pattern and camouflaged. One method is to park them against farm buildings and walls and cover them with snow-covered canvas.

Billets and bivouac shelters, depots, and vehicle parks outside inhabited localities must be established as far as possible in evergreen forests or in dense snow-covered deciduous woods. Trees may be chopped down only if timber is abundant. Clearings which may be visible from the air must be concealed from enemy observation by arching and tying branches together over the open spaces. Care must be taken that the branches are covered with snow. In open terrain, gravel pits, hollows, inclines, gorges, and ditches must be utilized as cover. Concealment of tents by digging them partly into the snow or ground may be necessary. This procedure also applies to vehicles.

Roofs, walls, doors, and windows of barracks must be painted white or covered with snow. Dumps must also be carefully integrated into the terrain. The rectangular

Figure 69.—Supplies concealed under trees and snow.

shapes of buildings must be concealed. Cone-shaped piles of supplies topped by a fir tree and plastered with snow deceive the enemy (fig. 69). In flat, treeless terrain, dumps must be distributed irregularly and must be covered with snow to make them appear like snowdrifts.

Billets and bivouacs should be heated, if possible, with dry wood, coke, or charcoal, which produce inconspicuous smoke. Chimneys must be covered at night to prevent the telltale escape of sparks. The soot which forms on the roof must be covered with snow from time to time. Strict blackout discipline must be observed.

e. Dummy Installations

Dummy installations of the simplest materials can deceive the enemy. They must be disposed logically from a tactical point of view and must be far enough from the real installation so that fire directed at them will not endanger the real position.

The dimension and shape of dummy trenches must be realistic. They are simulated by shoveling the snow until the ground becomes visible or, in case of deep snow, by digging them down to a depth of 16 to 20 inches. The trench floor is covered with fir branches, earth, or soot to simulate greater depth. Dummy roads and trails must lead to dummy installations. They are easily counterfeited in the snow and must be linked with the existing road net. After a snowfall, dummy trenches and covered dummy trails and tracks must be renewed.

Section IX. PROTECTION AGAINST COLD, SNOW, AND THAW

39. GENERAL

In addition to the fight against the enemy in winter, there is also the struggle against nature—against cold, snow, wind, poor visibility, and prolonged darkness. The soldier must master these difficulties, not only in permanent billets and field positions, but also on the march and, above all, in combat. To accomplish this, he needs experience and acclimatization as well as the capacity for improvising protective measures again and again. The knowledge of past experience in cold climates, however, is a valuable aid to every soldier. This experience must be supplemented with instruction and many practical exercises.

Knowledge of the following fundamental subjects is necessary:

(1) Clothing and equipment.
(2) Rations.
(3) Maintenance of health.
(4) Care of weapons, equipment, and ammunition.
(5) Care of motor vehicles.
(6) Care of horses.
(7) Heating facilities.

The troops should be trained in the following activities through practical exercises under simulated or actual winter field conditions:

(1) Conduct while on the march.
(2) Conduct in bivouac.
(3) Protection against cold in permanent billets.

(4) Protection against cold in combat and in field positions.
(5) Firing of infantry weapons.
(6) Artillery fire.
(7) Communications.
(8) Motor maintenance.
(9) Defense against gas and smoke.
(10) Care and evacuation of the wounded.
(11) Conduct during railroad movements.

Generally speaking, the danger of illness resulting from cold is slight, provided blood circulation is normal. It is impossible to warn too forcefully against the use of alcohol as protection against cold. Alcohol dilates the pores and merely simulates a feeling of warmth. It abets exhaustion and death by freezing and, therefore, must never be taken prior to physical exertion. If alcohol must be used, it is best administered in hot beverages such as tea. It may be issued only if a subsequent protracted stay in heated accommodations is expected. Those who must again go out-of-doors (sentries) must not receive alcohol.

40. CLOTHING AND EQUIPMENT

a. Regulations for Fitting Winter Clothes

For winter warfare in the east and in the north, the soldier is equipped as much as possible with regulation as well as additional clothing, the issuance of which is based on experience of needs and available raw materials. Nevertheless it is necessary that the unit should try to overcome the cold independently by using winter clothing as effectively as possible and by devising additional expedients. Protection against the wind is of equal importance.

A prerequisite for sufficient protection against the cold is the correct fitting of all clothing. Tight clothes impede the circulation of the blood, which might lead to frostbite. This is especially the case with tight footgear. Outer garments worn over heavy winter clothing must be large enough to assure a man freedom of movement. Only if there is an insulating layer of still air between and in the clothes can real protection against severe cold be counted on. Several thin layers of clothes will, in general, afford better protection than a few thick ones.

The field cap (*Feldmütze*) should be large enough to be worn over the knitted woolen muffler, and its flap should cover the back of the head and ears. The field blouse (*Feldbluse*) should be roomy enough to wear over the sweater and twill jacket. Motorcyclists and motorcycle riflemen must be able to wear a knitted woolen sweater in addition to sweater 36 [an issue garment]. If a man wears the knitted turtle-neck sweater, the collar of the field blouse must be wide enough so that the turtle-neck will fit between the neck and the detachable collar band. Sleeve-straps should be buttoned. Field jackets[1] (field-gray and black) must be long enough to protect the waist and kidneys. Riding breeches should not stop blood circulation in the calf, and they must allow the knees sufficient freedom of movement.

The pleat in the back of the regulation overcoat must be worn open, otherwise the coat will be too tight to afford protection against the cold. Overcoats for mounted men should be long. Surcoats and protective topcoats, which are designed to be worn over the regulation overcoat, should be long and roomy.

---

[1] Usually worn only by tank crews.—EDITOR.

Sweater 36 and the knitted woolen sweater should cover the waist and the kidneys. The sleeves should be long enough to keep the wrists warm. In extremely cold weather the steel helmet should be worn over the field cap and the knitted woolen cap. The ears must not come in contact with the metal of the helmet.

Footgear should be large enough to permit the toes to move freely when, in addition to inner soles, two pairs of

Figure 70.—Method of wrapping foot cloths.

socks or one pair of socks and one pair of foot cloths (see **b**, below) are worn.

b. Emergency Precautions against Cold

Put felt lining inside the steel helmet—preferably the crown of an old felt hat. If nothing else is available, use a handkerchief or crumpled newspaper. The strap should be worn loose so that circulation of the blood will not be impaired. The feet are especially susceptible to frostbite. Socks should be changed frequently. A proved measure for preventing frostbite of the feet is to use inner soles of straw, cloth, or paper; the straw should be cut to the right size and arranged carefully; if newspaper is used, it should be wrapped carefully around the foot to avoid wrinkles. Foot cloths (also paper "foot cloths") are warmer than socks (see fig. 70).

An especially effective measure for protecting the feet is to wear paper between two pairs of socks, and another layer of paper or foot cloths over the top pair of socks. All wrinkles must be smoothed out. If ski boots are worn, a piece of cloth should be sewed over the heels of the socks in order to prevent wear at that point.

Boot leather can be kept from freezing by covering the shoes or boots with the foot of a sock or a casing made of fur or similar material. Figure 71 shows how to make a toe protector of this type.

Clean underwear will keep the soldier warmer than underwear which has been worn for a long time. Therefore, all laundry facilities should be used. Special protective measures for the genitals should be taken if the weather is very cold or the wind very strong. The soldier should wear short trunks, if they are available, in addition to his underwear, or should place paper between his drawers and his trousers.

Mounted men should wrap cloth remnants, woven straw, or string around their stirrups. A protective cap for the toe of the boot, made of woven straw and fixed to the stirrup, is recommended. In case of a shortage of felt boots, sentries and drivers may wear shoes of straw over their regular

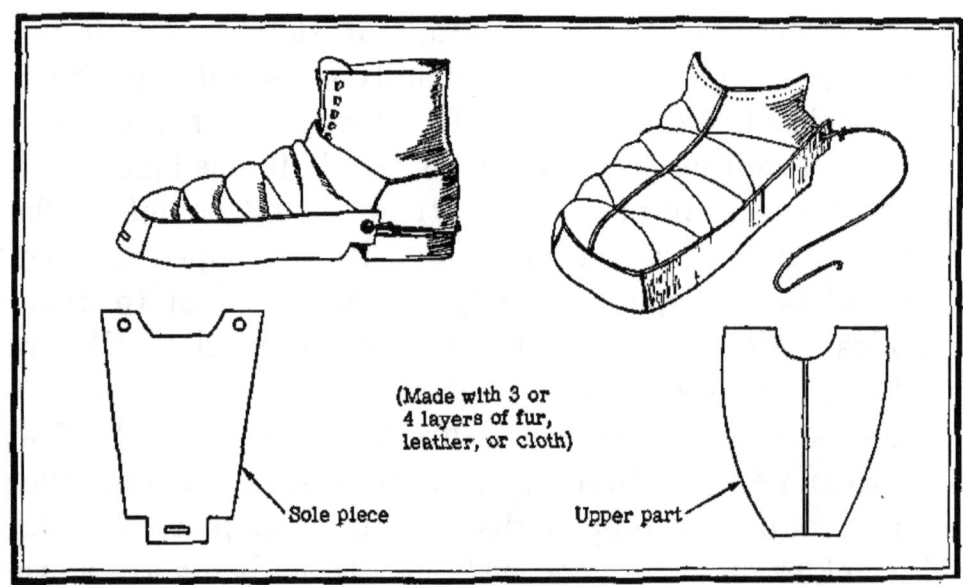

Figure 71.—Improvised protector for shoes and boots.

footgear. Use the natives to manufacture straw shoes. Motorcyclists should put layers of newspaper between the shirt and sweater to protect the chest from the wind. Wrap several layers of newspaper around the knees as protection against the cold, inserting them between the drawers and the outer knee-length stockings.

The sleeve straps of the field blouse should be buttoned or tied, and gloves should be drawn over the sleeves. Put paper, hay, or straw loosely in boot tops. Trousers should not be put into the boots flat, but should hang over the top of the boots, or outside the boots and tied at the bottom. Another method is to tie the sections of the skirt of the overcoat around the legs and wrap an improvised legging around them to keep them secure over the boot tops. The use of issue cloth for improvising wrap leggings is forbidden. Units which are not equipped with infantry boots should wear laced shoes with short woolen spiral puttees. If laced shoes must be worn without leggings, then the trousers should be pulled over the ankles, and the socks drawn over them. If the soldier wears two pairs of socks, he should roll down one pair, like ski socks.

As protection against the cold, units are provided with the following emergency paper articles in sufficient quantities: caps, vests and drawers (both of which are worn between the underwear and outer clothing), "foot cloths," sleeping bags, and bed sheets.

c. Care of Clothing and Equipment

(1) *On the march and in combat.*—On the march and in combat the following practices should be observed. Use breaks in the march and rest periods to exchange unserviceable articles of clothing and to make minor repairs. Garments left behind by wounded men should be collected and turned in without exception. In snowstorms wear the fur coat inside out and wrap a shelter half around it if it does not conflict with camouflage requirements.

Even during a temporary halt the troops should take time out to mend and clean their clothes. Particular attention should be devoted to drying wet clothes and, above all, footgear. Do not let boots or shoes dry near a fire or burning stove, because, in addition to the danger that they may burn, they may become hard and brittle. Wet footgear should be stuffed with straw or paper.

Snow is an enemy of leather, and the best protection is to keep the leather soft. Care of the footgear is especially important in preparing for a march. The uppers should be greased daily, preferably when damp. Leather which has been greased too much, however, chills the feet and permits water to seep through. This treatment should not be applied just before marches, but well in advance.

(2) *Procedure during rest in permanent billets.*—Instructions in cleaning and care of clothing should be given by noncommissioned officers. Fix a specific hour for cleaning and mending. Clothing should be cleaned, if possible, in commercial laundries; otherwise, field laundries should be established by service units or the units themselves. If even this is not possible, laundry details should be formed within the unit. Washing should be done by squads or platoons, under supervision. Prepare areas for washing and drying laundry and for drying wet outer clothing. Woolens should be washed in lukewarm, not boiling water. Clean fur coats frequently by heating and brushing them. Never dry wet furs in the immediate vicinity of a stove. Clothes which are infested with lice should be deloused as quickly as possible with hot air.

Clothing-repair shops must be established. If space permits, craftsmen of different sections of the same service units should be concentrated in one repair shop. Minor repairs should be made by the soldier himself. The mending of socks is very important.

(3) *Care of footgear during mud and thaw period.*—(a) *General.*—The troops should be taught that it is especially important to take care of footgear in order to assure good

health when the thaws occur. If the situation permits, inspections should be held as frequently as possible to make sure that methodical care is taken of footgear. Melting snow quickly penetrates shoe leather and damages it, especially the thread in the seams. Even though the leather may not be waterproof, it may be made so to a certain degree by proper treatment.

(b) *Leather footgear.*—Slight damage should be repaired immediately. Wornout hobnails should not be pulled out, because the holes they leave will let water through. New nails should be driven in beside the old ones. Do not allow shoes to wear until holes form in the inner soles. Wet boots should be changed. (Substitute laced shoes.) The inside of the shoe should be wiped dry with rags and stuffed with paper, straw, or other material which absorbs moisture. Let footgear dry slowly in moderately warm places only. The wetter the shoes, the greater the danger that the leather will crack if they are dried too quickly near stoves or open fires.

Footgear should be cleaned daily. The vamps should be slightly greased up to ankle height. Rub in the grease vigorously with a rag or, better still, with the hand. Warm grease penetrates leather more easily. Do not use too much grease, because it will penetrate the leather and soil the socks and feet. Grease should be applied freely in the groove between the upper leather and the sole in order to make the seam watertight.

Once a week clean the footgear thoroughly by using lukewarm water to wash off dirt and caked grease and polish. Then permit it to dry, and grease the leather. The leg of the boot need be greased only once a week. Treating shoe leather with dubbing keeps it pliable. Shoe polish alone has a tendency to make leather hard and brittle and clogs the pores of the leather. This causes perspiration to condense inside the shoe and might induce frostbite.

Impregnation material for leather shoes, if available, makes them tougher and more waterproof. It is applied when the sole is dry and clean. Repeat the treatment until the sole does not absorb any more of the preparation. Use it once or twice a month.

(c) *Rubber footgear.*—Rubber boots and rubber overshoes must be treated with special care because of the shortage of raw material. Do not wear them for marching on paved roads. They should be cleaned with a soft rag and cold or lukewarm water, never with hot water, oil, or gasoline. Do not use sharp instruments for scraping dirt off them. When drying them, hang them in moderately warm places, but never near or over hot stoves. Damage must be repaired with rubber patches.

(d) *Felt boots.*—Felt boots must not be worn after the thaw begins. Wet felt boots do not keep the feet warm; on the contrary, the evaporation of moisture in the felt causes the feet to lose warmth, and frostbite will easily occur, even at moderately low temperatures. Felt boots, because they have leather parts, must be dried only in moderately warm places.

Section X. RATIONS IN WINTER

41. GENERAL

All commanders and all units concerned with rations should always be conscious of the fact that they have the very responsible task of keeping their troops healthy. In the winter the troops should receive warm food and hot drinks more often than in summer. Hot soups should be served frequently with breakfast and supper. Always have hot water ready for preparing warm drinks. The colder the weather, the more fat should be included in the food. Food, especially cold cuts, must not be served if its temperature is under 50 degrees F. Cold easily causes deterioration or reduction of nutritive value; therefore, special attention should be given to the transportation, storage, and care of food which is susceptible to cold.

Alcoholic drinks should be issued only at night in bivouacs. Rum should not be given unless it is mixed with hot drinks, such as tea. If liquors like cognac and vodka are issued, care must be taken that some soldiers do not receive more than their regular share either as a gift from other soldiers or by trading.

If it is anticipated that serving from field kitchens will not be possible, powdered coffee, tea, and other rations should be issued in advance to enable the soldiers to prepare their own hot drinks and hot food. To prevent overloading the men, however, only essential rations should be issued. Otherwise they will throw away whatever seems to be superfluous at that moment. Every man must know how to cook and should be given opportunities to practice cooking.

Patrols and raiding parties should receive rations which are light and do not occupy much space.

42. FIELD RATIONS IN EXTREME WEATHER

In extremely cold weather, the following rations are especially suitable for the field kitchen: frozen and canned meat; hard salami; bacon; smoked meat; fresh vegetables, including beans and peas; spaghetti; macaroni; noodles; frozen potatoes; and frozen vegetables. Food which has a high water content should not be taken along.

Hot drinks should be issued. If the soldier cannot be fed from the field kitchen, he should be issued the following provisions:

(1) Bread ready for consumption and with some sort of spread on it. The men should wrap it in paper if possible and carry it in their pockets to protect it against the cold.
(2) Cracked wheat bread.
(3) Dried and baked fruits.
(4) Candies.
(5) Chocolates.

Drinks carried in the canteen will stay warm to some extent only if the canteen is well wrapped and then placed inside the bread bag or pack. If the canteen is carried outside on the bread bag, the contents will soon freeze. Never permit soldiers to eat snow to quench their thirst, or to drink cold water on an empty stomach. Snow water should be drunk only after it has been boiled. (Caution!)

43. EMERGENCY RATIONS

When on reconnaissance or isolated sentry duty, a soldier is often forced to be economical with his food. The following suggestions on how to make provisions last are based on Russian recommendations for emergency foods for guerrillas, stragglers, etc.

a. Frozen Meats

The simplest way to keep meat in winter is to let it freeze. Before being boiled or fried, it should be thawed over the range. If quick cooking is necessary, cut the frozen meat into little pieces and place them on the lid of the mess kit, after adding fat and a little salt. Keep the meat over the fire until a sample is at least tolerably tasty. During the thaw period, thawed meat will easily spoil. To prevent this, cut the meat into thin slices, dry them on a piece of sheet iron over a stove, and sprinkle them with salt. Meat thus cured will keep reasonably long.

b. Raw Fish

Cut the frozen fish into thin flakes, or, preferably, scrape the fish with a knife instead of cutting it, so that thin shavings are formed. If need be, it can be consumed without cooking.

c. Food from the Woods

The red bilberry grows in pine woods beneath the snow. Cranberries are found in mossy bogs. Fir cones and pine cones, when held over a fire, will open and yield nourishing seeds. Yellow tree moss is poisonous. Other tree mosses, especially Iceland moss (steel gray), become edible after several hours of cooking. The rushes which grow on the banks of rivers and lakes have root ends which can be eaten when boiled or baked. Wild apples or bitter fruits, like those of the mountain ash, become sweet after freezing.

d. Sawdust Flour

Flour rations can be stretched by adding sawdust flour, made preferably from the pine tree, but birch bark may also be used. For this purpose, carefully cut the outer layer of the bark from a young tree. Make two ring-shaped incisions in the inner layer of bark, about a yard apart, and vertical cuts between them. Then carefully lift off segments of the inner bark with a sharp knife, cut them into small pieces, and boil them, changing the water several times to eliminate the taste of tar. Next, dry the pieces until they are not quite brittle. Finally, mash and pulverize the pieces in the hand.

Usually sawdust flour is mixed with rye flour in a proportion of 25 to 100 or even 50 to 100. It is stirred into the dough with water added. Sour milk may also be added. The dough is rolled out very thin, and small flat cakes are baked.

e. Baking Bread in Mess Kit

Bread can be baked in the mess kit in hot ashes. This method is employed only when other bread cannot be obtained. The simplest and quickest way is to use baking powder. The ingredients are two mess-kit covers full of rye or wheat flour (about 540 grams, or 1 pound 3 ounces); one mess-kit cover about half full of cold water; one-half ounce of baking powder; and one-half teaspoon of salt, if it is available. Mix the ingredients slowly, add cold water, and knead the dough until it becomes medium stiff. This dough is shaped into a roll the length of the mess kit. Roll the loaf in flour and place it in the mess kit. Close the mess kit with its cover, and put it under embers and hot ashes, baking the dough for about 1½ hours.

44. EFFECT OF COLD WEATHER ON FOOD

The following articles of food will not spoil or at least will not deteriorate materially in extreme cold: bread; meat and meat products of all kinds, including canned meat; canned and fresh fish; fats; dried beans and peas; dried vegetables; dried fruit; macaroni, spaghetti, noodles, and other grain products; rice; coffee; tea; sugar; salt; spices; and dehydrated foods.

Canned vegetables; mixed fruit preserves which have been prepared in water or in their own juice, as well as sauerkraut and beans in cans or barrels; marmalade; and honey freeze easily but generally do not deteriorate. They should not be stored where the temperature is below the freezing point. Milk, fruit juices, mineral waters, wine, beer, and liquor in bottles or barrels should be protected against freezing; otherwise the bottles and barrels may break. Red wine will not keep in cold temperatures. Potatoes become sweet when frozen and their palatability is thereby affected. Both hard and soft cheeses lose flavor, dry out, and crumble after they are thawed out.

45. TRANSPORTATION AND STORAGE OF FOOD

In cold weather and snow it is necessary to adopt special measures for the transportation of food. The commissary wagons should be equipped with double walls filled in with hay, wood shavings, or sawdust for insulation against the cold. The floor should be well covered with straw, improvised mats, old baskets, or sacks. The food containers—crates, sacks, baskets, and bottles—should also be covered with straw mats, blankets, old but clean sacks, and fir branches as protection against the cold. The insulating material must be kept dry at all times, or it will not accomplish its purpose. If possible, food should be transported around midday, when the temperature is somewhat warm.

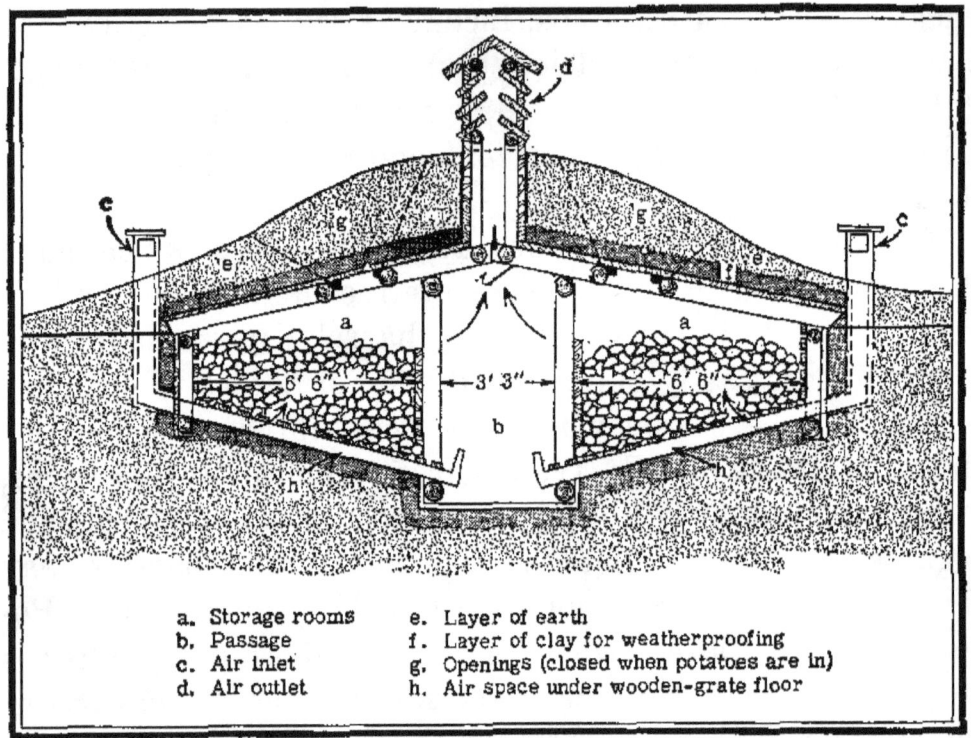

a. Storage rooms
b. Passage
c. Air inlet
d. Air outlet
e. Layer of earth
f. Layer of clay for weatherproofing
g. Openings (closed when potatoes are in)
h. Air space under wooden-grate floor

Figure 72.—Prefabricated rations hut installed underground for potato storage.

The precautions necessary for transportation also apply to the storage of small quantities of food. For the storage of larger quantities, use only dry cellars or frost-proof storerooms in houses or barracks. Where storerooms of this kind are lacking, the troops must improvise them before the cold weather sets in.

46. FREEZING AND STORAGE OF POTATOES

In order to facilitate the transportation of potatoes in very cold weather, they may be frozen. To transport them in weather that presumably will remain constant at least at 14 degrees F., potatoes should be taken out of storage and exposed immediately to the cold. They must be spread in one layer, not piled up, otherwise those underneath will not freeze. The freezing process should be completed quickly. Potatoes frozen at 14 degrees F. will acquire a sweet taste, but they will not lose much flavor or nutritive value.

If the potatoes are to be peeled, they should first be thawed out for 5 minutes in cold water. Potatoes and vegetables (all kinds of cabbages, turnips, kohlrabi, and celery), which will keep through the winter, can best be protected against freezing in an improvised cellar if appropriate frost-proof storage rooms are not available. Excavate a place large enough to erect the prefabricated rations hut below ground level (see fig. 72). Then cover the hut with a layer of earth about 3 to 6 feet deep. The entrance should be built like a sluice gate in order to reduce the penetration of cold. Experience shows that the temperature of this room will stay above freezing, even with an outside temperature of −13 to −22 degrees F.

Section XI. WINTER HEALTH MEASURES

47. HYGIENE IN BILLETS

a. Hygiene

(1) *Cleanliness and rest.*—It is best to wash oneself with cold water in the morning and with warm water at night. Wash cloths of rough fabric are desirable. A warm shower should be taken at least once a week. Finish it with a short cold shower; otherwise there is danger of catching cold. After washing, grease the face and hands with vaseline, boric-acid ointment, or water-free cold cream (*Vaseline, Borsalbe, wasserfreie Hautcreme*) before going outside. It is advisable to shave at night to avoid chapping of the skin. Hair should be cut short as a safeguard against lice. Regular brushing of the hair is very important.

In permanent billets, soldiers should work in shifts so that all will have rest periods. Duties outside barracks should be carried out around midday, when the sun is shining; duty inside barracks, when it is cold and dark. Loitering in the open air, especially after physical exertion and perspiration, should be avoided. Rest periods during fatigue in the cold, open air do more harm than good, as it is unwise to lie or sit down. During practice firing, soldiers should be relieved frequently, and huts and fires must be at hand for their comfort.

(2) *Prevention of disease.*—Vermin can communicate dangerous contagious diseases to human beings. The best method of fighting them is by keeping quarters, clothing,

and the body clean. Lice can transmit spotted fever, relapsing fever, and "five-day fever" (*Fünftagefieber*), a sickness which occurs frequently during the winter, when people live in close contact. Fleas from rats can communicate the plague. The sooner you fight vermin, the easier it will be to destroy them. Fix regular hours for delousing. Body lice usually are found in pleats and seams of clothing, bedding, and equipment. During inspection special attention should be paid to these hidden places.

Lice may be eradicated by washing clothing with a cresol-soap solution or with kerosene, and then pressing the garments with a hot iron. Regular use should be made of *Russla* louse powder. If clothes are too heavily infested with lice, they should be treated in delousing stations by means of dry heat or steam, or, in the case of underclothing, by boiling.

If bedbugs appear in great numbers, the quarters should be fumigated with gas. For this purpose, the men must move temporarily to other quarters, but only after having cleaned their bodies thoroughly and deloused their clothes. When returning to their original quarters, the men must observe the precautionary measures laid down by the fumigators.

Places where pipes have been removed should be especially protected against rats. Use traps continuously against mice and rats. Poisoned grain, meat, bacon, fish, and intestines should be used as bait. The bait and the location of the traps should be frequently changed. If rats or other rodents run around dizzily or let themselves be caught, or if a remarkable number of the bodies of these rodents are found, there is danger of an outbreak of plague. The unit medical officers should be notified immediately so that countermeasures can be taken in time. Each plague of human beings is preceded by a plague of rats.

Keeping animals for combating rats and mice is not advisable; dogs and cats can easily communicate rat-bite disease, tapeworm, and rabies to human beings with whom they live in close contact. Rabies is not infrequent in eastern Europe, because of the wolves indigenous there. Wolves and stray dogs and cats should be destroyed. If an animal which has bitten a person is suspected of having rabies, it should not be shot through the head because examination of the brain is necessary.

b. Sauna (Finnish steam bath)

If possible construct an emergency delousing station. Such a station consists of a steam bath, or *sauna* (common in Finland), which may be built in existing rooms that meet the necessary specifications. In field positions, these stations may be constructed in the form of log huts, but suitable drainage must be provided.

Heat-retaining walls and ceilings are essential. In the log-cabin type, for example, insulation is provided by filling all cracks with straw and earth, and insulating the roof with an upper layer of clay, with sand filler. Stone-lined ditches are installed under the floor for drainage.

A furnace of field stones, preferably granite, is made without cement on a solid rock foundation (see fig. 73). A chimney is not necessary; the smoke is drawn up through the ventilating pipe in the ceiling.

For fuel, use birch, alder, or pine wood. The furnace is heated for several hours until the room temperature reaches 140 to 158 degrees F. Then remove the fire from the furnace and pour a small quantity of hot water over the hot

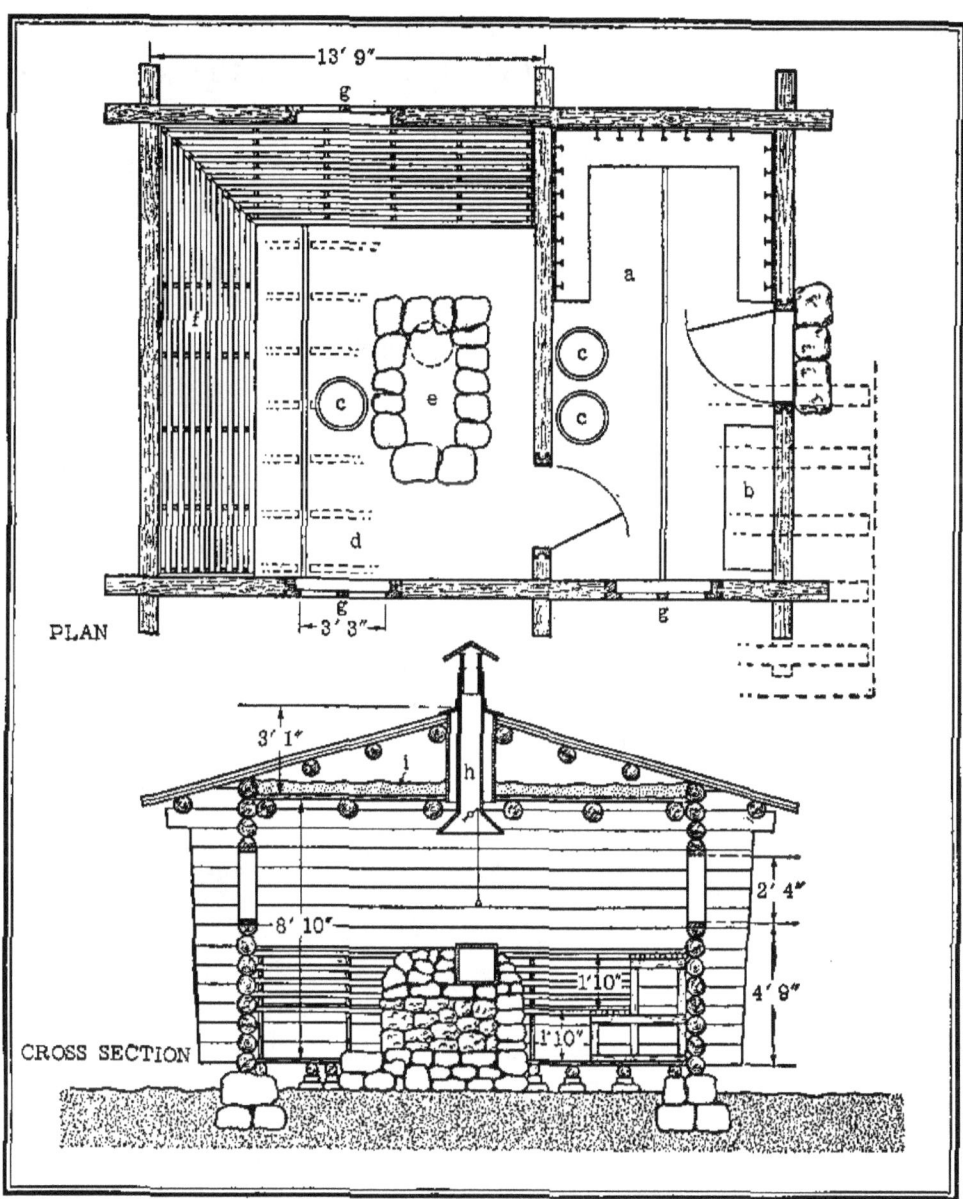

Figure 73.—Sauna (Finnish steam bath) in log cabin.

a. Anteroom with bench
b. Woodpile
c. Water tanks
d. Bathrooms
e. Furnace with hot-water tank
f. Benches in tiers
g. Windows
h. Chimney with vent
i. Roof insulation (humus and earth)

stones. The steam will drive the remaining smoke up through the ventilator in the roof. When the smoke has been cleared out, the ventilator vent is closed to prevent loss of steam. The *sauna* bath is then ready for use. During the bathing process, hot water is poured on the rocks from time to time in order to create more steam.

Section XII. EVACUATION OF WOUNDED

48. GENERAL

In general, speedy evacuation of the wounded to dressing stations in the rear is desirable. There final care can be given. Even men suffering from apparently slight wounds and freezing should not remain with the troops, because the degree of freezing cannot always be exactly determined at first and the effect of continued exposure to cold would be dangerous. It is necessary to provide dressing stations with heated rooms. Chemical warming bags should be given to every wounded man who is to be evacuated. When snowstorms or bad road conditions make it impossible to move the wounded, however, it is necessary to assign detachments of medical and surgical units to dressing stations for final care of wounds.

If the distance is too great from the dressing station to the ambulance stop and the main dressing station, and between the main dressing station and the field hospital, it is necessary to establish intermediate stations where the wounded may be warmed and fed and their blood-soaked or frozen bandages replaced. These stations should be located in farmers' huts, and similar shelters, and they should be operated by medical personnel. Warm drinks and warm food, as well as bandages to replace the upper layers of blood-soaked and frozen dressings, should be available in sufficient quantities.

At the intermediate stations, there should also be horses (with sufficient fodder rations) which can be used as reliefs for drawing ambulance sleds. Evacuation routes should coincide with supply routes which are continually kept free of snow and are marked with sign posts. When a great number of severely wounded soldiers are being evacuated on sleds, a medical officer and some medical soldiers should accompany them. When evacuating wounded men through territory infiltrated by the enemy, an adequate military escort should be provided.

49. MEANS OF EVACUATING WOUNDED

a. General

The particularly difficult conditions of winter warfare necessitate special measures for recovering and evacuating the wounded. Good skiers, if available, must be used for this purpose. Instruction in evacuation is an essential part of training in first aid.

By using shelter halves or litters and hand sleds a comparatively fast and safe evacuation is ensured. Whether the first-aid man uses snowshoes or skis depends upon the situation, terrain, and snow conditions. If time and circumstances permit, tracks should be prepared or a path trampled in the snow for an evacuation route. Provision should be made for high sleds, or, better yet, akjas, or boat sleds [1] (see par. **65b**, p. 198), for transporting wounded men and medical equipment even at the front and during a heavy snowfall. During the mud period, drags have proved to very effective.

At the unit dressing station and in the area back of it, a sufficient number of horse-drawn sleds should be available. Empty supply wagons returning to the rear may also be

---

[1] Finnish *ahkio*, literally "Laplander's sled."—EDITOR.

employed for the wounded. Heavy horse-drawn or motor ambulances can be used only on good, cleared roads. If a railroad is in the vicinity of a front dressing station, the wounded may be taken to the rear in passenger cars, freight cars, handcars, and trucks on rails. Airplanes can be used only in special cases for evacuating the severely wounded.

b. Hand Sleds and Improvised Means

In some circumstances it may be necessary for two skiers to carry a man between them for short distances. The wounded man is placed on a shelter half, oblique to the direction of travel. The two bearers grasp the shelter half at either end and carry the wounded man between them, leaving their outside arm free for the ski pole. The bearers change places when their "carrying arm" gets tired.

If only one bearer equipped with skis is available, the casualty is secured in the same manner. The skier pulls the wounded by means of a rope fastened to the point of the akja, or boat sled (see fig. 74 (1)).

A wounded man may be wrapped in a shelter half, secured with straps and belts, and dragged like a bundle (see fig. 74 (2)). This method may be useful for evacuating a casualty from a field of fire into a defiladed area.

Akjas, or boat sleds, are used in terrain under enemy observation or under direct fire. The wounded man is tied to the sled (which has been padded with woolen or fur blankets) with ropes or straps, and is pulled or pushed by the bearer while creeping (see fig. 74 (3)).

In easy terrain and under favorable snow conditions one skier is sufficient to haul a sled, but, as a rule, two men are employed to negotiate obstacles and slopes and to make greater speed (see fig. 74 (4)).

Figure 74.—Some methods of evacuating the wounded, showing (1) skier dragging an akja, or boat sled; (2) skier dragging a wounded man from a field of fire; (3) akja used for evacuation under fire; (4) method of evacuation in difficult terrain.

50. EQUIPMENT OF VEHICLES FOR WOUNDED

Every possibility of harm because of exposure must be avoided during transportation. While a casualty is being moved, the main object is to keep him warm in every possible way. It is important to equip all transportation facilities for the wounded with an abundant supply of woolen blankets, shelter halves, protective paper wrappings for limbs, and paper vests, socks, and caps. If possible, felt boots should be available for those wounded men who have none of their own. In horse-drawn sleds and ambulances foot-sacks of fur, or woolen blankets, should be available. All sleds and other means of transportation should have a bed of loose straw (in an emergency, fir twigs) or braided straw mats as protection against the cold and jolting. Straw mats should also cover the side walls. Horse-drawn sleds should, if possible, have a closed wooden superstructure with an observation window for the accompanying personnel.

All vehicles should be equipped with warming bottles, chemical warming bags, and, if necessary, bricks which can be heated at the intermediate stations. Sacks filled with hot sand may also be used. Care must be taken, however, that the patients are not burned, especially when they are unconscious or shell-shocked. It is very important that all vehicles be supplied with hot drinks in thermos bottles; in case of emergency, canteens filled with drinks may be kept hot in buckets of hot sand.

Section XIII. CARE AND USE OF WEAPONS AND EQUIPMENT

51. GENERAL

In winter, especially in extremely cold weather and during thaws, additional maintenance and careful handling of weapons and equipment is necessary. Frequent inspections and tests should be made.

Weapons should be kept in places maintained at the temperatures in which they are intended to function. If they are brought for a short time from a cold temperature into a warm one and then again into the cold air, they will sweat and rust, endangering the smooth operation of bolts, breech mechanisms, and other movable parts. Weapons, therefore, should not be kept in warm rooms. They should be kept in anterooms or shelters made of branches or other improvised materials, even snow. Spare parts should be stored with the weapons.

Weapons should, if possible, be cleaned daily. Use a cleaning wick or a soft rag lightly dipped in oil. A thin film of oil is sufficient. If too much is used, it will solidify and stoppages will result.

Parts which have frozen fast should not be forced. They should be moved gradually after careful warming and application of kerosene or of gun oil mixed with kerosene.

Before loading weapons, go through a few dry loading movements. If weapons are brought into heated billets for cleaning purposes, the sweat which will form must be dried

CARE AND USE OF WEAPONS AND EQUIPMENT

before the cleaning is started. The weapons should not be brought near hot stoves.

When firing, do not permit the hot parts of the weapons to come in contact with snow. When changing hot barrels, do not lay them in the snow, or they will warp. Take care that neither snow nor water enters the muzzle or bolt; otherwise the barrel may swell or burst while firing. Do not shoot with a barrel the bore of which is iced. Ice formations in the bore can be removed with warmed oil if normal thawing is not possible. The muzzle caps and antidust bags, through both of which firing is possible, prevent snow or water from entering the bore. Always keep bolts, lids of ammunition boxes, and dust-prevention devices closed in order to prevent the penetration of snow or water. Leave weapons in their covers, cases, or pouches whenever the tactical situation permits. Weapons should never be placed in soft snow; rest them on some solid foundation such as planks or snowshoes.

If possible, protect weapons in trenches from snow, rain, and shell fragments. Ammunition boxes for machine guns, ammunition drums, cartridge containers, magazines of all kinds, tool bags, and tool chests should always be kept closed in order to prevent rust. Frequent checking of these boxes and containers is necessary. Their contents should be examined frequently and cleaned, and all steel and iron parts covered with a light film of oil.

52. LUBRICANTS

Gun-cleaning oil can be used in temperatures as low as −22 degrees F. and lubricating oil as low as −4 degrees F. If the temperature is lower, kerosene should be added. The proportion of kerosene to oil in the mixture should be one to two. In very cold weather the troops in the east and in the north are issued frost-resistant cleaning and lubricating oils which are usable down to —40 degrees F. Containers with frost-resistant oils bear the label "frost-resistant" (*frostsicher*). In temperatures lower than —40 degrees F., even these oils should be mixed with kerosene in the given proportion.

Lubricating grease for elevating gears, rollers, and ball bearings can be used in temperatures as low as 5 degrees F.; if mixed with kerosene, as low as —58 degrees F. The amount of kerosene added (depending on the temperature) may be as much as six times the amount of the grease.

Oil for delicate mechanisms, such as the aiming mechanism, is frost-resistant down to —40 degrees F. The troops in the east and north are issued for winter use *Vacuum Servöl 222*, which is frost-resistant down to —58 degrees F. In case of emergency, gun-cleaning oil may be used. Complete greasing of the aiming mechanism, preceded by the removal of the old oil, may be done only by the armorer or the assistant armorer.

53. RECOIL LIQUIDS

The brown recoil liquid can be used for nonautomatic guns in temperatures as low as —40 degrees F., but for pieces with semiautomatic breech mechanisms, such as the 50-mm antitank gun 38 (*5-cm Pak 38*), only as low as —4 degrees F. At lower temperatures, the recoil brake and the compressed-air counterrecoil mechanism should be filled with cold-resistant recoil liquid in order to guarantee the opening of the semiautomatic breech mechanism and the expulsion of the cartridge case after the counterrecoil. The filling of the recoil brake and counterrecoil mechanism should be done only by the armorer or assistant armorer. Antifreezing solution, when used in guns, is cold-resistant down to −67 degrees F.

For guns whose recoil brakes are required by regulations to be filled with brake oil, Shell oil *AB 11*, which is frost-resistant down to −76 F., should be used. This oil can be mixed with captured oil without special precautionary measures.

54. CARE OF WEAPONS

a. Rifles and Carbines

If the triggers do not function satisfactorily in very cold weather, drop some pure kerosene from above into the opening for the trigger sear and from below into the opening of the trigger guard. Then pull the trigger several times until it works satisfactorily.

b. Semiautomatic Rifles

Care must be taken that snow and water do not penetrate the gas port or piston. If the trigger does not work, it may be made to function again by carefully putting drops of kerosene on it (but only in case of emergency). If, during combat, the gas-cylinder mechanism is found frozen fast, shoot until it has thawed out (with single shots, loaded by hand). This procedure also applies to the submachine gun (see **d**, below). Water which has penetrated must be removed later when the weapon is cleaned.

c. Pistols

Keep the magazine and cartridges dry (not oiled) and free from dust. In order to clean the cartridges, the magazine should, if conditions permit, be emptied and refilled daily. In doing this, check the magazine for warping and dents. Damaged magazines should be removed; as well as cartridges which are rusty or dented. After filling the magazine, press the top cartridge down several times and let it come up again so that the cartridges will be in proper alignment. Care should be taken that the cartridges do not jam in the magazine. The pistol holster will not protect the weapon and the magazine from damage caused by an abrupt change of temperature.

d. Submachine Guns

Whenever the combat situation permits, empty the magazines of submachine guns and take them apart in order to remove rust and dirt. This procedure should be followed daily, if possible. Separate those magazines which are out of shape or dented. Check the tension of the magazine springs; slack springs should be taken out. The springs should be at least two threads of a screw longer than the magazine chamber. Apply a very light film of oil to the magazine, both inside and outside, and then reassemble the weapon. Test whether the follower operates freely. Clean the cartridges and at the same time separate those with dents. Fill the magazines. After having done this, press the upper cartridge down several times with the magazine filler, always letting it come up again so that cartridges will be correctly aligned both horizontally and vertically. Test the operation of the submachine gun, frequently without the magazine. Just before firing, pull back the bolt behind the trigger sear or into the safety notch in order that no snow may fall into the housing and the attached

CARE AND USE OF WEAPONS AND EQUIPMENT 159

magazine. The inside of the magazine pouches also must always be kept dry and clean.

e. Machine-Gun Equipment

The steel cartridge belts should be checked daily to see that the cartridges are held in the belt with the normal amount of tension; that there is no clotted oil, rust, or ice between the cartridge cases; and that cartridges are in the proper position in the belt. If necessary, empty the steel cartridge belts, clean the belts and cartridges, remove the dented cartridges, rub the belt sections dry, and refill the belts with the cartridges. Iced web cartridge belts must be dried carefully in a warm room before being used again.

f. Machine Gun (M.G. 34)

Take special care that the bolt, belt-pawl, and top cover plate operate smoothly in extremely cold weather. Wrap up the machine gun and the barrel jacket and leave them wrapped when firing in a snowstorm. Prevent freezing of melted snow inside the barrel jacket, especially in front on the muzzle booster, by keeping it dry. Do not oil the barrel and inner moving parts when they are cold. If the trigger does not operate smoothly, use a few drops of kerosene.

Before each loading and during long lulls in firing, pull back the bolt and let it snap forward again so as to move the parts in the belt pawl. When firing a machine gun to warm it up, try to make it operate smoothly by pulling at the empty end of the belt. Then, when the weapon is warm, apply a thin coating of oil to the rubbing and sliding surfaces of the bolt, the belt-pawl cover, and the housing. During long lulls in firing, remove oil from the top cover plate, belt-pawl cover, and the sliding surfaces in the housing. When changing bolts, the new bolt should not be oiled.

All boxes and containers should be closed immediately after use. Any snow which may have penetrated must be removed as soon as possible. In cold weather the operation of the moving parts of the mount should be checked from time to time.

If possible, the telescopic sight should be protected from cold and dampness and should be carried only in the proper receptacle. It should not be mounted on the weapon until shortly before use. Frozen sighting instruments should be thawed only in a warm room.

g. Antitank Rifles

Wet cartridges should be rubbed dry. Dented cartridges should be set aside. Otherwise antitank rifles are protected just like other weapons.

h. Tank Guns

If the elevating gear is frozen fast, it should not be forced. It should be brought into operation gradually, by careful warming if necessary. The recoil brakes should always be kept filled to the proper point. Recoil and counterrecoil of the barrel must be normal. During long lulls in firing, test whether the breech operates smoothly and whether the point of the firing pin comes out all the way. Do not fire high-explosive shells through muzzle caps if the latter are iced. This procedure applies to the 20-mm tank guns 30 and 38 (*2-cm Kw.K. 30* and *38*), the 25-mm tank gun 35 (French) (*2.5-cm Kw.K. 35 (f)*), and the machine gun.

CARE AND USE OF WEAPONS AND EQUIPMENT 161

i. Antiaircraft Guns (2-cm *Flak* 30 and 38)

When the temperature is lower than −22 degrees F., the use of frost-resistant lubricating oil instead of ordinary machine-gun oil is necessary. Firing through barrel protectors is possible even if they are heavily iced. In extremely cold weather, automatic fire should not be started immediately; a few single rounds should be fired first.

If the weapon does not function precisely because the sliding parts are not operating smoothly, fire with the 41-mm muzzle brake; if they operate with great difficulty, fire without using the muzzle brake. In cold weather, the box with the data-calculating mechanism of antiaircraft sights 33, 35, and 36 (*Flakvisier 33, 35,* and *36*) should be kept in the billets until the alarm is sounded, if the sights cannot be kept warm with the weapon. The latest type of antiaircraft sights can withstand cold temperatures.

j. Artillery

During movements and long lulls in firing, the muzzle and the parts of the breech mechanism must be well covered so that snow and water cannot enter the breech or the breechblock mechanism. In temperatures below freezing, grease and oil the piece just enough to afford protection against corrosion and friction.

In extremely cold weather, frozen gears must not be forced but must be worked gradually, and, if necessary, they should be heated. The water containers for the recoil brakes must, if the temperature is below freezing, be filled with a mixture of brown recoil liquid and water in the proportion of 10 to 4.5. In temperatures below 22 degrees F., however, it is advisable to fire entirely without the use of water for cooling.

Recoil brakes and the counterrecoil mechanism should always be filled. The recoil and counterrecoil of the breech must be normal; otherwise too much strain is put on the gun mount, and the outriggers may crack. (For heavy antiaircraft and high-trajectory fire, there is a special steam generator.)

If the ground is frozen, guns should be emplaced on reed mats, or, if these are unavailable, on a soft foundation. When firing, use ice spades. At the same time, look for a soft foundation in order to spare the gun. The soil should be dug up at the lower edges of the outriggers so that they will not crack.

Before opening fire, remove with the barrel wiper frost and existing ice formations from the inside of the barrel. Heavier ice formations should be dissolved with warmed cleaning oil. Do not fire while ice is in the barrel. If firing has ceased, put the muzzle cap on the barrel to prevent it from cooling off too rapidly. Test the smooth operation of the breech and the complete protrusion of the point of the firing pin frequently during long lulls in firing in order to prevent misfires. The shells, especially the rotating bands, should be cleaned of frost and ice before loading; otherwise solid ramming is impossible. After firing and after cleaning the barrel, apply a thin coat of oil inside the barrel and to the breech mechanism. Do not wash the guns in cold places or in the open air.

k. Chemical Mortars and Heavy Projectors

(1) *105-mm chemical mortars 35 and 40.*—If the ground is frozen hard, replace the base plate with special rock and

ice spades. On a solid ice surface, do not use the ice or rock spades, but place the base plate in a hole filled with twigs or loose pieces of ice.

In extremely cold weather, fire off a few blanks of the 105-mm chemical mortar 40 (*10.5-cm Nb.-W 40*) in order to warm the barrel before firing the actual mortar shell. This precaution will prevent breaks in the barrel.

(2) *Heavy projectors 40 (wooden model) and 41 (metal model).*—The heavy projector 40 (*s.W.G. 40*) (wooden model) can be warped under some weather conditions to such an extent that lateral dispersion will be unpredictable. Therefore, if possible, heavy projector 41 (*s.W.G. 41*) (metal model) should be used instead.

Setting up heavy projector 40 (wooden model) and heavy projector 41 (metal model) in hard and frozen ground is, because of the necessary leveling work and pegging up, difficult and time-consuming. Wooden pegs cannot be used in frozen ground. The sound of iron stakes being driven into the ground can be heard at a distance of about 750 yards.

If the snow is deeper than 4 inches, the firing position must be cleared; otherwise the projectors cannot be securely pegged and consequently cannot be used. The detonating cables and ignition machines as well as the connection plugs and sockets of all weapons of the smoke-laying troops must be protected against water and ice. In very cold weather the detonating cables should be treated with special care because they might break if the insulation hardens.

55. FIRING OF INFANTRY WEAPONS

a. General

When the weapons are brought into position, they must be employed on a solid base. In low temperatures weapons shoot rather low at first, but after a few rounds accuracy returns to normal. During firing, the snow in front of the muzzle becomes black. During pauses in firing, fresh snow should be spread over the spot. To prevent snow clouds from billowing up and betraying the firing position, the snow in front of the muzzle of the weapon should be covered with planks, white sheets, or other suitable material.

Snow-covered terrain affords few reference points for target designation and range estimation. In clear weather, distances in snow-covered terrain appear much shorter, especially if the background is white. Therefore, target designation and range estimation should be practiced carefully. In dry snow the burst of high-explosive shells can usually be observed. Solid shots, however, can be observed only if the angle of impact is acute.

b. Rifle

The firing position for the rifle is the same as in the summer. If equipped with skis, cross the ski poles and slip each wrist thong over the opposite pole, placing the rifle in the fork. (This is feasible for the kneeling position.) In the prone position the knapsack may be used as a support. Assume this position by throwing yourself to the ground either with the legs spread out or with the legs close together and the skis parallel, their edges on the ground.

c. Light Machine Gun

Provide a solid base for the weapon by placing it in the gun rest or on a foundation of brushwood, a plank, skis, poles, an akja (see par. **65b**, p. 198), or snow plates (see **d**, below).

d. Heavy Machine Gun

In flat or packed snow, provide a solid position for the heavy machine gun by means of snow plates. In deep and soft snow, however, push the legs of the machine-gun tripod as far as possible into the snow, or mount the gun on the akja (see par. **65b**, p. 198), on reed wickerwork, or on planks. When the machine gun is fired in deep snow, the front leg of the tripod often sinks in deeper than the rear legs; therefore, repeated readjustments are necessary. Do not fire over the heads of friendly troops unless the legs of the machine-gun mount are on a solid foundation.

To prevent the machine gun from sinking into deep snow, snow plates should be provided for bipod and tripod legs. The troops can improvise these for themselves. Figure 75(1) shows a snow plate made of sheet steel 8 inches long by 7 inches wide. The metal is bent down about three-quarters of an inch around the edges. A rectangular opening is cut out of the plate to receive the spike of the front leg of the mount. Two straps are riveted to the plate for the purpose of binding down the tripod leg. The plate may also be made of wood.

Another type of snow plate is shown in figure 75(2). The outer ring, 10 inches in diameter, is made of band steel. The base plate, 4 inches in diameter, is made of sheet steel. Sixteen riveted straps of band steel hold the plate in the ring. A similar type, with a band-steel ring of the same dimensions, may be made with a heavy wire web to hold a 5-inch-square base plate (fig. 75(3)). A belt for strapping down the leg of the mount is braided through the wire in order to increase the carrying surface of the plate.

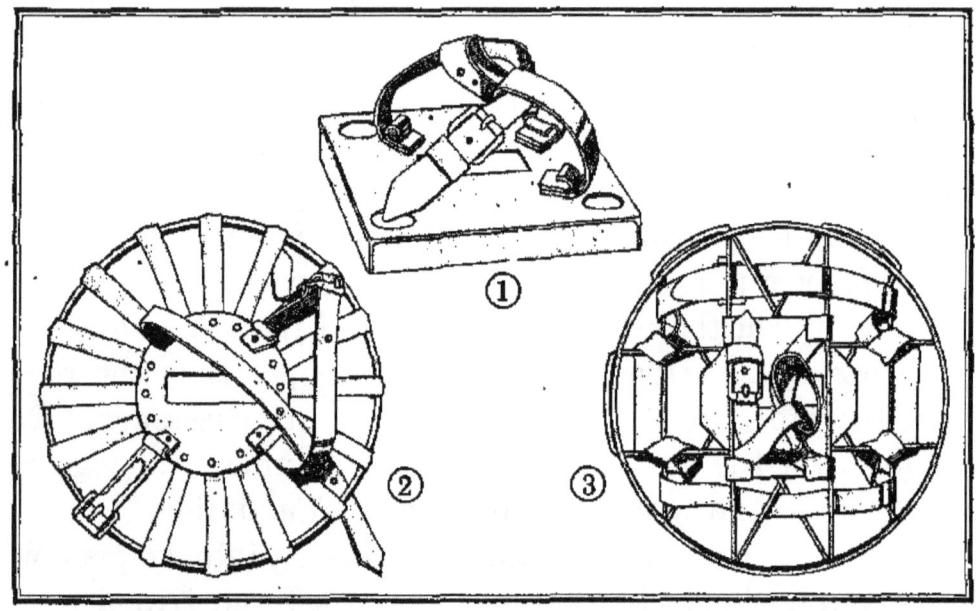

Figure 75.—Snow plates for machine-gun mounts.

It is advisable to paint the metal parts of the plate with red-lead paint in order to prevent rust.

e. 50-mm Light Mortar 36 (5-cm l.Gr.W. 36)

This mortar (5-cm l.Gr.W. 36) is brought into position after snow or excavated soil has been removed. In deep snow, provide a plank or other support for a solid foundation. The fragmentation effect of the shell is reduced in deep snow. Observation when the range is more than 200 meters (219 yards) is almost impossible. Follow the firing regulations exactly. Remove any snow or ice from the shell before inserting it in the barrel.

f. 81-mm Heavy Mortar 34 (8-cm s.Gr.W. 34)

In general, the instructions are the same as those for the light mortar. Commence firing with a greater range than the calculated range, and with the lowest possible charge. Use mortar shell 38 if it is available.

g. Infantry Howitzer

When moving over roads, the infantry howitzer (*Infanteriegeschütz*) is loaded on runners or on simple sleds and drawn by horses; off the road, on ski runners or on special sleds. When snow is on the ground, heavy infantry howitzers can be moved only on paved streets and roads.

When bringing howitzers into position on frozen ground, place them, if possible, on reed mats, or, if these are not available, on a soft foundation such as brushwood. When firing, use ice spades; however, provide a yielding foundation for the spades (brushwood or bundled branches) in order to spare the weapons. Do not leave the weapon loaded for a long period, or the projectile will freeze fast. Fire only after having carefully determined the brackets, but fire at a greater range than the determined one. It is advisable to start firing with the lowest possible charge. The barrel may be warmed by discharging a blank shell. If possible, fire ricochet shots. This can be done if the snow is soft and up to 16 inches deep and the ground is frozen.

h. Antitank Weapons

On roads the 37-mm antitank gun (*3.7-cm Pak*), the 50-mm antitank gun (*5-cm Pak*), and the heavy antitank rifles are drawn by motor vehicles. The 37-mm antitank gun may also be loaded on a pack sled or ski runner and can be hauled by horses or by the troops themselves. The heavy antitank rifle may be dismantled and the parts carried on light sleds.

56. STORAGE AND HANDLING OF MUNITIONS IN WINTER

a. Storage

Particular care must be taken in selecting enclosed spaces for the winter storage of ammunition. Wherever possible, select buildings, barns, sheds, and pillboxes which are not located near other buildings. If such buildings are not available, ammunition sheds must be constructed. Corrugated-sheet-iron huts and wooden sheds, covered with tar paper, are suitable. Special attention must be paid to camouflage and drainage. In the spring there is danger of flood because of the rapid melting of snow. Drainage ditches must be dug. Storage of ammunition in the open is prohibited if paper or tarpaulins are the only covering.

Storage sheds must have particularly strong protection on the weather side, and doors and windows must be located on the lee side. Snow fences must be constructed to prevent snow drifts. In order to keep paths open, snow-clearing equipment must be kept on hand. There must be air space all around the ammunition, and it must be stacked about 1 foot above the ground. Passages between the ammunition piles must be paved with stones, wood, or broken bricks. The ceiling must be leakproof.

Storerooms should be ventilated as often as possible, but only when the inside and outside temperatures are approximately the same. Otherwise moisture may condense on the ammunition.

Only clean, dry ammunition may be stored in regulation containers. Lids of containers and fasteners must be locked. The containers must be stored in such a manner that water cannot penetrate through the seams. Parts which are used for the protection of ammunition, such as fuze caps and ammunition belts, must not be lacking. Moisture carriers, such as wood shavings, woolen blankets, or rags, must not be used for packing ammunition.

Ammunition in airtight packing (paraffin) should remain, if possible, in the original packages. The dryest possible rooms must be selected for flare and tracer ammunition, fuzes, explosives, and cartridge-case wads. Ammunition with safety caps should be stored with the points slightly raised so that water can run off. Cartridge cases should be stored bottom-up so that no water will penetrate to the charge.

In winter, ammunition is especially exposed to dirt, moisture, and frequent changes in temperature. Therefore, particularly careful handling and continuous inspection of the ammunition are necessary. Inspections are particularly important after changes in weather and after rain or snowfall. If ammunition becomes moist on the outside, it must be dried by dabbing (without destroying the sealing material). Moist containers have to be airdried. Cartridges with moist powder or fuzes with signs of corrosion must be reported immediately. Shells with scarred paint must be lightly greased. The washers and cover plates of fuzes must be checked. Leather parts, belts, and felt plates must be examined in order to prevent mold deposits.

b. Ammunition in Combat Positions

Ammunition in emplacements and other combat positions should be stored on mats or grates. It must be covered to protect it against moisture and snowdrifts. Shells, before being loaded, must be cleared of all ice and snow. This precaution is particularly necessary with respect to rotating bands, as firm ramming of the shells would otherwise be impossible. To avoid the danger of sparks, use wooden, not iron, tools in cleaning the ammunition.

c. Handling of Shell Cases

Shell cases must be covered to protect them against cold, wind, snow, rain, fog, and dew. They should be wrapped in hair blankets. Very cold shell cases should not be brought into warm rooms, or moisture will form on them and "shorts" (*Kurzschüsse*) will result when the shells are fired. Special shell cases should be kept in their containers until they are actually loaded. Cartridge cases must always be placed on a clean base. They must be free of sand, dirt, gravel, and ice. Particular care should be taken with mortar ammunition, which can be seriously affected by moisture and cold.

In very low temperatures, special Arctic ammunition must be used. Wooden rocket-projection cases may be warped by the weather to such an extent that up to 25 percent of the rockets will be jammed. Because this warping may result in "shorts," changes of direction, or explosions in the firing position, the rockets should be packed, if possible, in iron cases during the winter.

CARE AND USE OF WEAPONS AND EQUIPMENT

d. Ammunition of Chemical Troops

Mortar shells and shells with rocket charges, as well as attached rimvent fuzes (*Randdüsenzünder*) and hot-tube detonator fuzes, must be protected against icing. Before loading, each round must be checked to be sure that it has been cleared of ice, particularly the vents. Ice must be removed without damaging the ammunition. Because of the danger of sparks, only wooden tools should be used for this purpose.

Ammunition for chemical mortars 35 and 40 can be employed down to a temperature of —31 degrees F.

The 280-mm HE rocket (*28-cm Wurfk. Spr.*) and the 320-mm incendiary rocket (*32-cm Wurfk. M Fl*) can be used in temperatures down to 5 degrees F. without special treatment. A shortening of the range of fire must be reckoned with at temperatures below this point. At temperatures below 32 degrees F., 320-mm incendiary rockets are effective only against buildings and other easily inflammable targets. If projectors are held ready for fire for a long time, they must be checked for ice formations before they are fired.

e. Special Experiences

All special experiences and observations concerning the behavior of ammunition in general at extremely low temperatures (—22 to —58 degrees F.) should be reported to the Army High Command, G-4, Ammunition (*OKH/Gen. Qu. 3/I*). All observations concerning artillery ammunition should be reported to the chief of field artillery of the army staff.

57. ARTILLERY FIRE IN WINTER

a. Effect of Weather

The conduct of fire prescribed in the gunnery manual and in memoranda is also valid in winter. The effectiveness of the projectiles is influenced by frozen ground as well as by the depth and firmness of the snow. Soft snow reduces the possibilities of ricochet fire and minimizes fragmentation to such a degree that it is almost without effect. Additional adjustment fire and fire for effect with combination fuzes, corresponding to each target area, become necessary.

A hard snow surface, frozen ground, and ice increase the possibilities for ricochet fire but make the course of the ricochet and the impact incalculable when delayed-action fuzes are used. These factors should be taken into special consideration in delivering fire near friendly troops. Changing temperatures and weather conditions make it necessary to check repeatedly the burst effect of the projectile in the same target area. Earth banked up against field fortifications has much greater resistance in very low temperatures; therefore, it becomes necessary to fire with heavy calibers in order to combat such fortifications effectively.

In order to avoid "shorts," prompt weather reports are very important. In case of observed fire, the effect of low temperatures on the chart range must always be taken into consideration. If fire is delivered near friendly infantry, it is recommended that an increased range be selected for the first two groups ("barrel warmers") in order to preclude the possibility of "shorts."

If a heavy charge must be used in howitzers which use a special shell case, first deliver several rounds with small and medium charges. It must be understood that medium charge means the highest charge which can be fired without the use of a special shell case. To engage distant targets use, if possible, guns which can reach the required range with small or medium charges. In organizing ammunition supply, the increased need of combination fuzes should be taken into account, and they should be requisitioned promptly from the services of supply.

b. Artillery Reconnaissance

Artillery reconnaissance by the observation battalion and the survey battery (armored) entails no special difficulties in winter. All telephone wires, which are most likely to be damaged in cold weather, should be supplemented by radio in order to prevent interruption of communications. Employment according to plan is always desirable.

If, during adjustment fire in deep snow, the impacts of shells fired by friendly batteries do not register, the sound-ranging battery should have the fire adjusted so that the points of the bursts are low, thus making it easier to register the detonations; or the flash-ranging battery should direct fire with high points of bursts on enemy batteries which have been located by the sound-ranging battery.

Captive balloons may be sent up in temperatures as low as —22 degrees F., while pilot balloons may go up for weather reports in any temperature. This also applies to the use of radio-sounding balloons.

c. Firing of Chemical Mortars

In firing mortar shells with fuze 38 (*Wgr.Z 38*) and combination fuze 38 (*Wgr.Z. 38 St.*) at a target area of uncrusted snow (powdery snow) or soft or swampy ground, remove the closing disk of the mortar-shell fuze. This increases the sensitivity of the fuze, reduces the number of duds, and is considerably more effective. The closing disks can be removed without danger by the troops themselves with any pointed object, such as a pocket knife or nail. The number of disks removed must not exceed the number of mortar shells to be fired during the day. The storage of mortar shells without closing disks for longer than 2 days is forbidden because of the danger that moisture might penetrate and cause a dud.

58. OPTICAL INSTRUMENTS

If possible, optical instruments should not be exposed to extreme changes of temperature. If a gun is kept in the open, the panoramic sight should be removed. It should not be kept in heated billets, but in a dry anteroom. To prevent the formation of moisture on the eyepiece and objective lenses, dust them off thoroughly with a soft cloth and then rub them with a *Klarinol* cloth. If the lenses of the eyepiece become covered with a thin deposit of ice, do not remove the ice forcefully, but melt it slowly and then polish the lenses with a soft rag. The instruments should not be warmed near a fireplace or a stove or moisture will form within them and on the graduated plate.

Instruments which bear the letters "KF" near the trade mark are greased with cold-resistant *Invarol*, which guarantees perfect functioning of the gears to −4 degrees F.

Instruments which, instead of the sign "KF" or in addition to it, have a light-blue seal, are greased with Vacuum grease 1416 (*Vakuumfett 1416*) or with a grease having the same qualities. These instruments can be used without trouble down to —40 degrees F. The grease in instruments which have not yet been provided with a cold-resistant grease and also those marked "KF" will harden in very cold weather and the gears will stick. The instruments, when not in use and in extremely cold weather, might be placed in rooms which are not too cold, or must be protected in another manner. While being transported, the instruments must be protected against extreme cold by wrapping them in blankets and shelter halves.

While in use, the movable parts—eyepieces, gears, and screws—should be kept functioning by moving them in both directions; forceful turning must be avoided. If the arms of a BC scope (*Scherenfernrohr*) are frozen while spread very far apart, they should not be forced back into the parallel position without warming; otherwise the eye-adjustment housing tube will break. Instruments which have a focusing dial or an eye-adjustment mechanism should be set once for use by one person, and, if possible, should not be changed thereafter.

59. CHEMICAL-WARFARE EQUIPMENT

a. Gas Masks

Filter elements and dry gas masks for both men and animals can be used even in very low temperatures. The rubber of the gas mask becomes somewhat stiffer. This, however, does not prevent the gas mask from being put on quickly or from fitting snugly. If it is worn for a long time in temperatures below 23 degrees F., an ice crust and icicles will form at the air outlets. But these are of no consequence. When the gas mask is being worn, the valves will not freeze, even if weather is extremely cold. Inlet and outlet valves, however, can freeze when the mask is taken off and exposed to extreme cold while it is still damp from the breath.

The freezing of the outlet valve is nothing to worry about, because, after a few minutes, it will thaw out and open. Until then, the exhaled air escapes at the sides at the fitting band. Fitting bands and the chin supports which have become wet can freeze stiff, and the mask will not fit snugly. If force is used, the fitting band or the chin supports may break. Frozen fitting bands and chin supports must be thawed before the mask is put on. The best remedy is to button the mask under the field blouse for 3 to 5 minutes. In very cold weather the antidimming disks may become covered with ice after the mask has been taken off, thereby losing their transparency. Therefore, if the mask has been worn for longer than half an hour, the antidimming disks should always be changed for new ones immediately after taking off the mask. The inner surface of the eyepiece should be dabbed dry before the new antidimming disk is inserted.

To prevent icing, the gas mask should not be placed in the canister after it is taken off, but should be worn under the overcoat or blouse with the carrying strap around the neck until there is an opportunity to dry the mask. It is not sufficient just to wipe off the mask: in the case of gas mask 30 (*Gasmaske 30*), the leather fitting band must also be dried properly. Iced gas masks must be thawed slowly (not near a stove). Until this is done, they must not be folded or packed into the canister.

b. Horse Respirators

A damp horse respirator will freeze and in such a condition is brittle. The respirator should therefore be adjusted carefully and the straps tightened only when the respirator bag has been thawed out by the warmth of the breath. In billets damp horse respirators should be kept in rooms which are free of frost.

c. Protective Clothing

The heavy gas-protective suit may become brittle in extremely cold weather. The repacking and reloading of the individual pieces should therefore be avoided until they lose their stiffness. When dry, the light gas-protective suit and the stockings for horses are almost cold-proof. When frozen, however, they become brittle and must be thawed out and dried before use.

d. Gas Detectors

As the effectiveness of persistent gases decreases with increasing cold, it also becomes more difficult to detect them. The register of mustard-gas test paper in cold weather becomes weaker than that of test powder. (Test powder registers a persistent gas chemical agent down to about 5 degrees F.) Crystallized poison gas cannot be detected by either.

The little testing tubes of the gas detector are effective in cold weather as follows:

Tube No. 1—For mustard gas, down to 27 degrees F.
Tube No. 2—For nitrogen-mustard gas, down to 5 degrees F.
Tube No. 3—For diphosgene and phosgene, almost all temperatures.
Tube No. 4—For chloropicrin, almost all temperatures.
Tube No. 5—For prussic acid, down to 23 degrees F.

e. Decontamination Materials

Decontamination agents, and decontamination materials for weapons, function effectively in temperatures as low as

—4 degrees F. The pocket container with the skin-decontaminating ointment should, in extremely cold weather, be carried in the trouser pocket to prevent freezing. Frozen skin-decontaminating ointment thaws upon application. Cleaning oil for the decontamination of weapons becomes pulpy at about 27 degrees F., and tallowy (hard) at —4 degrees F., but it still is usable. If necessary, use a pocket knife to take it out of the container in pieces, pulverize it, and then rub it in.

f. Smoke-Producing Agents

Smoke candles, rapid smoke candles, and smoke hand grenades remain fully effective even in extremely cold weather. In deep snow, however, the throwing or firing of the smoke-producing agent is ineffective because, while producing the smoke, they become hot and thus melt the snow and sink into it. However, if smoke candles are placed on supports, they are fully effective.

Ordinary smoke acid decomposes in very cold weather (below —4 degrees F.). It should therefore be protected against frost during the cold period. In the Russian winter the only smoke acid which can be used (*Arktik*—"Requisition No. Ch 10,300") is one which remains liquid at —22 degrees F., and upon which a thin ice deposit forms only when the temperature goes down to —36 degrees F. The effectiveness of this smoke acid (*Ark*) is superior to that of the ordinary smoke acid because it is not influenced by moisture in the air.

Section XIV. SIGNAL COMMUNICATION

60. PROTECTION OF SIGNAL EQUIPMENT

a. Housing

Most signal equipment can be used in low temperatures if difficulties peculiar to winter are anticipated and if the means of overcoming them are known. For operational purposes, signal equipment should be placed, if possible, in heated rooms. On the march, protect equipment from the wind by wrapping it in blankets. The soldiers' packs may be used for this purpose also.

b. Heating and Insulation

For the heating of enclosed motor vehicles and small rooms in which equipment is operated, use—

(1) Poronto stoves (*Porontoöfen*). The latest model can be used with all liquid fuels.
(2) Oil stoves. They are sensitive to drafts, and should be used only in enclosed rooms, exactly according to prescribed directions. Only refined gasoline can be used. (Regular motor fuel is not suitable.) These stoves give comparatively little heat.
(3) Electrical stoves or heaters. Where there is a voltage of 220, either alternating or direct current, electrical stoves or heaters can be used.

Heating with fuel which contains lead is forbidden because it is injurious to health. Large rooms in which equipment is operated should be heated with solid fuel. Provision must be made for a chimney. As long as there are fires in the stoves, they must be watched. Ventilation must not be overlooked. An open flame should not be brought near motor vehicles with storage batteries, or into rooms where such batteries are being charged, because of the danger from inflammable gas.

When signal equipment is operated in unheated rooms or in the open air, it should be packed in warming boxes with double walls. Make the boxes large enough so that heated stones or warming bags can be placed around the equipment. The heating devices should be separated from

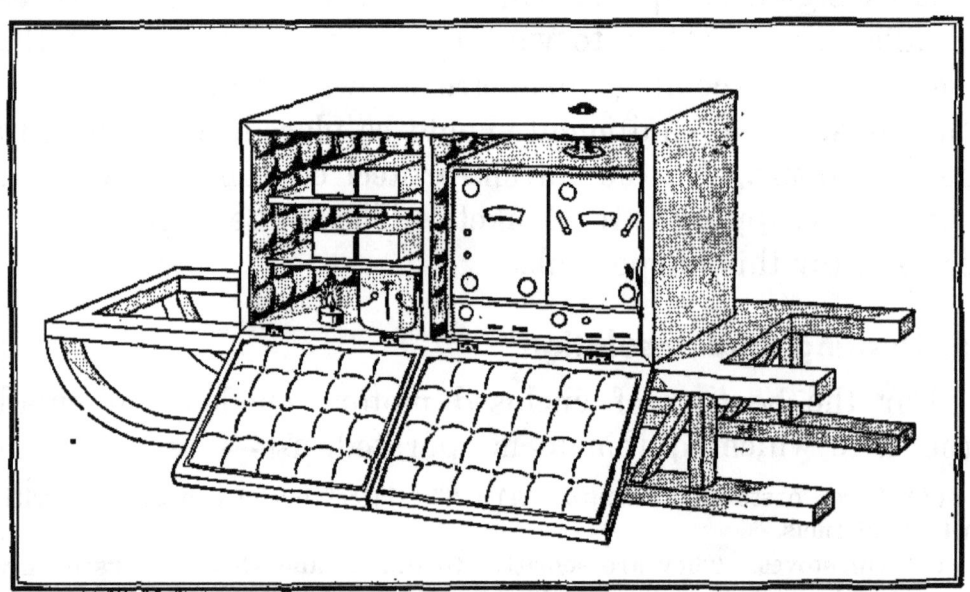

Figure 76.—Padded and heated box for a portable radio.

the equipment by sheets of tin or plywood. A nest box of tin or plywood is even better. Fill the space between the double walls with sawdust, peat moss, or straw.

An improvised box, padded and heated, and mounted on a sled, makes it possible to use the portable radio even in extremely low temperatures (see fig. 76). Rags, cotton wadding, or straw may be used for insulation. A candle provides sufficient heat to keep the battery warm.

When equipment is brought from the outside into a warm room, the condensed moisture should be carefully dried off. Do not place equipment in the immediate vicinity of a stove or in temperatures of more than 86 to 95 degrees F. (normal warmth of the hands). Microphones become covered with moisture when they are used in the open air or in cold rooms. They should be dried frequently to prevent freezing. Prevent moisture from entering the microphone by using a cover, and always have spare microphones ready.

c. Lubrication

Lubricants which are *not cold-resistant* will become hard if used on signal equipment in cold weather, and movable parts will jam. Do not use force under any circumstances to get the parts moving. Warm the equipment in heated rooms or boxes until the parts move normally again. It is better, however, to remove oil and grease which is not cold-resistant and substitute cold-resistant grease (*Calypsol*).

d. Grounding

Frozen soil does not make a good ground. Bury grounds for single-wire circuits to prevent them from getting coated with frost. Put your ground connection below the frost line in cellars and wells. It is better, however, to use full metallic circuits. In radio installations substitute counterpoises for the ground connection.

e. Protection of Crew

If the head set is worn without the rubber earpieces, there will be danger that the edges of the ears will freeze without the radio operator's being aware of it. If operating in the open air, put the knitted woolen cap over the earpieces.

61. PROTECTION OF POWER SOURCES

a. Storage Batteries

The stored-up power of storage batteries decreases with lowering temperatures. In very cold weather dead batteries may freeze, and in extreme temperatures the frozen liquid may break the battery case. Therefore, protect batteries by packing them in wood or by wrapping them in blankets or straw. If the storage battery is charged, however, this danger does not develop. The Edison storage battery (*Nickelsammler* or *Edisonsammler*) freezes somewhat more easily than the lead-acid storage battery. The colder it is, the more frequently storage batteries must be charged. If possible, storage batteries should not be allowed to discharge completely.

The specific gravity when the battery is charged must not be below 1.28 in the lead storage battery and 1.24 in the Edison storage battery, nor should the concentration be far above these figures. Check the batteries carefully. If there are no facilities for measuring the specific gravity during the cold-weather period, fill the lead-acid storage batteries with sulfuric acid and the Edison storage batteries with potash lye instead of distilled water. This may be done only when the batteries are charged. Storage batteries filled with a concentrated liquid should be marked with a "W." When the warm weather begins, the fluid should be diluted with distilled water.

b. Dry Batteries

Regular dry-cell batteries will not function if exposed for a long period to a temperature of –22 degrees F., but cold-resistant batteries have a performance rating of 25 percent at the same temperature. The latter batteries are marked with the sign of a snow crystal or with the designation *Ark*. Dry cells and dry batteries get completely cold in 4 to 8 hours. Therefore, warm them thoroughly before using them in the open air in order to prolong their life. From time to time exchange them for thoroughly warmed batteries.

In cold weather the voltage is reduced to approximately two-thirds of its original value and remains at this point for a rather long time. In order to prolong their use, connect two instead of one, or three instead of two batteries in series. This must not be done, however, with issue radio receivers (*Wehrmachtrundfunkempfänger*), because their tubes may be damaged.

c. Converters, Vibrators, and Generators

The ball bearings of converters are lubricated with cold-resistant grease (*Calypsol W 1a*) and function without difficulty in temperatures as low as –22 degrees F. In lower temperatures they start with difficulty; however, this may be remedied by warming.

Foot and hand generators function perfectly down to –22 degrees F. If the voltage is too low in very cold weather, increase the rate of revolutions per second until the correct voltage is reached. The vibrators function without difficulty down to –22 degrees F.

d. Power Units

The instructions in **b**, above, apply also to power units. Lead the exhaust gas into the open air by means of sectional pipes. If there are no other facilities, place all portable power units in tents, resting them on stones, empty cans, or other fireproof foundations. (A foundation also prevents the units from sinking into the ground and freezing fast when the machine is not running.) If more than one power unit is being used, group them so that they heat each other with the warm air which they release. When the power units are not in operation, they should be kept well covered.

Do not sleep in tents or small rooms in which power units are in operation, for their fumes may cause poisoning.

e. Network Markings and Safeguards

Exact diagrams of networks are especially important. Even before the beginning of winter, signboards and posters should be set up to indicate position, distance, and other information about cables. The text should be in code. Cables should not be bent at a sharp angle, because the insulating material breaks. If possible, wind cloth around the connecting wires to protect them against moisture.

f. Protecting Lines against Frost, Ice, and Snow

Frost and sleet storms occur when the temperature falls sharply, and snow falls at temperatures around 32 degrees F. Areas in the east where this happens frequently are Stalingrad, Saratov, Tambov, Voronezh, Ryazan, Tula, Orel, and northern and central Ukraine, and even more frequently in the southern part of the Ukraine, the Crimea, Rostov, Krasnodar, the Caucasus, and less frequently in

Leningrad. In weather such as this the wire becomes as much as 5 times heavier and 20 times thicker, thereby causing the breaking of wires and poles. Remove deposits of frost and snow by beating against the poles with wooden hammers, and deposits of ice by tapping the wires of cables with thin rods.

To avoid dampening of sound caused by deposits of frost, snow, and ice, install intermediate amplifiers along long stretches of wire.

Surface lines should be constructed firmly. There should also be shorter intervals between poles and more wind anchors. If the situation warrants, tripod supports, embedded in the soil itself, should be used instead of single poles.

Establish a frost-warning service in collaboration with the weather stations of the Air Force. Place motor vehicles or horses and sleds at the disposal of wire-repair crews; if near a railroad line, provide the crews with line-inspection trolleys, locomotives, signal-construction trains, and, if necessary, relief trains.

g. Laying of Cables

Cables which have been laid on the ground will freeze fast to the ground or the snow as soon as cold weather sets in, and they cannot be taken up without considerable damage.

If the snow is 8 inches deep or more, cables which do not have to be moved until the spring thaw should be laid under the snow. Then there is less possibility of their being molested, and they will suffer less damage than if they are strung overhead or are laid on top of the snow. As soon as the snow begins to melt, the cables should be strung overhead. Where deep snowdrifts occur, the poles of an overhead line must be high enough to permit uninsulated wires and cables to clear the drifts.

In planning the construction of lines, avoid places which will be endangered by floods during the thaw period. If this is not possible, barriers should be installed in front of the poles to protect them from floating ice. For the mud period, have mud-planks, boats, log-rafts, ropes, and anchors ready.

Heavy field cable should, in very cold weather, be tied to the poles with bands of thick cord. If clove hitches or other ties are unavoidable, select thick trees or poles for the purpose. For single-line construction, be sure to get a deep ground (for instance, by digging under the layer of ice, or in cellars, pillboxes, and wells). It is better, however, to have full metallic construction.

If the heavy field cable is wrapped in *Igelit* insulation (red color), the *Igelit* casing will, in extremely cold weather, become dry and break. It is not possible, however, to replace this cable completely with the heavy black field cable because of production problems and scarcity of raw materials. If the black cable is not available, the heavy field cable with *Igelit* insulation should be buried in the ground before the cold weather sets in. This will prevent strain caused by reeling and unreeling during very cold weather.

For surface-line construction of field trunk cables, the splices should be fastened with linen bands to poles or trees at a height of 5 to 6 feet and marked. This will help to eliminate line troubles by preventing sharp bands and cracks. Be very careful when taking up the field trunk cable, especially if it is frozen fast. For overhead-line construction, the cable should have plenty of slack and should be supported about every 50 feet. Slack must be correctly adjusted according to the slack tables in Army Manual 419/7 (*H.Dv. 419/7*). Check clamp couplings and loop-knot ties frequently because they become loose in marked changes of temperature. In line construction above ground, hang switch-boxes lid-down to prevent penetration by melted snow.

62. TELEPHONE, RADIO, AND MISCELLANEOUS EQUIPMENT

a. Telephone

If the field telephone is well cared for and properly handled, it will function in all temperatures. Switchboards are very sensitive to moisture; therefore, pay special attention to paragraph **60, a** to **e**. The bearings of movable parts, such as drop-shutters, should be covered with a thin film of very fluid oil. The repeating coils need no special protection. Repeaters can be set up in unheated rooms or in the open air because they function perfectly down to –40 degrees F. Repeater 38 (*Verstärker 38*), however, operates well down to 14 degrees F. only.

If the deposit of ice on the lines is very heavy, the amplifying range of a repeater (for instance, cable *MEK 8* with 3-mm bronze wire) decreases from the normal range of 260 km (161½ miles) to 100 km (62 miles).

The carrier-frequency equipment is very susceptible to moisture. It must therefore be installed under a roof, and, if possible, in a heated room. With deposits of frost, snow, or ice, its range decreases considerably. In the inverter, the supply of current may fail when the temperature is below 32 degrees F.

b. Radio Equipment and Sound Locators

(1) *Transmitters, receivers, and cipher equipment.*—For radio equipment it is especially important to follow the instructions in paragraph **60, a** to **e**. Make appropriate preparations in time: practice unloading of radio equipment of all types, including the 100-watt radio apparatus, from motor vehicles. Make preparations for transportation on sleds and operation in the open air.

In general, the electrical qualities of radio apparatus (sensitivity, selectivity, frequency calibration, individual performance) do not change in cold weather. However, radio apparatus may be damaged by water condensing on the equipment. Cold weather also tends to reduce the power of the generating unit.

Frequent testing of the frequency is advisable. Frequencies of more than 3,000 kilocycles in some sets will show the greatest frequency variations.

In older models of radio equipment, the operating handles may become immovable in temperatures lower than −13 degrees F. (For remedying this condition, see paragraph **60c,** p. 181.) More recent models, however, are provided with cold-resistant grease. The radio equipment of armored vehicles can, in general, be operated in temperatures down to −4 degrees F. In lower temperatures, the measures taken to keep the tank functioning are also adequate for the built-in radio equipment.

(2) *Aerials and accessories.*—The weight of ice can cause the aerial wire to break, and may reduce range. Therefore, frequent checking of antenna installations is advisable. Knock off icicles with thin poles. The parts of the aerial of portable radio sets must be completely dry and free of ice or snow before they are telescoped; otherwise they will

freeze fast. The grease should be washed from the surface of the individual mast pipes in a warm room, and then a very thin coating of cold-resistant lubricant should be applied.

In wooden houses without an electrical wiring system or iron beams, all portable radio sets can be operated without noteworthy reduction of range if the aerial is placed as far as possible from the ceiling and the walls. In other types of structures place the aerial outside.

c. Teletype Equipment

It is especially important to operate teletype equipment in heated rooms and to protect it against dampness. The teletype apparatus and the teletype code machines operating with perforated tape function only if the temperature is above 32 degrees F. At 32 degrees F. the former must be warmed up for 10 minutes before it will write clearly. Use the cold-resistant *Calypsol W.I.B.D.* instead of the prescribed operational lubricant.

Remote switching unit 38 (*Fernschaltgerät 38*), the teletype adapter, teletype switchboards *T37, T39, WTD, WTE,* and *WT40* can theoretically be used down to 14 degrees F., but in practice at best only down to 32 degrees F., because they are connected with the teletype machines. The tape (specially gummed strips) should be kept in moisture-proof tin containers (waxed paper is not sufficient); otherwise it will be useless because the paper will stick together or become tangled.

Wire-tapping receivers can be used in very cold weather, if pick-up loops are used instead of ground connections. When the ground is frozen, only limited use of the cable detecting equipment can be made, as ground connections are frequently poor. Wire-tapping receivers (small), pick-up clamps 35 (*Lauschzange 35*), special insulators, and *SAT* amplifiers are influenced by cold weather only insofar as the strength of the power sources decreases.

Recorder d of the propaganda equipment can be operated in very cold weather if it has been lubricated with cold-resistant grease. The loudspeaker is cold-resistant. All other equipment can be operated in an enclosed and heated motor vehicle when the weather is very cold.

d. Blinker and Heliograph Equipment

Blinker signal communication is possible even in low temperatures. Hand generators and fine-adjustment gears function perfectly down to —22 degrees F. For lubrication, only the cold-resistant grease (*Calypsol*) should be used.

In the use of heliographs, no electrical difficulties are encountered down to —40 degrees F. Fine-adjustment gears may function with difficulty at —4 degrees F., but this can be remedied by warming them.

e. Pyrotechnic Equipment

In temperatures lower than —13 degrees F., the illumination and the smoke of pyrotechnic ammunition last longer, without appreciable reduction of visibility. To prevent jams, remove the ordinary lubricant from flare pistols and grease the parts of the bolt with *Calypsol*.

f. Supply of Equipment

Establish a limited supply of the following materials in the army signal-equipment park well before very cold weather sets in:

SIGNAL COMMUNICATION

(1) Heavy black field cable.
(2) Cold-resistant field cells.
(3) Cold-resistant anode batteries (B batteries).
(4) Concentrated sulfuric acid.
(5) Power units and spare parts.
(6) *Calypsol*.

An increased demand for these items must be expected. Do not store heavy black field cable and cold-resistant field cable too early, for they may lose power during storage.

Section XV. SKIS, SNOWSHOES, AND SNOW VEHICLES

63. GENERAL

To assure mobility in winter warfare, regular troop units require skis and snowshoes as well as the special troops and individuals who are regularly supplied with them—reconnaissance troops, ski squads, companies, battalions, runners, signal personnel, headquarters troops, and medical troops. It is also necessary to equip man-drawn or horse-drawn vehicles with sleds or runners. The mobility of antitank weapons is particularly important in winter. Sleds and runners are prepared in the communications zone and are issued to the troops (in exchange for wheeled vehicles) upon command of the authorities. When converting wheeled vehicles into sleds, essential spare parts and accessories should be removed and placed in the sleds. It is to the interest of all troops that winter equipment be collected and turned in at the end of the winter in order that it may be properly repaired and stored for future use.

When adequate equipment is not available for issue, means of transportation can be either confiscated from local inhabitants or constructed by the personnel of the unit. If it is necessary for a unit to construct its own vehicles, particularly sleds, the vehicles of the natives should be used as models. These vehicles have proved their worth for centuries. Keep the width of runners standardized.

64. SKIS, ACCESSORIES, AND SNOWSHOES

a. Skis

Skis are issued if they are available; otherwise they must be confiscated from the civilian population. They should not be made by the unit, because the work is too difficult and consumes too much time.

The following are not suitable for use in the army:

(1) Special jumping and downhill skis (these are too heavy).
(2) Skis less than 6 feet in length.
(3) Skis narrower than 2 inches.
(4) Skis broader than 3½ inches.
(5) Unmatched pairs of skis.
(6) Skis with steel edges (these have not proved of value on the Eastern Front).
(7) Ski poles shorter than 45 inches.
(8) Metal or plastic poles.
(9) Light metal pole rings.

One set of ski equipment consists of one pair of skis with bindings, one pair of poles, one tube of ski wax (50 grams), and one pair of strap-on sealskins (special issue).

A great variety of ski bindings is available. A simple binding breaks less often and can be repaired or replaced more easily. Only one type of binding should be used in any one unit (platoon, patrol, etc.).

Some troops are being equipped with the new Army flat-terrain ski binding. With this binding, in combination with an overboot, any kind of shoe may be used; otherwise boots for ski shoes must be specially designed.

b. Ski Shoes

Because of the extraordinary shortage of ski boots, only laced shoes, with which every soldier is equipped, can be considered for mass skiing. (The infantry boot is less suitable.) The laced shoe can be adapted by attaching a metal strip to the sole and bending it up on each side of the toe. This protects the shoe against damage and permits it to sit better in the ski binding. Use thin metal (tin cans). Bend the metal strips lengthwise to an angle of 90 degrees and fasten them with small nails to the under side of the sole. Then bend out and flatten the edges of the metal to prevent them from cutting into the uppers. Into the back of the heel drive 3 to 4 nails to prevent the ski binding from slipping off. Do not remove nails from the soles; otherwise water will seep through.

c. Army Flat-Terrain Ski Binding

The Army flat-terrain ski binding is used for skiing in flat, rolling, and wooded terrain, and is not intended for mountainous regions. The binding fits all shoe sizes. The angle of its toe irons is standardized and is bisected by the longitudinal axis of the ski; the binding, therefore, may be used for either the right or the left foot. The component parts of the binding on the ski are toe irons; front throw, with lock; holding screws; 4 countersunk screws, with nipples for each; and 2 countersunk screws for the front throw. On the boot or laced shoe are 1 shoe cleat and 11 countersunk screws for fastening the foot plate.

In fastening the binding to the ski the distance from the front edge of the toe irons to the tip of the ski depends on the length of the ski, as follows:

Length of ski	*Distance from ski tip*
6 feet 6 inches	3 feet 1 inch.
6 feet 8 inches	3 feet 2 inches.
6 feet 10 inches	3 feet 3 inches.
7 feet	3 feet 3 inches.
7 feet 2 inches	3 feet 4 inches.

SKIS, SNOWSHOES, AND SNOW VEHICLES 195

The distance of the front throw (rear edge) from the front edge of the toe irons is 30 to 35 mm (1-1/10 to 1-3/10 inches). The toe irons must be screwed on in such a manner that their bisecting line coincides with the longitudinal axis of the ski.

To open the binding, the front throw is pushed forward. This makes room between the lateral locking lugs and the ends of the front throw for insertion of the shoe cleat

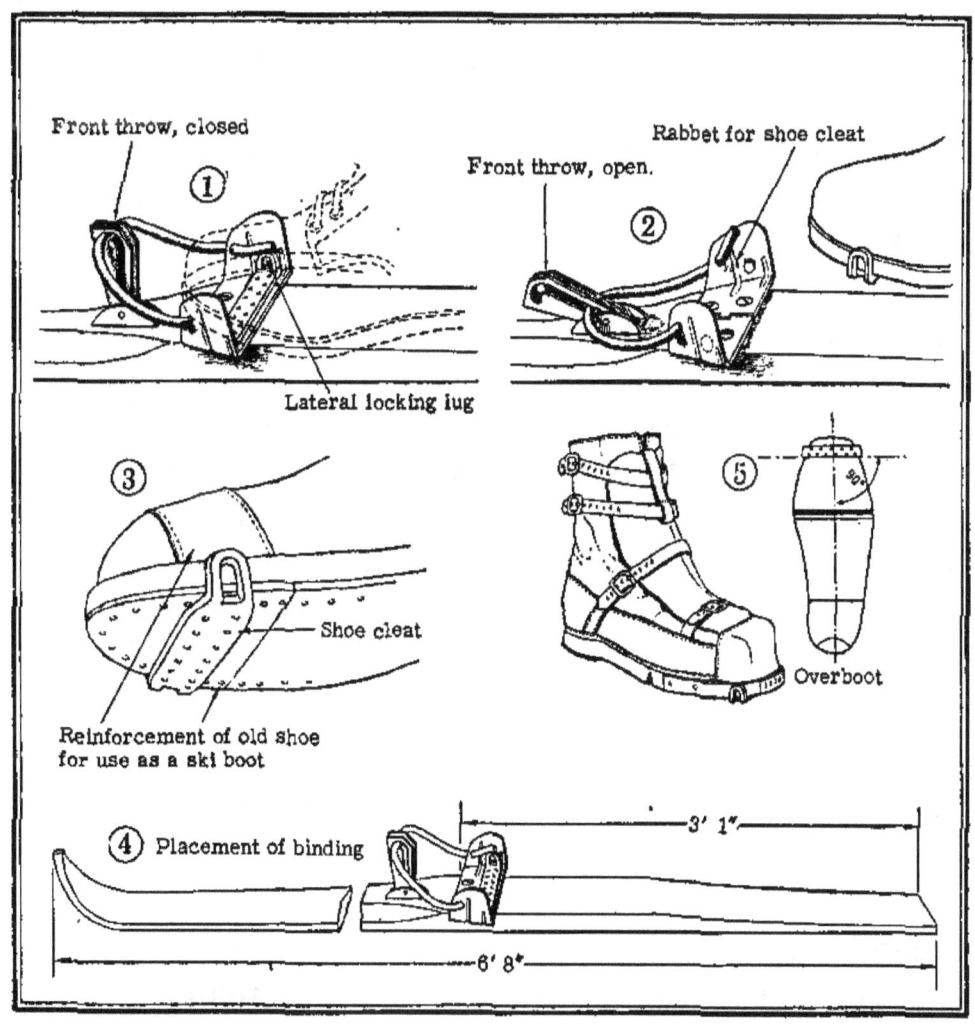

Figure 77.—Flat-terrain ski binding and the overboot.

between the toe irons. To lock the binding, raise the front throw vertically. The shoe cleat is thereby pressed snugly against the lateral locking lugs of the front throw and held in place; as long as the front throw remains in this position, the binding stays locked (see fig. 77).

The shoe cleat is at the balance point of the ski. It is screwed to the sole about 20 mm (about seven-tenths of an inch) from the tip of the shoe. Eleven screws are used for attaching it to the sole. The shoe cleat must be fastened exactly at right angles to the longitudinal axis of the shoe.

If a large number of shoes are to be fitted with cleats, it is recommended that they be prepared in the following manner. On the end of a piece of board, about 19 inches long and about as wide as a ski, a cleat is screwed on at right angles to, and bisecting, the longitudinal axis. The shoe is placed upon this plank and moved inside the cleat until it touches the ears on both sides. Care must be taken that the heel of the shoe is exactly in the center of the plank. The correct position of the cleat is marked on the shoe sole. In this way a large number of cleats can be fitted rapidly.

If the shoes are badly worn or if their soles are not stitched to the upper leather, the soles must be strengthened at the front with shoe pegs. Faulty shoes may also be reinforced by placing a leather strip about 1 inch wide over the upper leather and stitching it to the sole at the point where the cleat is fastened (see fig. 77 (3)).

d. Overboot

The overboot often replaces the ski boot, and is worn as protection against cold over laced shoes, marching and riding boots, as well as felt boots (see fig. 77 (5)). The overboot is issued in three sizes. A large size is better than a tight fit.

If the shoe has too much play in the overboot, the empty space can be stuffed with paper, excelsior, straw, hay, rags, and dry moss, which provide good insulation against the cold. The overboot is issued complete with cleat.

e. Ski Kit

With each 10 pairs of skis fitted with the Army flat-terrain binding, one ski kit is issued. Its contents are—

Binding complete with all parts	1 pair.
Front throw	1 pair.
Cotter pin (2 inches long and one-tenth of an inch in diameter, for ski-pole ring)	2
Shoe pegs	20
Screw driver with changeable blades (width of edges, three-twentieths of an inch and two-tenths of an inch; length of blade, 3 inches)	1
Awl (gauge three-twentieths of an inch)	1
Wire (0.039 inch)	16 feet (approx.)

f. Snowshoes

Snowshoes are issued, but in emergency they can be constructed of wood or branches interwoven with cords. Walking with snowshoes is easy to learn, but it is tiresome if long distances must be covered in deep snow. (Relieve men marching in front.) In flat terrain, walk with toes pointing in. When climbing a mountain, place the weight on the toes; when descending, keep the weight on the heels.

65. HAND SLEDS

a. General

Hand sleds and bobsleds of the types used for sports cannot be employed to any great extent for military purposes, particularly in the deep snow of the Eastern Front. All high sleds with broad runners have proved their worth in snow of medium depth. Akjas, or boat-shaped sleds of Finnish type, have also done well in deep snow.

b. Akjas

Akjas are provided for general use, but they are especially useful for ski troops and other mobile units.

The following akjas are provided:

(1) Weapons akja.
(2) Boat akja.
(3) Light akja (plywood).

The weapons akja made of pinewood (fig. 78(1)) is a flat, boat-shaped sled. It is open at the rear, but a detachable board may be used as a stern piece. At the top of the inner walls, loops are provided for the ropes used to lash the load in place and to fasten the tarpaulin. The weapons akja is used to transport light weapons (machine guns, mortars, light antitank rifles) and ammunition. The machine gun, light mortar, and light antitank rifle can be fired from the akja. There are two rings, one fastened to the front and one to the rear, for the towing and braking ropes. The weapons akja can be hauled by one to three skiers, depending on the load.

The boat akja (fig. 78(2)) has the same shape as the weapons akja, but it is closed on all sides. It is used to transport signal equipment, ammunition, hand grenades, mines, food carriers, radio equipment, heavy mortars, flame-throwers, etc. It may also be used for the evacuation of wounded.

The light akja (figs. 78(3) and 79) is a flat sled made of plywood and shaped like a boat. In the side walls there are

SKIS, SNOWSHOES, AND SNOW VEHICLES   199

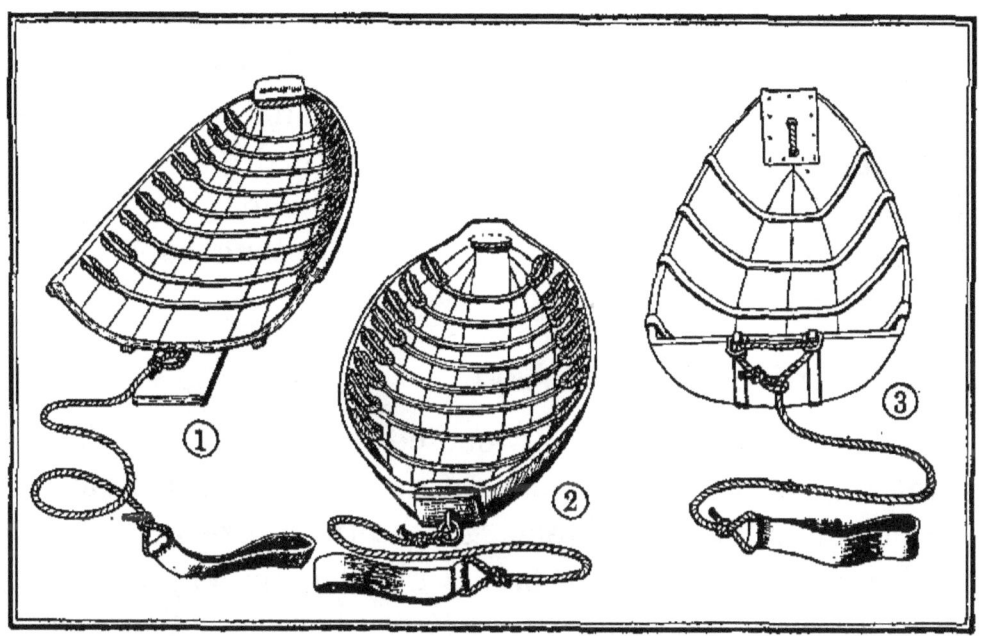

Figure 78.—Types of akjas: (1) weapons akja; (2) boat akja; (3) light akja.

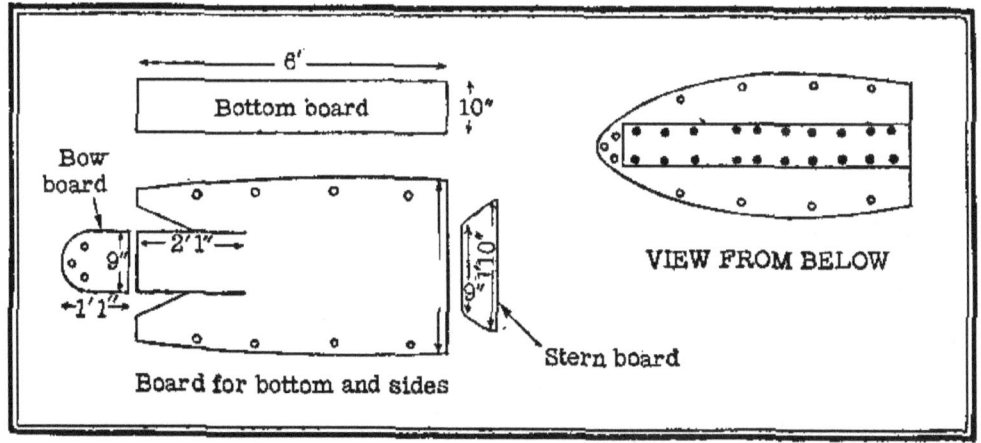

Figure 79.—Construction of a light akja.

four holes for lashing the load and four for fastening the tarpaulin. It is used to transport small loads similar to those specified for the boat akja. The light akja is also towed by one to three skiers. Two trained dogs may also be used. The leading dog must be on a lead. To stop and to steer the akja on steep inclines, a braking rope with a loop is attached to the rings in the rear.

c. Construction of Light Akja

To make a light akja, plywood consisting of three layers about 1½ inches thick is cut out as illustrated in figure 78 and put together with rivets. At the front a piece of board or plywood (five or more layers glued together) is riveted on. Two holes for the towropes are provided. These holes should be drilled as low as possible for greater ease in pulling the akja out of snow. The rear end is held together by a board and reinforced with a thin metal band. Two hooks are riveted to the top for the braking rope. A strong plywood board or a plank on which the sled will slide is riveted to the bottom of the akja. To strengthen the akja, an iron band is riveted underneath on each side and three sheet-metal ribs are riveted to the inside. Four holes must be drilled on both sides to receive the lashing ropes. Before being bent, the wood should be soaked in water.

d. Construction of Hand Sled

The light hand sled (Model Army Training School for Mountain Warfare) (*Modell Heereshochgebirgsschule*) has proved to be very useful on the Eastern Front in snow of medium depth. (See figs. 80 and 81.) It can be drawn by men, dogs, or horses and is made of old skis and other easily

SKIS, SNOWSHOES, AND SNOW VEHICLES

procurable material. No metal parts are used at the joints. The sled must be flexible and mobile, and the front part should be more lightly loaded than the rear. It has a weight of 9 to 11 pounds and can be drawn by one or more men, or by dogs. It can be used in trackless terrain. When drawn by skiers, the weight of the cargo should not be more than 80 kilograms (176 pounds); when drawn by dogs, not more than the total weight of the dogs.

A double shaft, which also serves as a brake, is used to tow single or tandem sleds. A towrope (preferably with a

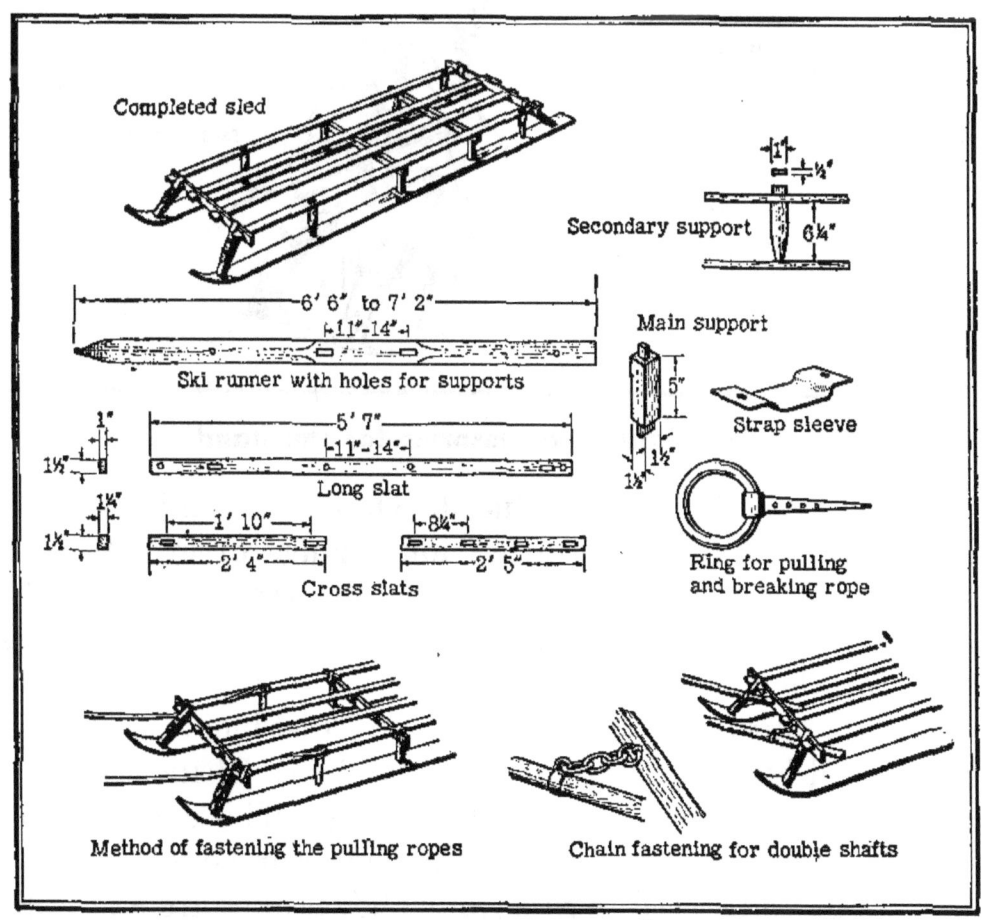

Figure 80.—Construction of a hand sled.

breast or waist belt) is used for sleds drawn by one or more soldiers or by dogs. Braking ropes are used in hilly terrain.

The materials necessary for construction are one pair of skis without bindings, or two old unusable skis, and hardwood for the frame. For the two lengthwise slats in the middle, softwood will do. As a substitute for hardwood, dried branches (birch or ash) can be used, but stability and

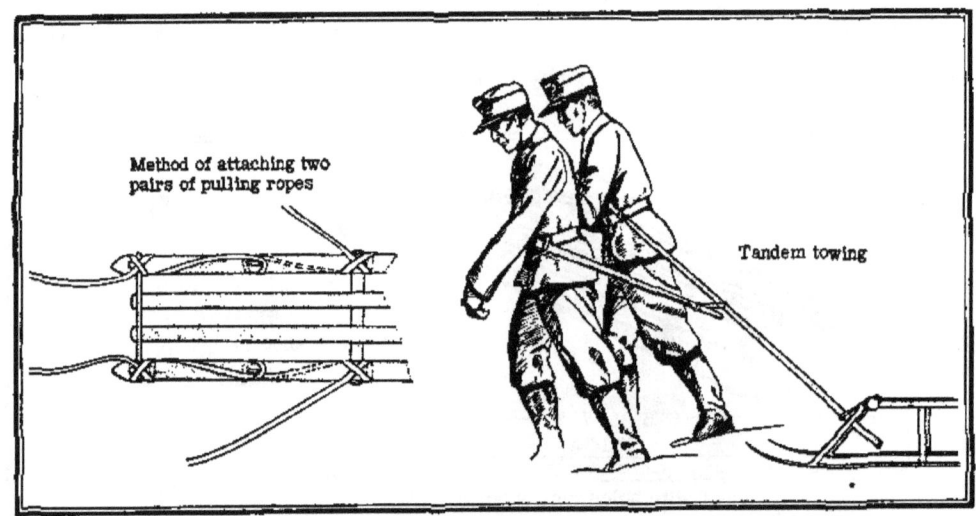

Figure 81.—Hauling accessories for the hand sled.

carrying capacity will be reduced. Other materials are four leather straps, about 10 inches long; rings or eyelets with screws for fastening the straps to the frame and to the runners; two rings for the towing device, and two rings each for the tandem and braking ropes; two poles (for a tandem); four poles, 6 feet 6 inches to 7 feet long, for shafts; one barrel hoop (two hoops for a tandem), 24 inches in diameter; ropes for towing and braking. The construction time required is 1½ hours for a carpenter and one assistant.

A similar sled used in Siberia is shown in figure 82. This sled is well adapted for towing by skiers, and may be used for transporting the wounded. The ski-shaped runners are 4 to 5 meters (13 to 16 feet) long. The width of the track should be about the same as that made by a skier (in no case more than 24 inches). The height of the sled is 28 inches; the height from the runners to the carrying board, 12 inches. The carrying board is flexibly fastened to the upper rails of the frame with ropes or cords.

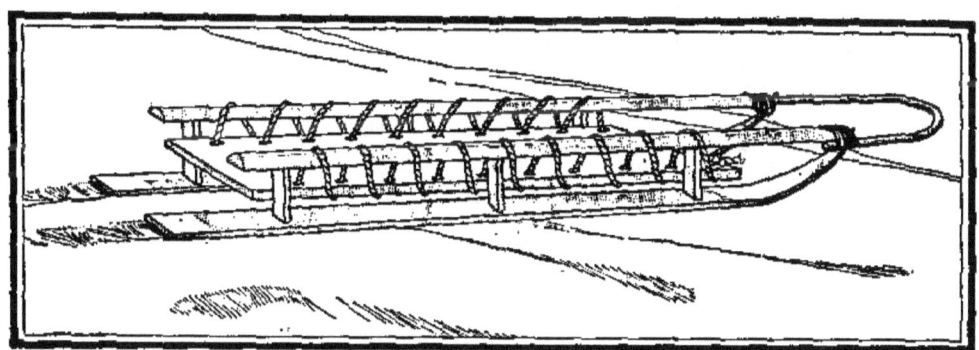

Figure 82.—Siberian type of sled.

66. HORSE-DRAWN SLEDS

a. General

The horse-drawn sleds used in central Europe, like the hand sleds of the same region, are too heavy and unwieldy for use on the Eastern Front. They cannot follow the troops, particularly ski troops, cross-country, and they are not built to a standard track width. The *panje* sled generally used in Russia has proved to be the best for the transportation of light loads. Its carrying capacity is small, being commensurate with the draught strength of the *panje* horse. In midwinter the capacity is frequently not more than 100 pounds.

	Army Sled No. 1	Army Sled No. 3	Army Sled No. 3/1	Army Sled No. 5	Light akja	Boat akja	Weapons akja
How drawn	Single or tandem	Single or tandem	Single or tandem	Single or tandem	Man-drawn	Man-drawn	Man-drawn
Weight (kilograms)	129 (284 lbs)	208 (459 lbs)	330 (728 lbs)	292 (644 lbs)	11.5 (25 lbs)	14 (31 lbs)	12 (26 lbs)
Maximum load (kilograms)	300 (661 lbs)	500 (1102½ lbs)	500 (1102½ lbs)	1,000 (2,205 lbs)	100 (220 lbs)	150 (331 lbs)	150 (331 lbs)
Length of box (millimeters)	2,100 (6 ft, 10 in)	2,270 (7 ft, 5 in)	2,120 (6 ft, 11 in)	2,885 (9 ft, 4 in)			
Width of box (millimeters)	740 (2 ft, 5 in)	1,100 (3 ft, 7 in)	1,250 (4 ft)	1,100 (3 ft, 7 in)			
Height of box (millimeters)	430 (17 in)	430 (17 in)	1,120 (3 ft, 7 in)	430 (17 in)			
Length of vehicle without shaft (millimeters)	2,760 (9 ft)	3,940 (12 ft, 11 in)	3,940 (12 ft, 11 in)	4,650 (15 ft, 2 in)			
Length of vehicle with shaft (millimeters)	5,337 (17 ft, 6 in)	6,370 (21 ft, 1 in)	6,370 (21 ft, 1 in)	7,150 (23 ft, 5 in)			
Total width of vehicle (millimeters)	950 (3 ft, 1 in)	1,200 (3 ft, 11 in)	1,410 (4 ft, 7 in)	1,200 (3 ft, 11 in)			
Width of tracks, measured from middle of runner to middle of runner (millimeters)	660 (2 ft, 1 in)	660 (2 ft, 1 in)	660 (2 ft, 1 in)	690 (2 ft, 3 in)			
Total length (millimeters)					2,130 (7 ft)	2,360 (7 ft, 9 in)	2,200 (7 ft, 2 in)
Width (millimeters)					660 (2 ft, 1 in)	620 (2 ft)	660 (2 ft, 1 in)
Height (millimeters)					160 (6 in)	170 (7 in)	160 (6 in)
Length of box with driver's seat (millimeters)			3,010 (9 ft, 10 in)				

Figure 83.—Table of specifications for issued sleds.

b. Army Sleds

Based on our own and Finnish army experience on the Eastern Front, the following Army sleds have been developed and prepared for issue to the troops, particularly for mobile winter units (see also fig. 83):

Army sled No. 1, carrying capacity 300 kilos (661 pounds).
Army sled No. 3, carrying capacity 500 kilos (1,102½ pounds).
Army ambulance sled No. 3/1, for severely as well as slightly wounded men.
Army sled No. 5, carrying capacity 1,000 kilos (2,205 pounds).

Army sled No. 1 (fig. 84) is a one-piece vehicle that may be used to carry freight and personnel. For bulky loads,

Figure 84.—Army sled No. 1, with side walls in place.

such as crates wider than the carrying surface, the side and rear boards can be removed.

The seat board in the front can be used as a driver's seat or to increase the height of the front wall, and other seat boards may be used similarly on the backboard. The shafts are two plain wooden poles, each with a ring for attaching them to the runners. The wooden whiffletree is attached

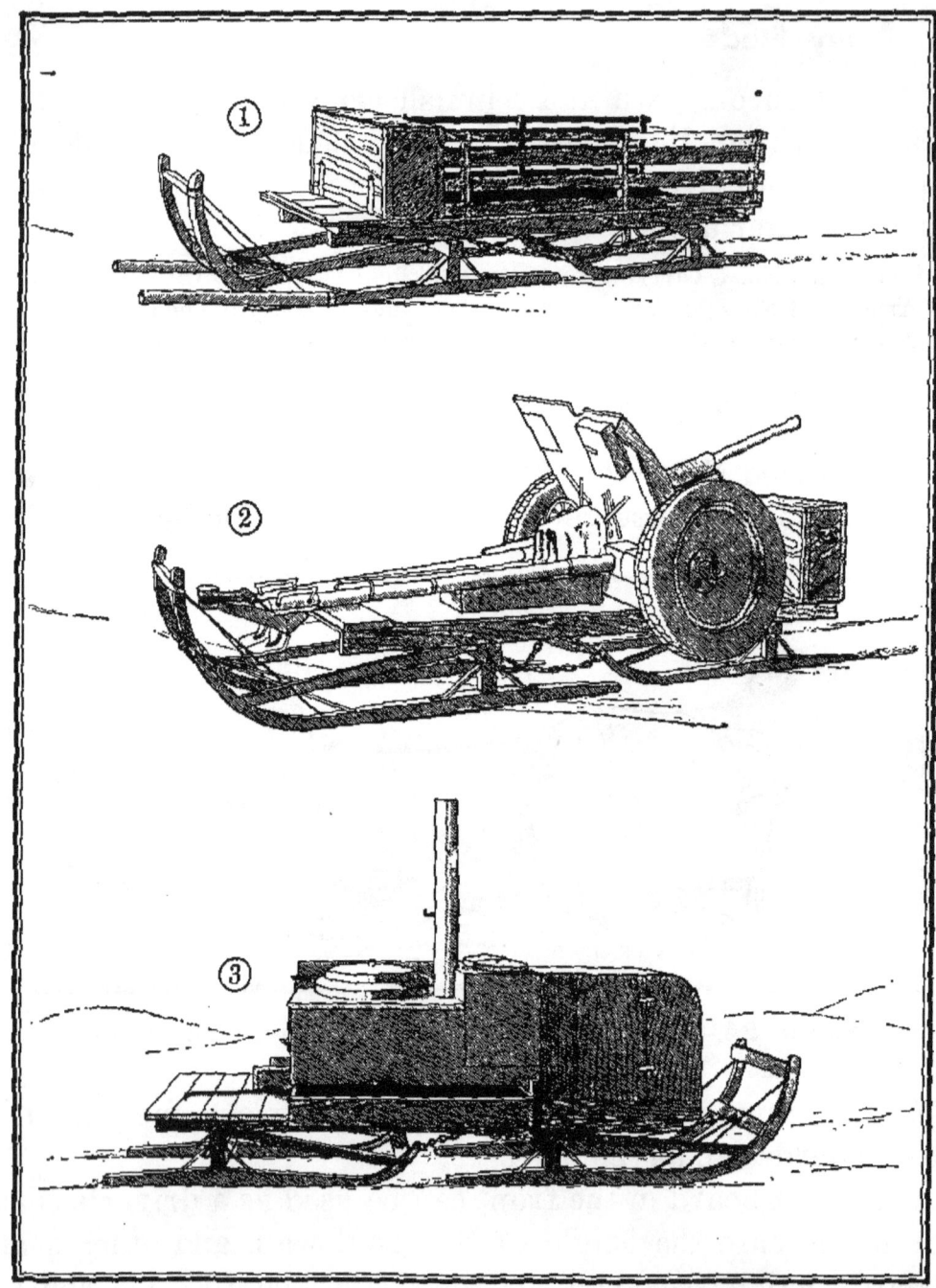

Figure 85.—Army sled No. 3, showing (1) the sled with the body in place; (2) an antitank gun mounted on the sled; (3) a light field kitchen loaded on the sled.

SKIS, SNOWSHOES, AND SNOW VEHICLES 207

to a hook on the upper cross bar of the front part of the sled. On the rear cross bar above each runner is a towing hook to which akjas or other light sleds can be attached. Army sled No. 1 can be drawn by a single horse or a tandem.

Army sled No. 3 (fig. 85) transports light field kitchens, 3.7-cm antitank guns, light infantry howitzer 18, signal equipment, engineer equipment, ammunition, and miscellaneous equipment. If a field kitchen, a light infantry how-

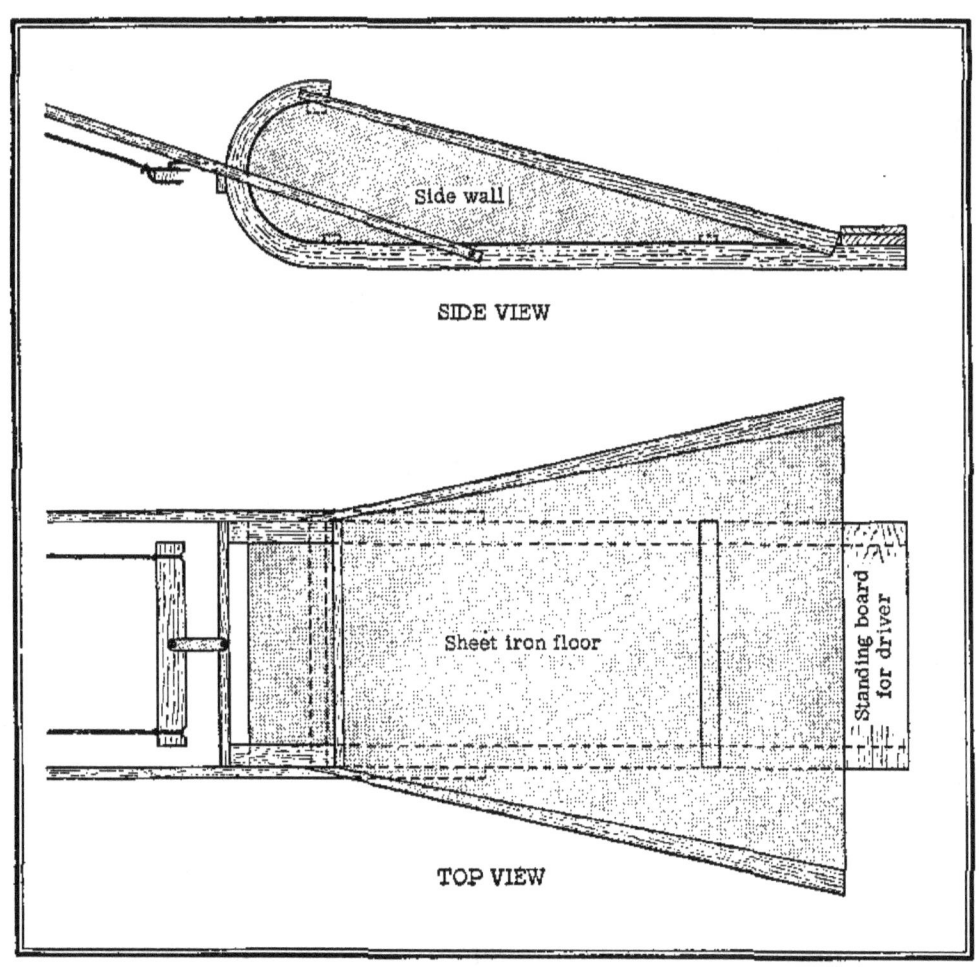

Figure 86.—Improvised horse-drawn toboggan type of sled.

itzer 18, or a 3.7-cm antitank gun is to be loaded on the sled, the body is removed and a platform is put in its place.

The sled is constructed in two parts. The front and rear parts are connected with each other by two crossed chains. The removable box is fastened to both parts with two pegs. The rear peg can move lengthwise. The side walls and the

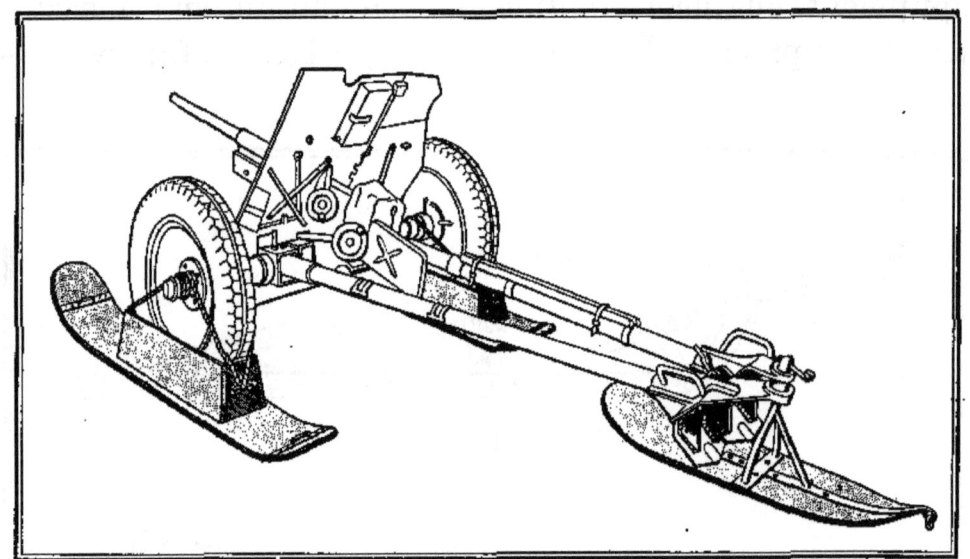

Figure 87.—Antitank gun mounted on ski runners.

rear wall of the box are removable. The shaft and the whiffletree are attached as in Army sled No. 1. Army sled No. 3 can be drawn either by one horse or by two horses in tandem.

The ambulance sled (Army sled No. 3/1) can carry two severely wounded men on stretchers or four slightly wounded men, who can sit on the three seat boards. The substructure is similar to that of Army sled No. 3.

The sled box has two windows, one on each side, equipped with swinging doors. It can be heated by a stove located in the front. The floor has two wooden slats with springs to which two stretchers can be attached. The ambulance sled is drawn in the same manner as Army sled No. 3.

The heavy transport sled (Army sled No. 5) is used to transport heavy field kitchens, large air compressors, engineer and signal equipment, ammunition, 100-mm chemical mortars, and other heavy equipment. The sled has the same

Figure 88.—105-mm howitzer mounted on sled runners.

form and superstructure as Army sled No. 3, but is of heavier construction and the superstructure is about 23 inches longer. The sled is drawn like Army sled No. 3, and also by three horses, one behind the other.

c. Loading Army Sleds

The 37-mm antitank gun is loaded on Army sled No. 3 as in figure 85 (2). The light infantry howitzer 18 is also loaded on this type of sled, while the 38-mm antitank gun and the 75-mm antitank gun 97/38 are loaded on Army sled No. 5.

The heavy field kitchen is loaded on Army sled No. 5, and the light field kitchen on Army sled No. 3. The following preparations are necessary. Remove wheels from the wagon body of the field kitchen. Reinforce the axle and axle springs. The side walls and the rear wall must be removed from the sled and also the boards in the middle of the floor in order that the wagon body of the field kitchen can be placed directly on the lengthwise boards of the floor of the sled. Fasten the wagon body to the lengthwise boards with wood screws and lock screws. Build a makeshift box of boards over the empty part of the field-kitchen floor, and put a small door in the right side of this box. (This box replaces the limber of the field kitchen, which is left behind.)

d. Toboggan Type of Sled

An improvised horse-drawn toboggan type of sled, about 6 feet 6 inches long, is shown in figure 86. It has proved its worth on the Eastern Front, particularly for evacuating the wounded, where enclosed, heated sleds were not available.

e. Runners and Sliding Troughs

(1) *Runners.*—In many instances runners have not proved effective, because they skid on slippery roads and do not have much carrying capacity in deep snow. They are, however, the only medium for the transportation of heavy material which cannot be loaded on sleds, particularly when guns must be brought into position. Runners have the advantage that they can be constructed by the troops, but a great disadvantage is that they do not fit into

the tracks of sleds (usually they must be built to a greater width). Ski runners (see fig. 87) and snow or sled runners (see fig. 88) are issued as equipment of combat troops.

The wheel pair of ski runners may also be used as gun supports during firing. The wheel and trail runners are issued with iron fittings but without wheel blocks; the latter must be constructed by the troops to fit the wheels. If the gun is to be hauled by troops, the runners must be pro-

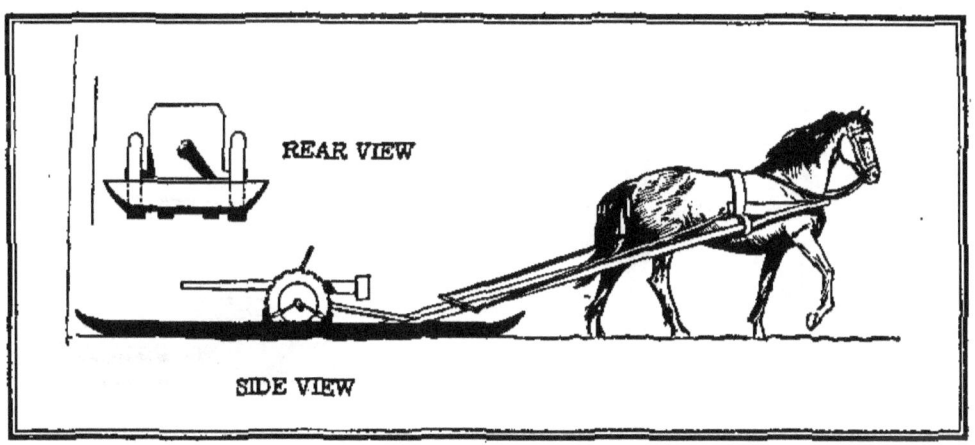

Figure 89.—Sliding trough for hauling heavy loads.

vided with fittings for towropes. The antitank guns (37-mm to 75-mm), smoke-shell mortar, light infantry howitzer, and the recoilless gun can be carried on this type of runner.

A set of snow or sled runners consists of two wheel runners and one trail runner. Both types are for hauling guns on roads with horses in tandem, and for supporting the gun while firing. The infantry howitzer, the heavy antitank gun, the light field howitzer, and the smoke-shell mortar can be carried on them.

Runners made of tree trunks have proved very valuable on the Eastern Front. They can easily be constructed by the troops. A set of tree-trunk runners can be used for transporting the same equipment which may be carried on sled runners.

(2) *Sliding troughs.*—Sliding troughs have proved to be very effective for transporting heavy weapons on trails in snowy terrain. A trough of the type shown in figure 89 has

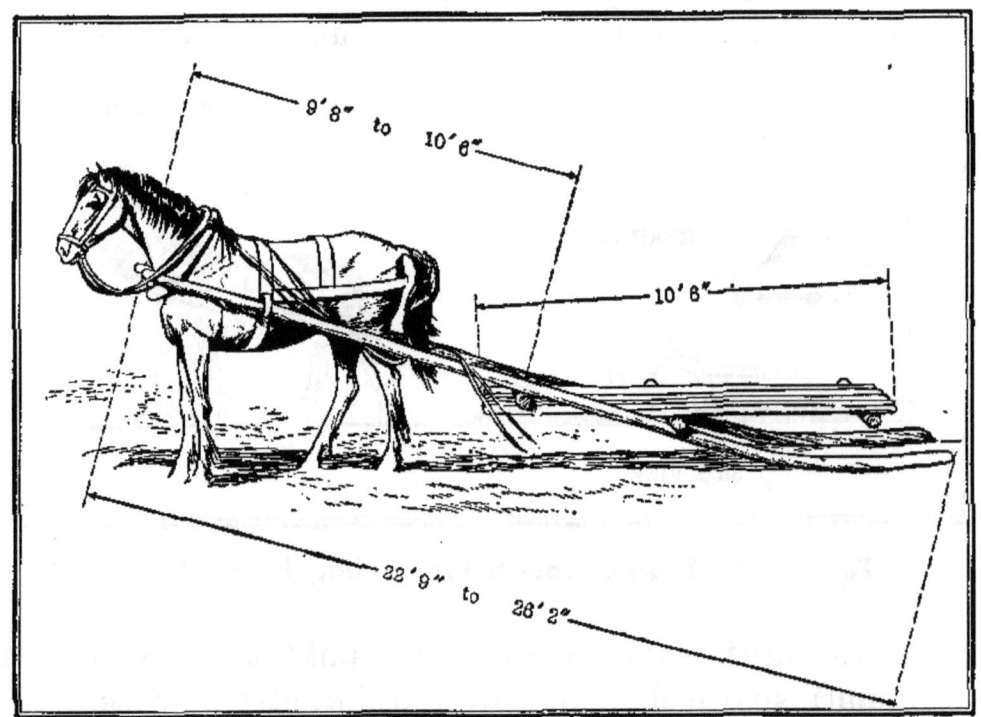

Figure 90.—Drag made of naturally curved tree branches.

proved good for antitank gun *M41* (28/20-mm), the 37-mm and the 50-mm antitank guns, and the light infantry howitzer. They are constructed preferably of several ash planks joined side by side. Curve both ends, while they are hot, over a mold, and smooth the sliding surface. If necessary, apply wax. The following measurements have proved practicable: for loads up to 150 kilograms (about

330 pounds), the length should be 7½ feet and the width 13 inches. For loads up to 300 kilograms (661 pounds), the length should be about 12 feet and the width about 16 inches. For loads up to 800 kilograms (1,764 pounds), the length should be about 17 feet and the width about 19 inches.

f. Drags

Drags are used for transportation in snow and particularly in mud. They make it possible to traverse entirely trackless terrain, and have proved useful for general purposes and especially for the evacuation of the wounded in the forests of Russia and Finland (in the latter country they are called *purilaat*). The type of construction varies greatly, from rough-hewn to neatly joined branches (see fig. 90).

g. Harnessing

Army sleds issued as winter equipment are usually drawn by one horse. If one horse is not sufficient for a load, the sled must be drawn by two horses harnessed in tandem. In exceptional circumstances three horses harnessed one in front of the other may be necessary.

67. PACK HARNESS

Two improvised carrying appliances for small west Russia rural cart horses and light draft horses can easily be constructed by the unit itself. They have proved their worth during the muddy season. A medium-sized horse of this kind, equipped with these devices, can carry a total load

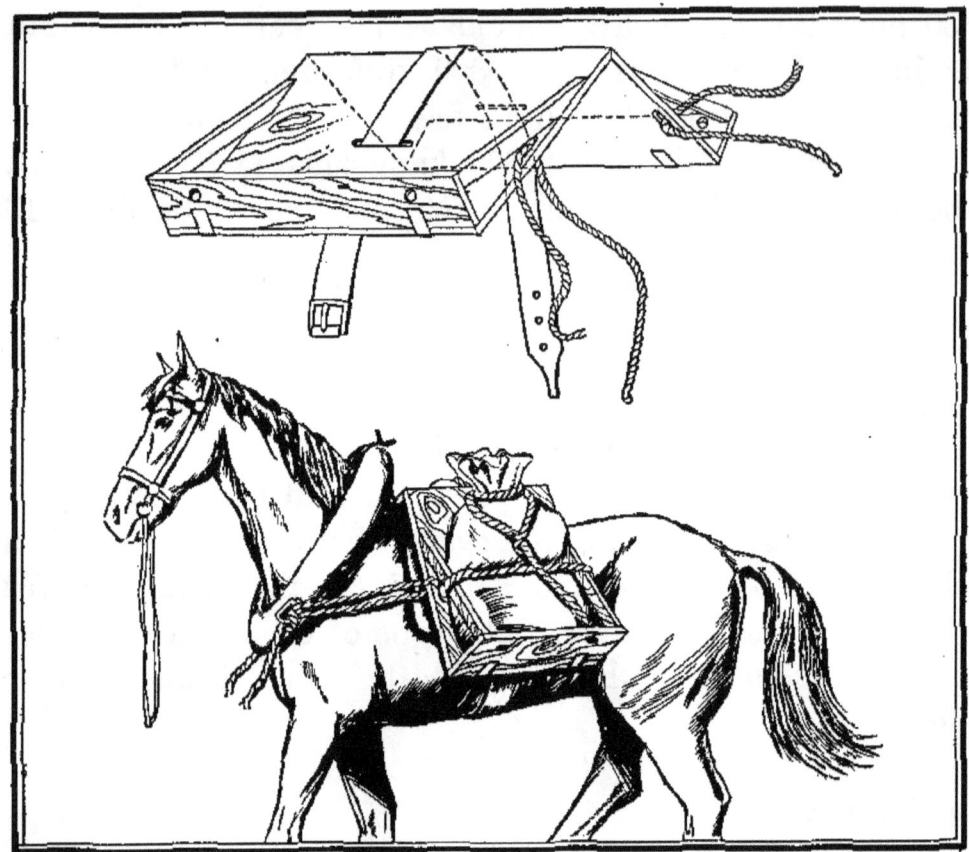

Figure 91.—Improvised wooden pack saddle.

up to 50 kilograms (110 pounds). Stronger horses can carry up to 100 kilograms (220 pounds).

Figure 91 shows a wooden pack saddle for ammunition boxes and other items of supply. The frame is made of wood, and the reinforcement of strap iron. The frame and the bellyband are fastened in front to the collar of the horse with two ropes or leather straps. Another type of pack saddle consists of a back pad and ropes or leather straps, as shown in figure 92. The loads are attached as high as possible and close to the back pad.

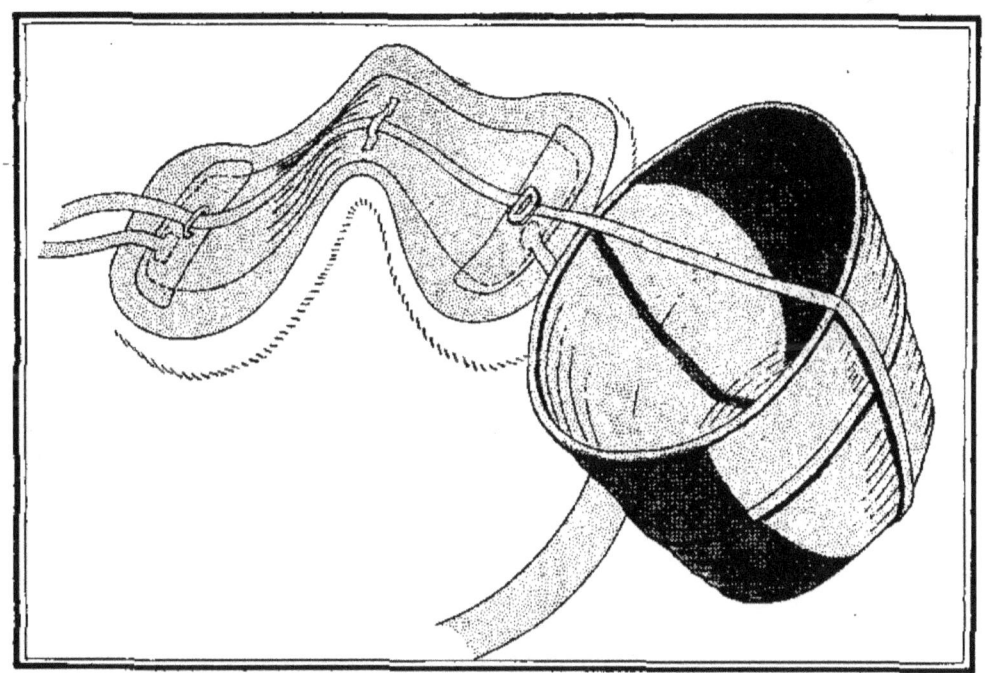

Figure 92.—Pack saddle consisting of a back pad and basket.

To avoid bruises, a saddle blanket, folded six times, should be placed under both pack saddles. It is also important that the load be distributed equally on both sides of the horse.

www.ingramcontent.com/pod-product-compliance
Lightning Source LLC
Chambersburg PA
CBHW081834170426
43199CB00017B/2725